the
catch me
if you can

Brightly colored buildings line the streets of Bo-Kaap, my favorite area in Cape Town, South Africa, and the historic center of Cape Malay culture.

the
catch me
if you can

One Woman's Journey to Every Country in the World

JESSICA NABONGO

NATIONAL GEOGRAPHIC

WASHINGTON, D.C.

For Rose and Ephraim
Webale nnyo

◆

contents

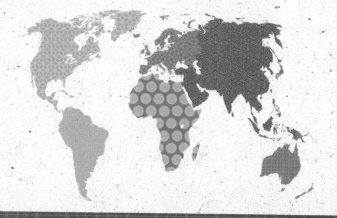

> "To live is the rarest thing in the world.
> Most people exist, that is all."
> —OSCAR WILDE

introduction

I GOT MY FIRST PASSPORT WHEN I WAS four or five years old. What I didn't know at the time was how generous life could be and that I was being handed the world to explore. I could not have imagined that little blue book would lead me to a carpet seller in Afghanistan or that I would fall in love with a mosque in Iran. How could I have guessed that I would form lifelong bonds on a road trip in Namibia? Or that kissing a giraffe

in Kenya would be as memorable as walking next to one in Niger? That little girl could not have known she would climb Japan's Mount Fuji or swim with whales in Tonga.

I grew up in a home with hundreds of books, two sets of encyclopedias, an atlas, and a globe that, though now inaccurate, still sits on my countertop. I am a geography nerd. Always have been, always will be. My parents never put boundaries on me and my sisters. We were raised to feel like anything truly was possible. So it's no wonder I developed so many wild dreams; visiting every country in the world was just one of them.

Let me back up a little. I have lived many lives—some short, some prolonged, all vastly different—and I've enjoyed each one. In my childhood, I was engaged in sports, music, ballet, and tap recitals, and I had sleepovers with people who became lifelong friends. In high school, I was voted "Class Trendy" and was quite the social butterfly.

In college, at St. John's University in New York City, I graduated magna cum laude, helped establish the Africana studies minor, held internships at both Time, Inc., and Pfizer, and was accepted into a competitive summer program at Harvard Business School. My first full-time job was at Pfizer, where I was given pay and benefits that flirted with six figures. Company car, check. Base salary that was on

For my adventure to the Edge of the World (*Jebel Fihrayn*), towering cliffs in the Saudi Arabian desert, the team at Four Seasons Riyadh set up the perfect camp to enjoy lunch.

par with my friends slaving away on Wall Street, check. Cell phone and home internet paid for, check. Expense account, check. Stock options, check. 401(k), check. As a 21-year-old, what more could I ask for?

I had laid the foundation to take the corporate world by storm. My path ahead was clear: a successful career, someday married to a six-foot-three, perfectly chiseled partner, two brilliant children, and a sprawling home with two luxury cars parked outside.

Everything was going according to plan. I had relocated back to Detroit, and with the freedom of adulthood and disposable income, I let loose. Weekends often consisted of trips to Miami or New York. I spent too many weeknights having martinis downtown. I was excelling at work, and for my 22nd birthday, I bought myself a two-bed, two-bath condo with views of the Detroit River and Canada. I had a custom closet built for my shoes and designer jeans. Life was good. Very good.

Then, one day something in me snapped. In the parking lot of a doctor's office I checked my email on bonus day only to see a three-digit figure that still makes me cringe. I was doing all that I could to reach my sales goals. I was going above and beyond and had become a favorite sales rep among the doctors in my territory. But my bonus was a reflection of the pharmaceutical marketplace, not my effort. I realized in that parking lot that life is not a meritocracy.

I captured this image of a group of young monks near the Kakku Pagodas in Myanmar after I discovered them sneakily taking pictures of me.

I went home and Googled teaching jobs in Japan. Japan came to mind because I had a friend living there and I had always been fascinated by the Japanese language because it has similarities to Luganda, my parents' native tongue. I applied for a job and was hired to teach English in a small community. I began preparing for a move to a country and continent that I had never visited. This was in 2008, before I had Twitter and before Instagram was even launched. There was no "Black travel movement." At this point in my life, I had traveled to nine countries and one territory across three continents. And I had never traveled solo, save an awful eight hours in Paris. I packed my bags and put the contents of my condo into a storage unit, and then I had an unforgettable going-away weekend. As a final preparation, I shaved my head, knowing I would not find anyone to do my Black hair in a small city outside of Kyoto.

My move to Japan ultimately changed the trajectory of my life. Unwilling to go back to the life of working nine to five in the United States, I decided to continue living abroad. When I left Japan, I started

a blog called The Catch Me If You Can, began focusing on my photography, and traveled until I ran out of money. Subsequently, I called London home while I earned my master's degree at the London School of Economics, then I worked for a nonprofit in rural Benin, and I followed that with a post at the United Nations in Rome. I often quit jobs because while I was unsure of what I wanted to do in life, I always quickly figured out what I didn't want to do.

Celebrating my 32nd birthday in the vibrant streets of Cuba's Old Havana

Americans, including me, have been socialized to believe that a successful life is finding a high-powered and high-paying career, buying a huge house and fancy car, and having a beautiful family. Although this fantasy works for some people, it didn't work for me, so I tried to find what *would* work for me.

In February 2017, I finally figured out what I wanted to do to find fulfillment in my life: travel to every country in the world. I said I would do it, and so I did. In October 2019, I sat on the shores of the Seychelles, surrounded by family and friends, having checked the 195th country off my list.

Entrepreneurship helped bring me to this goal and the life of freedom I was seeking. After leaving my last corporate job in 2015, I founded Jet Black, a boutique luxury travel agency that worked to promote tourism in Central and South America, the Caribbean, and Africa. Its initial goal was to change the narrative about countries in those regions, and it evolved to also promote Black tourism. As a content creator, I

Pyongyang is the surprisingly colorful capital of the Democratic People's Republic of Korea (North Korea).

partnered with brands on social media, and in November 2019, after my journey was complete, I founded the e-commerce site The Catch with the aim of giving artisans from around the world access to a global marketplace. Entrepreneurship is certainly not for everyone—I'm exhausted thinking about my day-to-day balance—but the freedom that comes with it makes it the right choice for me.

Fourteen years after that life-altering decision to move to Japan, life looks a lot different. Now, life is dreaming, creating, and achieving the impossible. It is experiencing new foods and new cultures, learning new languages, and turning strangers into friends. It is experiencing the world with my closest friends and inspiring people to live alternative lifestyles. I traded that traditional nine-to-five for all of this and more.

People often make assumptions about my life based on the swoon-worthy photos on social media. They assume I am always on vacation or that what I do is not "real life." I assure you, it is. I have created the type of life that I want to live: one that excites me every single day when I wake up. I changed my belief system around what "real life" is and what it can be.

After living an unconventional life for so long, I've realized the most important thing to me is my freedom—freedom of movement, freedom of time, freedom of location. I rarely know what day of the week it is. My body is now incapable of getting jet lag. I strive to create a life in which I say yes and no whenever I want. I found happiness only once I started choosing what I *actually* wanted and stopped letting others or circumstances choose for me. Now, I very rarely do things that I do not want to do (including when my mother asks me to cook a dish for Thanksgiving. *Not doing it!* Love you, Mommy!). I am focused not on money but rather on having enough to do the things that interest me.

This freedom and indulgence in all life has to offer means it's now nearly impossible for me to name a favorite thing. I have neither a favorite country nor a favorite food. Life is too full of amazingly beautiful things, places, and people to pick just one.

I have visited the world's 195 countries and 10 territories. Through these travels I learned two key lessons: First, most people are good. My journey was made possible by the kindness of strangers—some who opened their homes to me and others who donated money to help me reach the finish line. I do not know when we started to assume the worst in each other, but if you consider yourself to be a good person, why would you assume that a stranger is a bad one? I always assume the best of people because that is what I received nine times out of 10 in every corner of the world. The few bad experiences will never outweigh the good.

The second lesson I learned is that we are more similar than we are different. In the end, neither race, gender, social class, religion, sexual orientation, body type, education level, nor nationality make you better than the next person. The French philosopher Pierre Teilhard de Chardin said, "We are not human beings having a spiritual experience; we are spiritual beings having a human experience." Once you fully accept that, you realize how much our differences simply do not matter.

A lush background and brightly colored swimsuit helped create the perfect drone selfie in Samoa.

As travelers, we have a duty to tell the stories of the places we visit with dignity and respect, to share our adventures without patronizing places or people. There is always danger in a single story. One person's experience in a country can cause others to follow in their footsteps or swear to never step foot in a destination. If I am going to tell a single story, I seek to find the positive. I travel with a lens of curiosity and a desire to understand what everyday life is like. I am looking to learn rather than confirm biases. When traveling, and really in life, you will find what you are looking for. If you look for joy, you will find joy. If you look for beauty, you will find beauty. Alternatively, if you seek misery, you will find that. Life gives you what you seek. What are you seeking?

For far too long we have seen the world only through one lens, and I am here to offer an alternative. Most of the people who have visited every country in the world are white men, and there is no question that our experiences are very different.

I am a Black woman, but beyond my Blackness, my travels are shaped by my Africanness. I am unmistakably African, and I am identified as such no matter where I am in the world. Upon exiting the Accra airport in Ghana recently, an immigration officer referred to me as an African princess—even to other Africans, I am stereotypically African.

I have had many issues with immigration due to the negative perception of Africans globally, and yet, somehow, I have managed to keep going, persevering through tears and anger. But through the pain, I have always felt that the behavior at border control was not reflective of the population of the countries I have visited. And although these challenges are frustrating, the privilege of the journey is not lost on me.

I want to change where the world travels to and how the world sees travelers. For too long, a homogeneous group—a group that does not look like me, or much of the world for that matter—has chosen Eurocentric top 10 lists. These lists are determined by people who often have barely scratched the surface of global destinations—very few of whom have been to 50 countries, let alone 195 like me. Although those destinations are often aptly beloved, if you rely on them alone for your bucket list, you're leaving an entire world left to be explored. That world is full of natural beauty, kind people of diverse backgrounds, cultures worth engaging with, and histories that should be learned. Whether or not you make it to these places isn't the point. My hope is that even if you couldn't find these countries on a map before reading this book, you will understand the joys and riches they offer and the way they changed me for the better.

In Balkh, Afghanistan, a woman walks past the Khwaja Parsa Mosque, built in 1467, wearing the blue burka that has become synonymous with Taliban rule.

I have wanted to travel to every country in the world since my 20s simply because of my curiosity. But the journey that I completed was so much bigger than me. It morphed from a personal goal to being about changing narratives and ensuring that people who look like me are seen equally as tourists around the globe. It is about normalizing our existence, because, yes, even in 2022, I am often the only Black person on a plane of 300. I can travel for days and *never* see someone at the same end of the color spectrum. My mission is to create space. To shake shit up. To say, we are here and we belong.

The intention of this book is not to convince you to travel to every country in the world, though it might. That was my dream. My intention is to show everyone—not just Black women and men, but all women and men—that your dreams are valid. Your dreams are achievable.

Would I do it again? Probably not. While I am proud of this journey, it was not easy. There were a lot of lonely nights. There

were tears of frustration. There was anger from being treated as less than equal. The resilience required to complete this feat could only be bestowed by the universe that selected me for this particular mission.

World-renowned Haitian metalwork artist André Eugène gives me a tour of his studio in Port-au-Prince.

Now you're ready to dive into the story of my journey—or at least some of it. In these pages you'll follow me to 100 countries, in the order I visited them. I have been to all 195 UN-recognized countries, so you're probably wondering how I decided on these 100.

I had a cultural experience in each place I visited, but, honestly, they were not all impactful enough to share. I left out some countries because I want to experience more of them, including some of the world's most visited, like Mexico and the United Kingdom. How can I write about Mexico without visiting Oaxaca or Guadalajara? Though I lived in London for a year, how can I write about the United Kingdom having never seen Scotland or Wales?

Most of the countries that made it into this book are ones I fell in love with, countries that upon arrival found a special place in my heart. They are where I met characters whose stories needed to be told or strangers who became immediate friends. Many of these destinations do not immediately come to mind when people create a bucket list, but I believe you should consider them for yours.

This book is a collection of countries that make my heart smile. I hope my stories make you laugh, cry, feel something, and ultimately make you think differently about the world in which we live.

SNAPSHOT FROM CROATIA: The walled Old Town of Dubrovnik, Croatia, perched on the Adriatic, is one of the Mediterranean's most iconic cities.

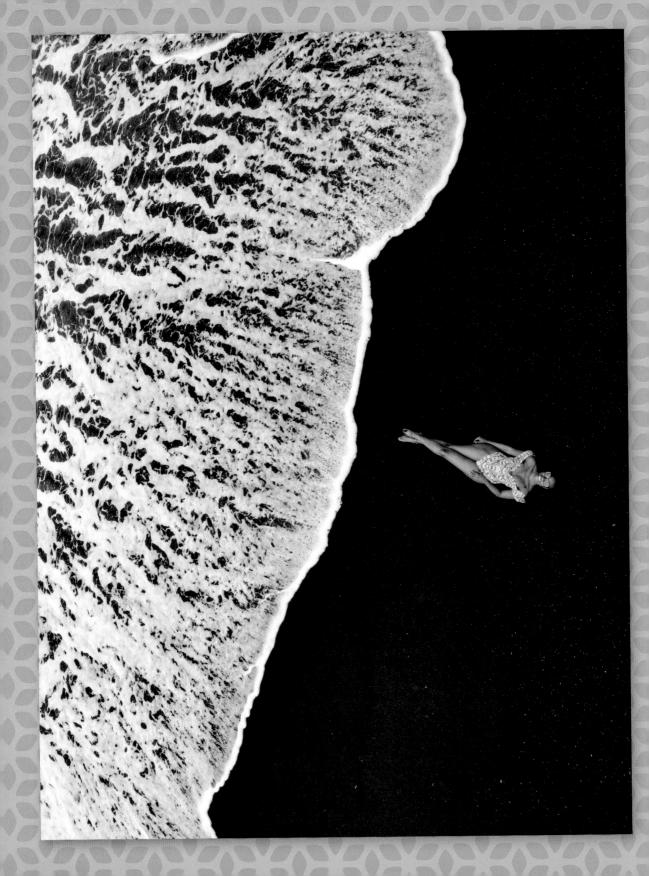

united states

I WAS BORN IN DETROIT, MICHIGAN, at Grace Hospital on the city's west side. My parents—Ugandan immigrants who permanently settled in the United States in 1969—brought me home to a beautiful two-story brick house with a manicured lawn and white picket fence in the Grandmont neighborhood. A young chemist and a nurse, my parents laid the foundations of a beautiful life for me and my two older sisters, Joyce and Christina. ¶ Throughout the 20th century,

Detroit was one of the most important cities in the U.S., thanks to the auto industry, Motown, architecture, and design. Detroit is also home to Woodward Avenue, the first paved road in America.

When the auto industry collapsed in the early 2000s, most Americans felt the city of Detroit did, too. And although the city did go through a bankruptcy and substantial population loss (it was once home to 1.86 million people), with more than 639,000 residents still there, not all of our stories are being told. Many people hold a skewed view, thanks to news articles and plenty of shows and movies that depict Detroit as run-down and less than stellar. I've found these, like all destination biases, to be untrue. I can assure you my hometown has much to offer.

My upbringing in the city was a microcosm of the world that I would one day travel through. I went to Catholic school in the suburbs alongside Jewish and Chaldean children. One of our go-to restaurants was a Japanese establishment, Kyoto, where I learned to eat with chopsticks. We ate *pączki* (doughnuts) from the Polish bakery, Greek-style gyros from Coney Island (a Detroit-style diner, not the New York amusement park), chicken shawarma from a Lebanese restaurant, and fresh tacos in Mexicantown. Some of our dearest family friends are Kenyan, Congolese, Filipino, and Indian.

Detroit's rich history is best explored through its museums, Charles H. Wright, Henry Ford, and Motown being my favorites. The Detroit Institute of Arts and Museum of Contemporary Art Detroit hold beautiful collections. And visiting in summer is best, when Hart Plaza and

NORTH AMERICA

Wai'anapanapa State Park's black sand beach in Maui, Hawaii, offers a beautiful juxtaposition of the volcanic sands and the cool Pacific waters.

the entire riverfront are alive, buzzing with cultural and music festivals that celebrate the city's rich diversity. Should you choose to visit in winter, I will not take any responsibility for your experience with the frigid temps, but do go ice-skating in Campus Martius.

No trip to Detroit is complete without trying a Coney dog: a hot dog smothered in beef chili and onions. I prefer chili cheese fries—but you have to try the dog, paired with a bag of Better Made chips (barbeque is the best) and an ice-cold Faygo pop. (Yes, *pop;* we don't have "soda" in Detroit.) I was today years old when I found out my favorite ice cream, Superman, originated in Michigan. I can't tell you what flavor the blue, yellow, and red concoction is, but I can tell you that the only place I'll get it is at Ray's Ice Cream. Finally, you must eat Detroit-style pizza from the iconic Buddy's Pizza. Thank me later.

The U.S. is the third largest country in the world—by area and population. I've been lucky enough to visit nearly the entirety of the country. With more than 50 million immigrants, it is fundamentally shaped by the rich cultural texture of migration. With all its flaws, it also has countless treasures to see and people to meet. From the Black cowboys of Oklahoma to the people of Appalachia to the Somali community of Minneapolis, visiting each state can be like seeing a new country.

So far, I have driven through 38 of the country's 50 states. My longest road trip was in July 2009, when my Australian friend, Matyas—whom I met at a McDonald's in Japan—and I embarked on a 16-day, 5,615-mile (9,035 km) road trip through 10 states and Vancouver, Canada.

In downtown Detroit, Michigan, the work of local artist Sheefy McFly brightens up the city, with the iconic Renaissance Center in the background.

I didn't plan any of our interstate road trip in advance, but as a seasoned traveler I always come prepared. I packed three maps and a bunch of AAA tour books, which paid off. When we left our first stop, Las Vegas, all we knew was that we had 16 days before our respective flights home from Los Angeles.

Our first stop was the Hoover Dam, which is massive. Walking across the dam in 101°F (38°C) desert heat, though, was absolutely, beautifully miserable. From the dam, we drove six hours east to the North Rim of the Grand Canyon. Understand this: No picture, video, or retelling of stories can ever compare to seeing the Grand Canyon for yourself.

At the Grand Canyon we finally made our game plan using the maps I brought and the book *1,000 Places to See Before You Die*. Only then did we realize we would be driving for more than 100 hours and well over 3,000 miles (4,828 km)!

This road trip exposed me to so much of America's natural beauty. Following the Grand Canyon we visited Monument

Valley and Salt Lake City in Utah; Coeur d'Alene and Idaho Falls in Idaho; Grand Teton, Jackson Hole, and Yellowstone National Park in Wyoming; Glacier National Park in Montana; Seattle, Washington; Vancouver, Canada; Portland, Oregon; and we drove along the Pacific Coast Highway to Napa Valley, San Francisco, Yosemite and Sequoia National Parks, and, finally, Los Angeles.

America's National Park System—with 63 national parks and more than 400 sites—is a true treasure. I highly recommend Acadia National Park in Maine, Zion and Bryce Canyon in Utah, and the Great Smoky Mountains in Tennessee. My dream is to see all 63 parks, but I've got a long way to go.

My next big road trip was in July 2013, when my sister Joyce had the idea to take a southern U.S. civil rights road trip with her two young kids to celebrate the 50th anniversary of the beginning of the civil rights movement. Our trip took us through six states: Florida, Alabama, Tennessee, Arkansas, Mississippi, and Louisiana. In Louisiana, we made a stop in New Orleans, which I have visited two times since and love. New Orleans is *hands down* America's best food city. From the char-grilled oysters to the po'boys, jambalaya, beignets, gumbo, and fried catfish, just eat everything. I'm begging you.

"Are we there yets?" from my five-year-old nephew and seven-year-old niece notwithstanding, we had an amazing trip full of heartwarming and heartbreaking American history.

My favorite ice cream flavor, Superman, originated in Michigan, and the only place I get my fix is Ray's Ice Cream, just outside Detroit.

SOME OF MY FAVORITE PLACES
IN THE U.S.

1. Detroit, Michigan
2. Horseshoe Bend, Arizona
3. The Ranch at Rock Creek, Montana
4. Amangiri, Utah
5. Black Sand Beach, Maui, Hawaii
6. Glacier National Park, Montana
7. New England
8. Brooklyn, New York
9. Great Salt Lake, Utah
10. New Orleans, Louisiana

In Oklahoma, Tory (on the horse), a third-generation cowboy, taught me the history of Black cowboys across the country.

One of the saving graces of a road trip is it makes travel possible when the world shuts down. Having made my way to some of the most inaccessible countries around the globe (hello, North Korea!), I could never have imagined a world in which travel came to a complete halt. But 2020 and the coronavirus pandemic brought the unimaginable.

While I was grounded, I still had the urge to get out and see more of the world. So, in July 2020, my friend Nyanquoi and I embarked on a road trip through New England. Armed with negative COVID tests and a carful of sanitizer, wipes, and masks, we hit the road for two weeks to visit Connecticut, Rhode Island, Maine, Massachusetts, New Hampshire, Vermont, and upstate New York. This is one of my favorite trips in all of the U.S.—mostly because of the food. In Rhode Island, we had the best oysters ever at Matunuck Oyster Bar. Maine became the love of my life for its lobsters, landscapes, people, and architecture. In a past life, I am sure that I lived there. Dinner at the White Barn Inn in Kennebunkport is unmissable.

In the fall of 2020, still unable to travel internationally, I took a road trip that included West Virginia, North Carolina, South Carolina, Georgia, Tennessee, Kentucky, and Ohio. I fell in love with Charlotte, North Carolina, where I met Chef Greg Collier, who instantly became family and introduced me to Chef BJ Dennis, who in turn became my local guide in Charleston, South Carolina.

Seeing Charleston through Chef BJ's eyes brought me face-to-face with Geechee and Gullah culture. I will never forget going to a juke joint and seafood boil in his friend's backyard, where the fish, crab, oysters, and shrimp were fresh, the drinks were strong, and I shucked my first oysters. Chef BJ also recommended we visit the McLeod Plantation. Our guide, Toby, a Charlestonian, passionately shared intimate and gruesome details of the enslaved Africans who lived and died on the property. When you travel, you are always learning.

I could go on and on about what I love in the U.S., but America is a complicated country, and I cannot talk about it without talking about race and my personal experience as a Black woman. In fact, some of my worst travel experiences have been in my home country.

Consider this: I have been to every country in the world, and that includes North Korea, Afghanistan, South Sudan, and Venezuela. People often ask me about "dangerous" countries, no doubt thinking of the headline makers, the countries on the "do not travel" lists. I always respond that no country in the world is completely unsafe and no country in the world is completely safe. For me, a Black woman living in America, the U.S. has proven to be the most dangerous.

ROAD TRIP
TIPS

1. If you are going to more than three national parks in a year, buy the $80 annual pass in advance.
2. Set a loose itinerary to have the right amount of time in each place, with wiggle room for exploring.
3. Stop in small towns for meals.
4. Look for off-the-beaten-path places to explore.
5. Prep your playlist, podcasts, or audiobooks in advance.
6. Go solo or with someone you really, really like. Weeks-long road trips can be stressful.

Utah's stunning Bryce Canyon National Park is one of the state's five national parks.

Let's start with U.S. Customs and Border Protection, which gives me anxiety. From the first time, in 2009, that I was sent to a secondary security screening (see Honduras, page 52) to when I exited a flight only to find an armed U.S. military officer asking for my passport, assuming I wasn't American, I have been through the ringer. There was the time returning from a work trip to Ethiopia that I was stopped and asked for my passport, which had already been checked and put away. After examining it, the officer asked me for a second form of identification, claiming she couldn't tell if it was me in the picture. The last instance—and there are plenty more in between—was in February 2021, when I was returning from a five-day trip to Senegal. The immigration officer at JFK airport asked how much luggage I had. When I told her that I had three checked bags, she flagged me immediately, saying I had a lot of luggage for such a short trip. I explained I had brought back two baskets for my house—that was not good enough.

The challenge with this type of discrimination is that it occurs under the guise of "doing one's job." Really, it is rooted in racism. I am the first to admit that I live a very privileged lifestyle. But my privilege will always come head-to-head with my oppression. It does not matter that I came out of a first-class seat before walking to immigration control. To those security officers, I am just another African to be suspicious of. I purposely denote African because most of my Black American friends have never experienced what I have with American immigration—even those who have traveled with me on the same flight.

Outside of my experiences with border control, the scariest thing that has ever happened to me while traveling occurred in Miami, Florida. My friend Crystal and I returned to our friend's apartment only to find ourselves locked out. Dressed in beachwear and leaning against the hallway walls, we chatted as a locksmith attempted to open the door. A couple of neighbors opened their doors to see what was going on. I yelled, "Sorry for the noise. He's a locksmith. We left the keys inside." A little later, I saw police officers enter the building, but I didn't give them a second glance because I knew they weren't there for us. Next thing I knew, I heard yelling and turned to see a gun held to my face at point-blank range. Scared and nervous, we all threw our hands up and I shouted, "He's a locksmith! He's a locksmith!"

The police officer said they'd gotten a call that the apartment was being broken into. Speaking as fast as Twista, I explained the situation. Eventually, he put down the gun and asked for our identification. Once I handed it over, I asked him if it had been necessary to pull the gun out. He replied coldly, "We shoot first, ask questions later." The harassment stopped only after a *white* neighbor told the cops that he had seen us staying there all weekend. That was one of my most traumatizing travel experiences—and it happened to us because we are Black. It was the only time and place I have ever had a gun pointed at me. Along with all its natural beauty, *this* is also America.

In 1963, Malcolm X said, "American propaganda is designed to make us think that no matter how much hell we catch here, we're still better off in America than we'd be anywhere else." That message has created fear of traveling abroad in many Black people.

It's time we break those chains. Yes, we live in a globalized system of white supremacy. Yes, you *might* experience racism abroad—I certainly have. But I've also experienced it the most at home. You shouldn't always expect to be met with racism, no matter where you are in the world. More times than not, I have been met with nothing but kindness from strangers around the globe. If I can find beauty and kindness in America, where I've also faced some of the most harrowing travel experiences of my life, I am certain I can find it anywhere.

Although there is so much to explore right at home in the U.S., after traveling to every country in the world, I urge you to go to the places you dream of visiting, near and far, no matter who you are. Do not let the fear of something happening keep you from going where your heart desires. I certainly haven't.

In New Orleans, America's best food city, Perino's has my favorite chargrilled oysters.

canada

LIKE MANY DETROIT NATIVES, my international travels started in Canada, our neighbor to the south, whose border was a mere 12 miles (19 km) from my childhood home. Yes, you read that correctly: Detroit is the only city in the contiguous United States where you drive *south* to get to Canada. When I'm actually home, I wake up to views of Windsor from my window in Detroit—just four miles (6.4 km) to the tunnel to Canada.

NORTH AMERICA

Canada is a great destination, especially for Americans, because it offers a similar feel to the U.S., has almost no language barrier, and has far less violence. Growing up, Canada was easier to get to than Mackinac Island. You did not even need a passport back then. My parents took us often, starting from the time I was four. We explored some of what the country had to offer for family-friendly fun: Canada's Wonderland, an amusement park in Ontario; the iconic Niagara Falls bordering New York; and Wheels Inn, a family resort in Ontario. We had family and friends in Ottawa and Windsor. We even visited Montréal, whose exquisite architecture and French language made me feel like we were in Europe. (Make no mistake: The French spoken in Montréal is distinctly different from the French spoken across the Atlantic—but the French snobbery there is real.)

Like most teenagers in Detroit, when I turned 19 I went to celebrate in Windsor, where the legal drinking age is 19. Also, Windsor Casino existed long before the casinos in Detroit.

In my 20s and 30s, Canada became a destination that I *chose* to visit rather than frequented out of convenience. In Vancouver I had some of the best Japanese cream puffs I have ever tasted outside of Japan. East Asians make up 23 percent of the population in Vancouver, which explains the robust and lively Chinatown and the beautiful Japanese botanical gardens.

I visited my friend Katie in Montréal and braved the winter-like temps of April for my first ever Lianne La Havas concert; she is now one of my favorite artists. I visited Ontario's wine country and enjoyed a meal at Ravine Vineyards overlooking vines that I hadn't known

Banff's Lake Louise, which freezes completely in winter, is nestled in the Canadian Rockies and is one of the region's most stunning locations.

existed until that trip. The architecturally stunning Calgary Central Library and the renewed sense of community around it spoke to my soul. And at Cluck N Cleaver in Calgary, I ate the best fried chicken of my life—in Canada, imagine that!

It's safe to say I have a lot of Canadian memories. But two stick out the most. En route to Cuba for my 32nd birthday, my friends and I spent a night in Toronto (at the time, you couldn't fly to Cuba from the U.S.). We maximized our 24 hours in the area and went to see Niagara Falls. It was the first time I'd laid eyes on the iconic falls since I was a child. As I sat mesmerized by the crash of water, I looked down at a boat of tourists disappearing into the cascade and thought, I would never do that. My fear of boating under that veil of water should have been a hint at what was to come on a later Canadian adventure.

Three years later, in January 2019, I invited myself on a trip to Banff with my friend Wes. The timing was perfect: I needed a break from running around D.C. trying to obtain visas ahead of an upcoming 20-day trip through North and West Africa. I was in the throes of making it to country 195, and the beauty of Banff seemed like the ultimate way to get a reprieve from the madness. I took it a step further and temporarily deleted my Instagram, deciding to take a complete mental escape and live in the moment. During my journey around the world, I did this from time to time when I had the opportunity to slow down and turn things off. The weight of maintaining an online presence while also trying to meet my goal added to the exhaustion and stress of my hectic travel schedule, managing my businesses, and always jumping from one time zone to another. I learned early on to take time to unplug whenever I could find a moment to do so.

As my bus from Calgary neared our destination, I was completely stunned. Located in the Bow River Valley, Banff is surrounded by the snow-covered Canadian Rocky Mountains, some of the most beautiful peaks I have ever seen. The jagged tops cut effortlessly into the blue skies, and white clouds danced around them.

A few days later, Wes and I drove into those mountains during a snowstorm. I still can't believe I trusted him to drive on mountainous roads in blizzard-like conditions. After about an hour, we came upon Spray Lake and decided to go for a walk. Visibility was roughly 50 feet (15 m), and it wasn't until we were on the frozen lake that we actually saw a number of ice fishermen. Always the curious traveler, I approached a few of the fishermen to chat with them about their day and their sport. I learned a thing or two about ice fishing that

The design of Calgary Central Library is a nod to nature, including entry arches inspired by the shape of clouds formed by chinook winds.

day—namely that the ice was about 10 inches (25 cm) thick and that beer helps get through hours of sitting in the cold.

The following day we went skiing—the first time I had been in more than a decade. I started on the bunny slopes and felt like it was a waste of money, the simple course more suitable for the four-year-old in front of me. Wes, meanwhile, was flying high on the other slopes.

Our second ski day, I got a pass for the real slopes. We took the chairlift to the top, where the views were insanely beautiful. I stopped to express gratitude to the universe for the moment and then looked down. I was a little hesitant, but Wes assured me I would be fine.

Partway down, fear took over and I suddenly lost control. I fell and my head bounced off the ground as I used my whole body as brakes to come to a screeching halt. As other skiers whizzed by, I tried to gather my poles and skis. Wes pulled up alongside me, expertly coming to a purposeful stop. He asked if I was OK. I nodded yes, but I wasn't. He couldn't see my tears behind my cute new reflective ski goggles. In an effort to give me the time I needed to get myself together, Wes sat down in the snow near me and took a call from his sister. Wes was chatting with her about finishing the SATs while I sat feeling like I'd just survived a near-death experience.

My entire body was shaking. I couldn't stop crying. Part of me truly believed I was going to die. The rational part of my brain, somehow still intact after the fall, was trying to convince me I would be OK. After about 10 to 15 minutes—or 48 hours, who really knows—I stood up, took a lot of yoga breaths, and hyped myself up for what seemed like a three-mile (5 km) vertical descent. I could do this.

Wes gave me some pointers, and off I went. Of course, I fell again. I didn't see Wes nearby and had a moment of panic thinking I'd have to get down the rest of the mountain all alone. Thankfully, a moment later Wes pulled up next to me and asked why I was going so fast. While heavily focused on getting down, I didn't realize that I had flown right past him.

I managed to get up quicker this time and focused on moving side to side to slow myself down. Repeating "turn, turn, turn" to myself, I managed to reach the bottom of the slope in one piece. I was seriously shocked I was alive. It was then that I saw we had taken a blue intermediate run—no place for beginners. I should have been sticking to the greens.

Somehow, my stupid self went back up to the top with Wes, but I never went down that run again—or any other run, for that matter. Instead, I took the chairlift back down to the bottom of the mountain, which I hadn't known was an option until that very day. Since then,

I have not put on a pair of skis, but next time I will be sticking to the beginner slopes.

I have learned something new in almost every place I've traveled, and that ski trip to Canada cemented a truth about myself: I am not an adventure traveler, at least in the traditional sense. While I have certainly put myself in many precarious situations (crossing borders by foot, traveling to a new country with relative strangers), adrenaline-rushing thrills aren't for me. I will never jump out of a plane for fun. One million dollars would never make me bungee jump from the bridge that crosses Victoria Falls. I have, however, sat on the edge of Victoria Falls and felt the rush of the water from what's called the Devil's Pool. I have gone ziplining and surfing and ridden on the backs of motorcycles through heavily clogged streets, hiked mountains, gone horseback riding, white-water rafted on the Nile, explored volcanoes, and driven a dogsled. Thrilling, yes. Death-defying, no. That fall down the mountain in Canada affirmed something for me: I see no need to risk life and limb to find adventure. I can get my thrills in other ways—meeting locals, visiting beautiful and historic landmarks and architecture, tasting new foods, sampling local drinks and delicacies in small villages, and haggling in markets, just to name a few.

The road from Calgary to Banff is framed by the massive, imposing, snow-covered Canadian Rockies.

uganda

ON THE BACK OF A *BODA BODA*, I whiz through the streets of Kampala, passing women with baskets of mangoes on their heads and men selling secondhand shoes. There is a mix of cultures in the city as people from all over the country and region descend on Kampala for economic opportunity. There are Baganda, who are right at home, Luo from Kenya, Acholi from the west, and many more.

After 10 minutes of dodging cars and people, my driver drops me at my favorite pork joint on Entebbe Road. I hop off, pay my 1,000 shillings, and head to pick out my meat. The pork is fresh. I am sure it has not been dead for more than 24 hours. The wait is long, but my taste buds are made patient by memories of meals past. The pork is served with a side of avocado, tomato, and onion, with a little pile of salt, and I devour it all using my hands and wash it down with a Tusker Malt Lager imported from Kenya.

My name is Jessica Nambowa Damarie Nassaka Nabongo. I am an American-born Ugandan. I am a native Detroiter. I am a member of the Mutima clan, a Muganda. I am both an American and Ugandan citizen, but the world sees me only as an African—a nonspecific, nondescript African. Before I speak, my American identity is often erased by my haircut, dark skin, high cheekbones, wide nose, and big lips. I am unmistakably African, but I have only briefly lived on the continent.

My mother, Rose Mary Namubiru, from the Mamba clan, is from the Southern Hemisphere, from a village called Mbale, near Masaka. My father, Ephraim Mukasa Nabongo, from the Mutima clan, is from the Northern Hemisphere. He grew up in Wampeewo, a neighborhood on the outskirts of the capital, Kampala. To visit my mom's side from my dad's side, I cross the Equator.

For those of us born to foreign parents, the question of identity and home often has an elusive answer. I carry both a Ugandan and American passport (the former coming in handy to enter countries

AFRICA

My *jaja* (grandmother) Nambowa, who I am named after, in front of her home in Namawojjolo in February 2020

that have a tense relationship with the U.S.). Though born in the United States, I grew up in a Ugandan household, eating Ugandan food, listening to Ugandan music, and being yelled at in Luganda. When I return to Uganda, though I am connected, I sometimes feel like an outsider. I am often called *mzungu* (a white person) because of my accent.

Having lived outside of the U.S. for nearly seven years, I view things differently now. Although many people want to put me in the American box, I cannot simply wash away my Ugandan heritage and upbringing. So when I'm asked where I'm from, I always answer, "I was born in the U.S., but my family is from Uganda."

Being born in America is a funny thing. Many people simply consider anyone born there to be American, with no regard for their parents' countries of origin. If I were born in China, no one would refer to me as Chinese. I'd simply be Ugandan. In Peru, the same thing. However, when I tell Americans that I am Ugandan, I am often dismissed with a "whatever, you're American."

Although Detroit will always feel like home, it will never feel like my ancestral home, nor will the U.S. I cannot reminisce like my friends about visiting cousins in the South during the summer. My memories are of celebrating Ugandan Independence Day or having *binyebwa* (ground peanut sauce) and *matoke* (boiled green bananas) when we found the perfect green bananas at the grocery store. My American childhood was very different from those who are third-, fourth-, and fifth-generation American. I don't know what this will mean for my children. My niece and nephew have a parent who was born in America to Ugandan parents and a parent who was born and raised in Uganda. What does that make them? A generation-and-a-half American?

My first visit to Uganda was in 1991. I was seven years old and I remember getting the necessary vaccinations. My mother insisted my dad go first. He winced when he got the yellow fever shot, leading me to scurry under the chair in hopes of avoiding the pain. Fully vaccinated, I boarded my first transatlantic flight. I do not remember much from that first trip, just the

During my first trip to Uganda in 1991, my sister Christina and I (center) rode around my mother's village with my uncle John.

joys of playing with my cousins in my mother's village and the baboons climbing on our safari jeep in Queen Elizabeth National Park.

My second trip was in December 1994, for my uncle's wedding. That trip gave me in-depth insight into so much of Buganda culture, including *kwanjula,* a huge ceremony where the families of both sides are introduced to one another. Gifts are exchanged and the partying seems to never end.

My third trip was an unexpected visit in 2003. My father died on May 17. That June, we took him to be buried in Uganda. It was my first time visiting Uganda as an adult, and although the whirlwind 12 days were largely accompanied by grief, I also discovered the cultural importance of *lumbe* (last funeral rites) and selecting an *omusika,* or heir (in this case, my dad's nephew). I was introduced to cousins, aunts, a half sister, and uncles I had not previously met. My large family was even larger than I had known.

Since 2003, I have been back five times. Though I rarely spend time in Uganda as a tourist, for my 29th birthday, my mom, a few of her friends, and I visited the Ssese Islands in Lake Victoria, a beautifully peaceful destination with unending lake views and a sunset on my list of top five favorites.

In 2013, I visited a grad school friend in Gulu, in northern Uganda. I was building my skills as a photographer and, inspired by the people

Uganda has some of the world's most beautiful sunsets, best viewed from the shores of Lake Victoria, where the colors reflect on the still waters.

Both my parents are from Uganda, my mother from the Southern Hemisphere and my father from the Northern Hemisphere.

of Gulu, started a new photo series called "I am." I wanted to use the images to change the perception of Africans. So many of the stories that I see about Africans point to poverty, famine, lack of education, unemployment, AIDS, malaria, corruption, civil war . . . need I go on? But to me, the word "African" evokes the world's most beautiful people, our skin shades of brown similar to a box of chocolates. I think of the wisdom of elders, smiling children playing with simple toys, a sense of community. I think of the expression "It takes a village."

In Gulu, I took a blackboard and chalk and asked people to write whatever came to mind when prompted with "I am." Their answers were as beautiful as they were: "I am educated." "I am happy." "I am bright like the sun." I posted the photos to my Tumblr page, hoping to drum up conversations about being African and change the way many people in the world unfairly think of the people throughout this great continent.

Then, in 2017, I traveled to Uganda with my friends Rosie and Ashley. It was fun to be both a tourist and a host, laughing as Ashley took her first *boda boda* (motorcycle taxi) ride and finding that they loved the roasted pork as much as I had hoped. Ashley convinced us to go white-water rafting on the Nile, an activity that my entire family thought was reserved for mzungus. We spent our day with White Nile Rafting, the first Ugandan-owned rafting company in the country. It was a joy to learn from Ugandans how to navigate the Class V rapids.

I—always a hesitant adventure traveler (see Canada, page 24)—had never been white-water rafting, and this was an exhilarating yet frightening first go. As we floated down the Nile, we spotted baby crocodiles perched on rocks. When we hit a rapid and our boat flipped over, it felt like being tossed and turned in a washing machine. As we resurfaced, Ashley came eye to eye with an otter in the incredibly still water. After that one huge rapid, everyone was expected to swim to the designated location. I chose to hitch a ride on one of the rescue kayaks, clinging to it like a panda on a tree.

Named the Pearl of Africa by Sir Winston Churchill—for good reason—Uganda has so much to love: Full of lush landscapes, one of the world's largest lakes, and the source of the Nile, the country also has perfect weather year-round thanks to its equatorial location.

But my favorite memories all reside in my mother's village. The first two times (ages 7 and 10) that I went to Uganda, I was excited to play with my cousins and run around chasing the pigs and chickens. The lack of electricity and running water didn't bother me. The two times after that (ages 19 and 21) were much less exciting. After two nights,

MUST-DO:
RIDE A *BODA BODA*

A *boda boda* is a motorcycle taxi and the most efficient way to navigate through the streets of Kampala. You will see them whizzing about town with a single passenger to a family of four, or carrying furniture and bundles of *matoke*. A ride on the back can be both exhilarating and frightening, but necessary if you want to avoid sitting in traffic in the densely populated capital. As with most things in Uganda, be prepared to negotiate the price. Ask someone in a café how much the journey should be so you have a clue if the driver is giving you a fair price. Be sure to bring a helmet!

Matoke (boiled green bananas) are common in Ugandan cuisine. Here they are wrapped in banana leaves and steamed for a large family event.

WHAT TO DO
IN KAMPALA

1. Eat freshly roasted pork.
2. Eat *matoke* and *binyebwa* with your hands.
3. Visit the National Theatre market and say hi to my aunt Rachel in stall 14.
4. Drink *waragi*, a triple-distilled Ugandan gin.
5. Party until the sun comes up at any club.
6. Watch the sunset over Lake Victoria.
7. Take a *boda boda* ride.

I exploded in a fit of spoiled-bratness, demanding a shower with hot water and my iPod.

Let me paint a picture of the village for you. In 2005, after a bumpy ride over the hill and through the woods, to grandmother's house we went. We arrived after sunset in the pitch-black, save for a few lanterns and powerful LED lights that my mom brought with her. Since my *jaja* Namayanja, my maternal grandmother, died in 2003, no one had been living in her house. The women in the village had cleaned it for our visit, but my allergies were keenly aware of dust still in the air. I spent the days sneezing, with a runny nose and red eyes.

The joy, beyond the company of family, was eating in the village, which meant lots and lots of fresh fruits and vegetables. We ate jackfruit, bananas, avocado, pineapple, and sugarcane. Lunch and dinner consisted of matoke, binyebwa, and a stew of beef or chicken, whichever was fresh that day. People also snacked on recently caught, peeled, and panfried *nsenene* (grasshoppers).

The thing I dreaded most in the village, though, was waking up in the middle of the night to use the bathroom. We had two options: Go outside to the outhouse or use the bathing room, never knowing what might be lurking in the dark.

One night, I headed to the bathing room with my LED light, only to spot a medium-size flying object—a bat! Too scared to face it, I opted for the outhouse. I walked to the back door and pulled before realizing it was locked. With the urgency intensifying, I went back toward the bathing room, but the bat was still there. At the back door again, I played with the locks and pulled. Still nothing. It had been locked from the outside.

In one last desperate attempt, I made a beeline for the bathing room. Thankfully, the bat was gone.

No sooner had I climbed back into bed than that bat flew right over my face. Thinking I imagined it, I made no real adjustments, though my heart was racing. Five seconds later, it came back around. I quickly hid my face under the blankets and slept that way until morning.

Experiences like this are why I often think about my mom's village when I travel. I am reminded of how different my life would have been had I been born there rather than in the United States. The dichotomy of my life as an American and a Ugandan has shaped my view of the world and the lens through which I travel. I do not view anyone's lifestyle as better or worse. Our lives are just different. Though a culture or a person's lifestyle may differ from my experiences and choices, who am I to judge another way of living?

Uganda was the last country I visited before the global shutdown in 2020 caused by the COVID-19 pandemic. Visiting as an adult makes everything different: I hear the language differently, see the city differently, taste the food differently. Having worked in the development industry, I am more critical of how I view Uganda, recognizing failures of the government, global markets, and the development industry. But with every visit, I fall deeper in love. I fall deeper in love with the matoke that my aunts make in the village, to which no restaurant can compare. I fall deeper in love with my family—particularly Aunt Ruth, my father's sister. I tolerate her badgering me to get married because she always spends time with me and teaches me more about our family. On my last trip she gave me the name Nassaka, the Mutima name that I had been missing for 35 years. My namesake, Jaja Nambowa, is 92. She and her sister raised my father after his mother died when he was 13. The highlight of each of my trips to Uganda is visiting her, my last living grandparent.

The market at the National Theatre in Kampala is a must visit for incredible Ugandan handicrafts.

jamaica

I FIRST VISITED JAMAICA when I was 10 years old. It was the summer of 1994 on a family vacation with my mom, dad, and sisters. I'll never forget the vibes of the Holiday Inn in Montego Bay. The entire time we were there, reggae music blasted from speakers and people were always dancing at the pool. One night I watched middle-aged Americans attempt to move in sync with the music, doing their deepest backbends

NORTH
AMERICA

during a limbo contest. My middle sister, Christina, and I spent what seemed like all day in the water, enjoying the sunshine and lively spirit. *No worries, mon.*

My parents taught us how to travel well from an early age, balancing resort life with off-site and cultural excursions. We took a trip to the famed Dunn's River Falls, where I slipped on a rock and grabbed my sister Joyce's arm before falling into the cool water, pulling her in with me. We visited the Bob Marley Museum in Kingston, where Joyce, 12 years my senior, developed a lifelong love for the global icon and his music. We ate jerk chicken paired with rice and peas, learned how to wine our waists, and became indoctrinated in all things reggae.

Fast-forward to 2020 as I joined my friend Wes in Kingston on the set of the film *Zion*, which he was directing for Universal Music and the Bob Marley estate. I was eager to experience the country again. It had been 26 years since I first heard the singsong charm of a Jamaican accent. Twenty-six years since the country's unmistakable energy wrapped me in its arms.

Kingston is a vibe. It effortlessly pulls you in and relaxes you. It doesn't feel touristy, like its beach resort counterparts on the west side of the island. Instead, the city is like a chill house party, with endless rum punch on deck and mellow reggae music on blast. Its people are decidedly unassuming and welcoming.

After visiting Tuff Gong International, the music studio founded by the legendary Marley, we called a taxi. I asked the driver, Victor, to take us to his favorite place for jerk chicken. With hunger nibbling at my insides, we drove through the city for 25 minutes to a "restaurant" that turned out to be his friend cooking "pan chicken" on the side of Red Hills Road. We placed our orders. It'd be another 20 minutes before I'd be able to quiet my stomach rumblings. This, I guess, is what people call island time.

To pass the time, we did what anyone would do in Jamaica: walked across the street and into a bar. I was looking for rum punch—a blend of fresh fruit juices and light and dark rum—but absent that I found myself drinking an "overproof" white Jamaican rum called Wray and Nephew mixed with Ting, a "sparkling grapefruit flavored beverage." Drink in hand, I wandered out of the bar and over to a table of men playing dominoes, a scene similar to ones I have seen across the globe in Saudi Arabia and Cuba, among other countries.

I love to see people from various places engaging in the same activity. It reminds me of how similar we are despite differences in language, culture, and nationality. Dominoes, no matter where you are in the world, is seemingly always played outside by four older men, while other men stand around watching. Such was the scene here in Jamaica. As reggae hummed in the background, the men played a game they have surely played hundreds of times in the same spot.

Across the road, our food was ready. Still hot from the pit, Miles, the grill master, began chopping the chicken, which had been marinating in spices and taking in flavor from the charcoal beneath the grate. It was served with white bread in a piece of foil. As I sat beside Victor and ate, I was in heaven.

Twenty-six years after my first visit to the country, I was surprised how much Kingston maintains its authenticity despite the commercialization of the rest of Jamaica and its culture. From the fresh coconuts sold on the side of the road to the wafts of marijuana in the air to the murals local artists painted downtown on Fleet Street to chicken on the side of the road and a friendly game of dominoes, Kingston remains the heartbeat of the nation.

Twenty-six years after my first visit, I returned to Jamaica, and after four days of exploring Kingston, I fell in love with the country.

france

FRANCE, PARTICULARLY PARIS, is one of those places that appear time and time again on must-travel-to lists. In fact, the country is the most visited in the world. But this is not a love letter to France. It is not an ode to buttery soft croissants, or my preferred *pain au chocolat*. I will not be whispering sweet nothings about champagne and cognac, even though they are two of my favorite drinks. I will not sing the praises of

French cuisine or the beauty of the language, which I consider to be my second. This is a story of a country that has chewed me up and spit me out—twice.

In November 2007, I was less than two years out of undergrad and working a very well paying job as a pharmaceutical sales rep. By this point in my life I had visited seven countries across three continents, and my wanderlust was only growing, but I was bound by my company's vacation policy—don't get me started on corporate America's vacation policies. Instead of a Thanksgiving at home, I took advantage of the free vacation days by visiting friends and family in London, then stopping in Paris to meet my friend Maurice.

It was my first time flying across the Atlantic solo. The plan was to call Maurice and meet up when I landed in Paris's Orly Airport. I called repeatedly for an hour but had no luck getting through. To top it all off, my luggage was lost. Frustrated, I hopped on a computer in the airport terminal and booked a four-star hotel. I needed a bit of comfort. I was already dreaming of taking a steaming-hot shower and falling into a plush, king-size bed. I sent Maurice an email, then made my way to the train to get into the city.

I studied French in middle school, high school, and undergrad. Although my language skills were far from perfect, I was confident that my sentence structure was correct, even if my accent was trash. As I attempted to make my way to the hotel, I sought help in the subway but was met by the turned-up noses of Parisians who couldn't be bothered to help this young, lost American. After three failed attempts, including asking a booth attendant for help, I exited the subway with tears streaming down my face and hailed a taxi.

EUROPE

The best way to enjoy a sunny day in Marseilles is with a glass of champagne on a rooftop overlooking the Old Port (Vieux Port).

The man at the front desk of my hotel informed me that the subway station I had come out of was only a five-minute drive away. My ride took 15 minutes. Considering the exchange rate was $1.42 to €1, that deceitful ride was another blow to my budget—and ego.

When I entered my hotel room, I was taken aback by the tiny quarters: two hard-as-wood twin beds and a tiny shower. This was not the large American hotel room that I was used to. My exhaustion and frustration hit me like a Mack truck. I grabbed a bottle of white wine out of the minibar and drank until Maurice finally arrived.

After I got past the series of unfortunate events that was my arrival, the trip was the epitome of a "First Time in Paris Checklist": Eat baguettes under the Eiffel Tower, visit Notre Dame, and tour the Louvre—kind of; we arrived after closing, but the illuminated pyramid was glorious.

I did not fall in love with Paris on my first visit. I felt in many ways that the city was inaccessible. As a lover of culture, I felt blocked from experiencing anything beyond food, wine, and sightseeing.

Paris struck again on a weekend trip from Rome, in 2012. On the RER B train through the suburbs to Charles de Gaulle—notably one of my least favorite airports in the world—I found myself nodding off. Because I knew a lot of theft happens on this train, I pulled out my cell phone to play a game to help me stay awake. More than halfway to the airport, I spotted a young man, and something seemed off. I watched as he got off the train, then just as the doors began to close,

Astoux et Brun is my favorite restaurant in Cannes. Be sure to try the *moules* (mussels) and *huîtres chaudes* (hot oysters).

he reappeared and reached in for my phone. I held on with an iron grip. He pulled back, the door closed, and fortunately I still had my phone. Even though I was physically unharmed, save a ripped bag, I was shaken. I kept replaying the incident in my head on the flight back to Rome. I was scared to take the train into the city when I landed, but I had to.

That fear stuck with me for several months. I kept wondering what could be lurking around the corner. I cursed that man for making me feel uncomfortable in my own skin. As someone who lives life freely and does not fear strangers, I was frustrated he stole that sense of security from me. Eventually, the incident no longer haunted me on a daily basis, but I have never again taken the RER B to or from the airport. I never have to be taught the same lesson twice.

Whenever people ask me about dangerous countries, I mention France. I think it offers perspective on other countries that we do tend to write off. France lands on

the top of every must-travel list again and again, yet I have had some of my most harrowing travel experiences there.

Though I never fell in love with the City of Lights, I've been able to see Paris under the hood, thanks to the help of local friends. I toured the charming neighborhood of Le Marais before it was gentrified. I visited Château Rouge, a district imbued with African culture that felt and smelled like a blend of Cotonou, Kinshasa, and Dakar rather than a European capital. Aunties walked around in sandals in late fall, and the sounds of Wolof and Fon filled the air. I spent New Year's Eve dancing in a penthouse overlooking the Eiffel Tower. I ate too many macarons from Ladurée and drank enough champagne for a lifetime.

My last trip to France was to the uber-glamorous French Riviera. This is the part of France I find sublime, with its chic cities and charming small towns. Starting in Nice, my friend Rene and I drove to Cannes in a rented Mercedes—we fit right in! Cannes is an impossibly chic city. At Astoux et Brun we dined on delicious *moules* (mussels) and *huîtres chaudes* (hot oysters). We went to St. Tropez and partied at the trendy beach club, Nikki Beach. The champagne and cocktails were flowing, the people were beautiful, the music was banging, and I was grateful that life could be full of moments like these.

As a lover of champagne, cognac, and luxury fashion, I cannot deny the impact of French culture on my life. And France taught me a truly valuable lesson: After I conquered my first solo trip to Paris, I knew I could survive anything and anywhere.

The iconic Louvre Pyramid, made of glass and metal, was added to the centuries-old museum in 1988.

japan

DISHEARTENED BY THE REALITIES of my corporate job, on February 17, 2008, I lugged three suitcases—two of which were 100 pounds (45 kg) each—to the Detroit airport, ready to board a flight to Japan. Wanting to travel, and always having considered becoming a teacher, I had signed on for a semi-spur-of-the-moment year abroad to teach English and figure out what I wanted to do with the

ASIA

Kyoto's Kiyomizu-dera, which dates back to A.D. 778, is one of the most beautiful temples in the country for experiencing cherry blossom season.

rest of my life. Having heard that toothpaste and deodorant were different in Japan, I packed a year's supply. Hearing that English-language books were expensive and hard to come by, I packed 20 books. I was proud I had only brought 17 pairs of shoes.

Just before leaving, my best friend, keondra, and I got tattoos to celebrate both of our departures from the U.S. The small tattoo to the left of my clavicle is an Adinkra symbol: "Ese Ne Tekrema," or "the teeth and the tongue." It denotes friendship and interdependence. Originally created by the Bono people of Gyaman, a subgroup of the Akan, Adinkra symbols are used throughout Ghana to represent proverbs and maxims. I got this tattoo long before I made it to Ghana and fell in love with the country.

I was distressed when the Northwest Airlines agent told me my suitcases were over the 80-pound (36 kg) weight limit and that I could not pay an overage fee, either. After buying a $10 cardboard box to off-load some of my belongings, my very patient mother and I began the painful process of removing what I thought I could live without. It left me frustrated and rushed to say goodbye to my mother. I didn't know when I would see her again. I was in tears as I made my way to my gate, about to fly to the other side of the globe.

Sweaty and drained from unpacking and repacking and a light jog to the gate, I was one of the last to board the flight. As I walked to seat 34G, I glanced around the plane and noticed no one looked like me. I realized this would be my life for the next year. I was heading to a very homogeneous country—more than 95 percent of the population being ethnically Japanese.

Ohanami, or "flower viewing," is a time of year where people enjoy sakura (cherry blossoms) during their brief period in bloom in spring.

MUST-TASTE: *YAKITORI*

The Japanese know how to do food—very well. Japanese street food is some of the world's best. One of my favorite dishes is *yakitori*, or "grilled bird." Throughout the country you will find the delightful chicken skewered and set to cook over a charcoal grill. At a typical yakitori restaurant, every single part of the chicken is on the menu. I opted out of a few choice pieces. *Yaki onigiri*, a fried rice triangle, is the perfect complement, along with grilled vegetables. Everything is topped with a distinct teriyaki-like sauce.

When I landed in Osaka and looked out the window, I could not read anything. Though I'd familiarized myself with Japanese via Rosetta Stone, I could by no means speak, read, or understand this very foreign language. In countries that use the Roman alphabet, I can often make out words. But this was the land of kanji, katakana, and hiragana, the three writing systems that compose Nihongo, as the language is called in Japanese.

Japan, known as Nippon or Nihon in Nihongo (I still don't understand why we say Japan), is 14 hours ahead of Detroit. As I looked at those indecipherable signs, I realized I was on the opposite side of the world from everything and everyone that I knew, both literally and figuratively.

Following a week of training and Japanese cultural lessons in Okayama, I was sent to my new job in Kusatsu-shi, Shiga-ken, a small suburb outside of Kyoto. Like the rest of the country, it wasn't very diverse. In my year there, I only spotted one other *gaijin*, or foreigner, besides my four co-teachers. I am a Black female, with no hair. To say I was a spectacle wouldn't even begin to convey the shock, awe, and curiosity of students and parents that first month of teaching. Though people were generally respectful, there were lots of stares. I felt like I was in a zoo.

My apartment was small. Rather than a bed, I had a futon—the Japanese version is a thin mattress on the floor. From my kitchen, which was part of a narrow walkway, I could reach into the bathroom and flush the toilet. What I miss most about my flat is the recycling program. On the wall was a clear chart identifying which bin for every single type of waste and a calendar for pickup dates. Fourteen years later, with a climate change crisis looming, I still have yet to see a recycling system such as this.

The first few times I went into a grocery store, I was overwhelmed. Very little was in English. I used the pocket translator my mother had given me to find what I needed. At checkout, I never took off my headphones because I couldn't understand the cashier.

Japan, the land of brands like Muji, Uniqlo, Bape, and Toyota, was so . . . Japanese. The local Italian restaurant was a Japanese take on Italian, which I eventually came to love. Starbucks had a size smaller than the American tall to meet more familiar serving sizes. And the cell phones! Japan has always been ahead of the tech curve: In 2008, contact information was beamed from one cell phone to another—like AirDropping today—no need to type anything. And the Japanese gave us our beloved emojis (the first of which—a smiling poop emoji—I received while living there). Most people even had cell phone jewelry, as I called it—little charms that hung from the top of their phones. I still have several of my own, some in unopened packages.

When you live in a foreign country that maintains its culture as strongly as Japan does, your mannerisms change; you adjust. I learned to sit comfortably on the floor with my legs folded underneath me for an hour. I began bowing at appropriate times without having to think. I knew how to use chopsticks before I arrived, but after one year I could proudly pick up single grains of rice. To get around town, I bought an orange bicycle. No matter the weather, I would take it out, bag in basket and headphones in ears. I even mastered riding with an umbrella in hand when it rained, just like the Japanese.

I took so much pleasure watching my students grow over that

When I left Japan at the end of my yearlong contract, each of my students gave me notes and drawings, all of which I still have today.

Though the souvenir shops were all closed when I visited the city of Obama, I managed to barter with this young man for his shirt.

year. The youngest, at six months, did not speak at all when I started. By the time I left, they had several English words in their vocabulary. I became close with other students, namely Rio and Seina, who wiped my tears with her sleeve when I said goodbye, and Taiga, named after Tiger Woods. Etsuko and Miki, two of my adult students, quickly became friends.

One of the best parts of living abroad is the access it gives you to explore nearby places. I spent my weekends in the closest cities, Kyoto and Osaka. Stunning Kyoto is still an absolute favorite: On its charming narrow streets you can spot a geisha in iconic white makeup, perfectly coiffed hair, a bright and custom-fit kimono, and traditional slippers that lead to a shuffle rather than a stride. The streets are lined with traditional wooden Japanese homes, each with sliding doors and paper lanterns.

I explored as many of Kyoto's 2,000 temples and shrines as I could. Kiyomizu-dera, one of my favorites, sits atop a hill offering stunning views across the eastern portion of the city. Its name means "pure water," an homage to the complex's waterfall that spills in three streams, each one offering a different benefit to drinkers. It is most glorious during *hanami,* the cherry blossom season. I got a tattoo of two sakuras, the quintessential Japanese flower, to honor my time in the country.

Just a 49-minute train ride away from Kusatsu, Osaka was where I spent weekends partying. I sang at *nomihodai* (all-you-can-drink) karaoke; spent late nights turned early mornings at Onzieme, where my friend David, a lawyer and DJ, was spinning; had drinks at Club Life (owned by a Nigerian named Chuks who let me DJ once); spent nights in capsule hotels when I missed the last train home; and drank Chu-Hi (a canned alcoholic drink) from the *combini* (convenience store).

You're probably wondering about Tokyo. I went a few times, but I didn't love it. It was like Times Square on steroids. I did, however, thoroughly enjoy some other uniquely Japanese experiences: I climbed Mount Fuji in the middle of the night and watched the sun rise from above the clouds. I had Kobe beef in Kobe on my birthday. The beef was so tender it tasted like butter melting in my mouth, but the portion was so small that I went to McDonald's afterward. I visited Hiroshima, which was heartbreaking; played with deer in Nara; and spent time on a beach on the Sea of Japan, where summer temps made the water feel like a hot tub.

The flip side to living abroad, and traveling in general, is all the stuff you miss back home. Though I never felt homesick, I missed my

WHAT COLOR IS AN EGGPLANT?

One day as I was talking through hiccups, I gave a class summary to one of my student's parents. Via my co-worker, who was serving as translator, the mom asked, "What color is an eggplant?" I thought it was a random question but assumed she wanted to know the name of the color in English. I responded, "Purple." She then asked if my hiccups were gone. Magically, they had disappeared. Now whenever someone has hiccups, I ask them, "What color is an eggplant?"

My colleagues made *takoyaki* (octopus balls), a famous Japanese street food, at my house one evening.

friends and family. At times, the language barrier made me feel like I was living in a void. I remember sitting on a train and wondering what the passengers were talking about. I had forgotten what people say to each other in public! It took until I learned the Japanese language and could talk to taxi drivers and other people I met more easily that the world opened up to me. Until then, it often felt isolating.

This was years before FaceTime and long before international text messaging was affordable or the invention of WhatsApp. I had to talk to people in the mornings, when the 14-hour time difference worked in our favor. Before I left, my mom bought a camera to prop on her computer so we could video-chat. I ultimately started my first blog just so people at home could see and read about what I was doing.

International travel wasn't as common then—and Japan was far from home. The only people who visited me while I was abroad were my mom and sister. They came for Thanksgiving. We invited my Japanese colleagues over for a Thanksgiving dinner of sorts—they brought *takoyaki* (octopus balls) and my mom made spaghetti and tacos. It was the perfect dichotomy of my American and Japanese lives, and nice for both my family and Japanese friends to experience it with me.

One of my few regrets living in Japan was that I wasn't in the U.S. when Barack Obama won the presidency. I tried to celebrate from afar: I took a picture in the Japanese post office of the man holding my ready-to-mail ballot to mark the historic moment. Between classes on election night (daytime for me), I kept running to the computer to check the results. But my celebration was contained to a small dinner alone and a single glass of wine. I'm thankful that social media wasn't as big at the time—the FOMO would have destroyed me.

I did get my own unique Obama experience, though, when a few friends and I visited the beaches in Obama—yes, that is the real name of the city. Excited to share the name with the world's most famous politician of our generation, the city was proudly producing Obama-related souvenirs. Unfortunately, we visited on a Sunday when stores were closed. But I spotted a young man in an Obama shirt. I take pride in both talking to strangers and haggling, so I cheekily asked to trade his shirt for my white tank top. Surprisingly, he agreed! My Japanese life was full of unexpected adventures.

Japan is where I first learned to explore a country fully and deeply. Where I purposefully sought authentic experiences rather than just the tourist hot spots. Where I freely roamed off the beaten path. I discovered happiness in solitude. I began to love my life, which was more carefree and less stressful.

Ultimately, Japan helped me realize there was nothing to fear in being away from home for a long time. I decided to get past any fears and dream big. To find new and amazing experiences. Uninterested in returning to the typical American nine-to-five and ready to see more of the world, I decided I wanted to live outside the U.S. for at least three years; that three turned into seven. Inspired by my Ugandan background and desire to improve the lives of people in poorer countries, I entered into the master's program for international development at the London School of Economics.

But I had seven months between Japan and London—a good window to visit a number of countries, including Australia, Fiji, and Costa Rica, among others. As my globe-trotting began, people kept asking me, "Where are you now?" and comparing me to Carmen Sandiego. Inspired by their questions, I launched my blog, The Catch Me If You Can, and began writing about my adventures around the world. My life on the road (or in a plane) had really just begun.

I spent many weekends enjoying Osaka. Pictured here is Dotonbori, a tourist attraction known for its bright lights and entertainment options.

honduras

ONE OF MY FIRST TRIPS BETWEEN living in Japan and moving to London for grad school was to Honduras. Though some of the other destinations I planned to make it to before grad school would have been closer to Japan, I had already planned a trip to visit my childhood friend, Elton, in Miami, Florida, for his birthday. Timing worked out that he found a $69 Spirit Airlines deal to Honduras scheduled to depart around

NORTH
AMERICA

The waters of Roatán's West Bay Beach are bright blue and flanked by lush mountains. It instantly became one of my favorites beaches in the world.

the time of my visit. He asked if I'd join him. Uh, duh! That trip was the first of our global adventures; we subsequently visited 30 countries together.

I charged Elton with the planning duties, a decision I later regretted. Our flight was scheduled to land in San Pedro Sula after 2 a.m. At the Fort Lauderdale airport, I asked Elton where we would be staying, only to be met by a look on his face that said, "Eeek." As we stood in line to board our plane, he hastily booked a hostel. I am not a fan of hostels, generally speaking, but we had to take what we could get. What we got was a shabby private room with no warm water. Thus began a series of unfortunate events.

When I mentioned that I was looking for a little more luxury, someone at the hostel recommended a place in the countryside and pointed us to the bus station. After a few hours on the bus, we realized that we had missed our stop. The bus driver kindly dropped us on the side of the road, leaving us to find a ride back in the other direction. After just a few minutes, a local bus that looked like a typical yellow American school bus picked us up. We stood out like sore thumbs among the locals and several chickens aboard.

Dropped off in another town, we found a taxi. The first resort was fully booked, and along the way to another resort, the taxi broke down—*yes, this really happened.* A man passing by happily offered to take us to a hotel that he built and ran with his wife. We breathed a sigh of relief and hopped in his van, only to arrive at what I would call a "two-star" hotel. It was rustic and run-down, not a place I was eager

The colors of Honduras—from the multihued buildings to the murals painted on their walls—drew me in immediately.

to stay. I lost it. I am not an incredibly patient person, but up until then, I had rolled with all the bloody punches—a cold shower to start the day, the ill-fated bus ride, the chickens, and a broken-down taxi. I put my foot down. I demanded luxury.

The proprietor was not thrilled but nonetheless handed us the Yellow Pages—remember those? We reached a hotel on an island called Roatán and were told to head to the dock, where we could catch the ferry. We wasted no time. On the dock, we bought delicious fish burritos from a food stand before boarding the ferry.

I'd been on boats in choppy water before, unaffected even as people around me hung their heads over the side. The ferry to Roatán, however, was a different story. Before the boat even began to move, an attendant handed everyone a barf bag. When he came to me, I said, "No gracias," but he insisted.

Let me be clear: This boat ride was a torture chamber developed by the devil himself. It was the choppiest boat ride I have ever taken (the ride between Cartagena and Islas del Rosario in Colombia is a close second). Barely 10 minutes in, people were putting their barf bags to good use. At the 15-minute mark, Elton left me for the tiny ferry bathroom: The burritos did not agree with him, nor did the boat. A pregnant woman was crying and ill, vowing to take a tiny plane back to the mainland. A gentleman behind me sat completely unfazed; he lived on the island and was used to seeing the horrific scene unfolding on the boat. My own stomach was dropping a bit, like I was on a roller coaster. I spent the last hour of the ride with my head between my legs. But I did manage to keep the burritos in my belly.

Though getting there was horrific, Roatán was a literal paradise. An island off the northern coast of Honduras, Roatán is mountainous, lush, and has some of the bluest waters I have ever seen. The second we disembarked, all of the day's annoyances melted away.

We made the most of our short time on the island. I went ziplining for the first time. We went snorkeling, too. Roatán has the best underwater beauty in the world, as it is located near the Mesoamerican Barrier Reef, the second largest on Earth. The crystal clear warm waters of the Caribbean Sea gave us a front-row seat to nature's marvels. The scene just beneath the surface was full of thriving coral reefs and schools of fish in nearly every color of the rainbow.

Though our time in Roatán was magical, the trip to Honduras was my first and last attempt at backpacking. Trying to be easy-breezy and convenient, I had only packed a regular-size backpack for the trip. I realized early on that if backpacking meant crappy hostels, local buses, and only eating street food, it wasn't the life for me.

After a series of unfortunate events, I was able to find a few good moments of relaxation on our unplanned visit to the beautiful Caribbean island of Roatán.

My return from Honduras marked my first negative run-in with American immigration officials. We arrived in Fort Lauderdale so early in the morning that the immigration office wasn't even open. After waiting on our plane for nearly an hour, I approached the immigration window and gave the woman a very chipper—for 5 a.m.—"Good morning!" After receiving a less than joyful response, I said, "Or not good morning." Though we had been on the same exact trip, Elton went through immigration easily and quickly exited the airport. I, however, was sent to a secondary inspection—a first for me. When I asked why, no one gave me a response. I wondered if it had been my cheery greeting that set off alarm bells. During the inspection, officers went through my backpack and asked me a barrage of questions, including "How did you pay for the trip?" "Why did you travel for only three days?" and "Why do you only have a backpack?" I replied, "I have money in the bank," "Because that's how long I wanted to go," and "Because I was only gone for three days." When they found nothing in my bags, I was finally on my way.

Turkey

VISITING A PLACE I KNOW little about is one of my favorite ways to travel. It allows for so many surprises. But with the advent of social media, international tourism skyrocketing thanks to Instagram, and low-cost international flights, it is now nearly impossible to visit a country completely blind. We are constantly bombarded with images of influencers in the most popular tourist attractions, present company

included. Things were very different in 2009; it feels like several lifetimes ago. I had been living in London for three months, attending grad school at the London School of Economics, when four friends and I decided to take a trip to Egypt and Istanbul for our December break. I hadn't yet set the goal of being the first Black woman to visit every country in the world, but living abroad had secured my sense of wanderlust. Though Istanbul was not high on my list, I was open.

I had never been to the region, so I was excited. Having not traveled to many places in the world, I was open to going everywhere and seeing anything. At the time, I did not know much about Turkey other than the glory of Constantinople (present-day Istanbul) and döner kebab, the delightful snack that had been perfect for soaking up alcohol after late London nights.

The historic city of Istanbul, Turkey's largest city and the country's economic center, straddles the Bosporus, the strait that forms the continental boundary between Europe and Asia. Istanbul is firmly planted in both continents. Once one of the most important cities on the Silk Road, Istanbul's location has contributed to its greatness and wealth. More than 13 million visitors travel to Istanbul each year, making it one of the most visited cities in the world.

The architecture of Istanbul is a mash-up of its Ottoman and Byzantine roots, seen in the intricate and colorful tiles, the typical arches on buildings, the skilled ironwork on many doors, the stained glass windows shedding colorful light in rooms, and the Arabic calligraphy that is a significant part of interior decor.

ASIA

From a small window inside of the Hagia Sophia, there's a clear view of Istanbul's iconic Sultan Ahmed Mosque, better known as the Blue Mosque.

Istanbul is also a place where all of the tourist hot spots are actually worth visiting. And that's exactly where we spent our time. The Grand Bazaar is one of the largest and oldest covered markets in the world. Its construction began in the 1400s under the Ottoman Empire. The 330,000-square-foot (30,658 m²) market teases all of your senses. The colorful ceramics please the eyes, aromas from all the spices tickle the nose, and the buzz of different languages colliding tantalizes the eardrums. As I ran my hand over fabrics of various materials, I began negotiating with a vendor who offered me a delicious apple tea.

The many vendors in the Grand Bazaar have to be creative to get you to choose their stalls over the others. The following were all actually yelled at us as we walked by: "Everything is free today!" "How can I help you spend your money?" "I want to sell you fake stuff!" "I want to sell you things you don't need!" Although none of the attempts were effective, they definitely made for a fun afternoon.

Then there is the Hagia Sophia. Initially built as a Christian church in A.D. 537, it was the world's largest indoor space at the time of its completion. For centuries, it stood as the largest cathedral in the world. In 1453, after the Ottoman Empire conquered the city, it was converted into a mosque. In 1935, it was made into a museum. In 2020, it was converted back into a mosque (but you can still visit). Unfortunately, our visit in 2009 coincided with construction—and huge scaffolding—right in the middle of the building. While we could not get a true sense of the space, what we experienced more than sufficed. The beauty of the Hagia Sophia is in its conversion from a Christian to an Islamic space. On the walls of the dome, the Christian mosaics are juxtaposed with large disks illustrated with calligraphic Arabic text—it's nearly impossible to separate Islam from Christianity. I found beauty in the harmony between these religions in such a distinguished space.

Turkey was also the first country where it was made clear, through stares and people asking for pictures, that many locals had never interacted with Black people. Sure, I stood out in Japan, but people wouldn't ask for a picture or yell things at me like "Obama" or "Halle Berry" as they did in Istanbul. Even in the grandeur of the Hagia Sophia, a group

The Spice Bazaar of Istanbul dates back to the 1660s; it has 85 shops selling spices, Turkish delight, dried fruits, nuts, and more.

of Turkish high school students excitedly asked to take pictures with me and my friend Jahmil.

While the Hagia Sophia is renowned, the majestic Sultan Ahmed Mosque, better known as the Blue Mosque, is the crown jewel of Istanbul. Completed in 1616, the mosque boasts five main domes, eight secondary domes, and six minarets, all of which can be seen from many spots throughout the city. Its nickname comes from the hand-painted blue tiles adorning the interior walls. The Blue Mosque was the first mosque I ever visited. I remember being surprised that we had to cover our heads and remove our shoes. Its beauty inspired me to visit mosques in all of the Muslim countries I have visited since.

At the airport for our flight back to London, I had a run-in with immigration that still makes me chuckle. I had shaved my head to travel, but I had hair in my passport picture. The first Turkish immigration officer looked at my passport, then at me, then the passport, then me, then back to the passport. Confused, he called in someone else who performed the same perplexed examination. When a third officer was comparing real me to passport me, I made a different face every time he looked up. I could have been annoyed with the whole ordeal, but I chose to find the humor in it all. The three of them eventually agreed I was, in fact, me—and I was on my way.

The Hagia Sophia has remnants of both its Christian and Islamic roots, as seen in the Christian mosaics and Arabic script.

egypt

SOME PLACES IN THE WORLD BELONG
on the bucket lists of everyone—all 7.8 billion of us. Although the Great Pyramid of Khufu makes the list of Seven Wonders of the Ancient World, the entire country of Egypt is bucket list–worthy. Following our trip to Istanbul, my friends and I spent six days in Egypt, but it feels like I've only dipped a toe in its wonders. As young children, we all learn about

Egypt, and the images of its architecture vary only slightly across centuries. Its mysticism feels as real in person as it does in history books.

The trip, though, didn't start out that way. As we made our way to the center of Cairo, my hopes were dimmed by the grungy and run-down feeling in the heart of the city's downtown. Cairo is densely populated. Because it was very early on in my travels, I had never been to such a place. I was a bit shocked. To top it off, as broke graduate students, we stayed in a hostel I can only describe as a very "two-star" experience. But nothing about the rest of the trip let me down.

Egypt is an easy country to navigate. It has catered to tourism for an extensive period of time and offers plenty of guided tours. But my friends and I easily figured things out on our own.

From Cairo, you can see the Pyramids at Giza, which date back to 2600 B.C. I still don't understand how they were built without modern technology. I know enslaved people were involved, and a significant loss of life, but the feat is incomprehensible, especially after seeing them firsthand.

Our Giza pyramid adventure started early in the morning, on the outskirts of the capital city. We traveled by camelback to get better and more varied views. I was flabbergasted as we passed a small soccer field with the famed structures as a backdrop. People play soccer with the pyramids *right there* overlooking their game. No big deal.

You cannot grasp the pyramids' full magnitude until you are standing face-to-face with these unreal structures.

AFRICA

The oldest and largest of the Pyramids at Giza, also known as the Great Pyramid of Khufu, dates back to 2600 B.C.

The Mortuary Temple of Hatshepsut, in Luxor's Valley of the Kings, is a masterpiece of ancient architecture.

No matter how many pictures you've seen of the pyramids, nothing can prepare you for seeing them up close. We are minuscule compared to them. The Great Pyramid of Khufu was originally 484 feet (148 m) tall, but over time the original limestone casing was removed to bring it to its present height of 454 feet (138 m). It is built of approximately 2.3 million blocks made of a mixture of limestone, granite, and mortar. Although the limestone was mined fairly close to Giza, the granite came from Aswan, more than 560 miles (900 km) upstream. Again, how? On the lowest level of the pyramid, the stones are just shy of five feet (1.5 m) tall. The sheer size, accuracy of measurements, and engineering acumen is enough to leave my head spinning more than a decade after visiting.

To visit the Pyramids at Giza is to understand the great wealth of the pharaohs of ancient Egypt. Unfortunately, European pillaging has taken much of the riches outside of the country. At the Egyptian Museum, we were met with small placards that noted the foreign museums that held many of the country's ancient artifacts. It felt problematic that I traveled all the way to Egypt to see the pyramids, but I would have to travel to London and New York to see the best items from their chambers. (Fortunately, at the time of writing this in 2021, many artifacts have been returned, and the most coveted items will no longer leave the country.)

The Sphinx, perched on the west bank of the Nile, was equally impressive. While sites like these are often overrun with tourists, the experience of seeing these architectural feats in person is unmatched and worth the crowds. It was truly like a dream.

Aside from the pyramids, we visited Coptic Cairo, an area of the capital that remains predominantly Christian and is home to eight churches, including the famous Hanging Church, so named because it was built on top of the gate to a Roman fortress. Portions of the church date back to the third century.

As a lover of markets, I could not leave Cairo without visiting Khan el-Khalili, the oldest market in the Middle East and the main spot today for handmade gifts and all your shopping needs. Our guide told me that it is the area of the world where the most languages are spoken in a single place. If you consider that people visit Cairo from all corners of the globe and the sellers are very motivated to appeal to shoppers in their native tongues, it is a plausible assertion. We zigzagged through the stalls as men yelled "My African sister," trying to sell me their wares.

From Cairo, we headed south to the city of Luxor. The fastest way to make the journey is by plane, but limited funds dictated our trip. We bought a travel package for about $90 that included a "first-class"

MUST-EAT:
FALAFEL

Falafel is found throughout North Africa and the Middle East, but it is thought to have originated in Egypt as early as the fourth century. Typically, falafel is made of chickpeas, though here it is made from fava beans and flavored with spices like coriander and cumin. It can be eaten plain or placed in a pita with tomato, onions, and tahini. When I was in Egypt, each sandwich cost roughly 20 cents, perfect for those on a budget like we were at the time.

As we set sail for a felucca ride on the Nile, a local man worked to ensure that the wind would catch the sails.

train ticket, a hotel, and a guide in Luxor. I learned to travel on a budget as a grad student. When we got to our train cabin, we were shocked by what they considered the best accommodations. The 14-hour overnight ride on the old, dirty, and smelly train was miserable.

The ancient city of Luxor was a stark contrast to our transportation. This is the home of the city of Thebes, the Valleys of the Kings and Queens, and the temple complex at Karnak, among other ancient Egyptian sites. In the Valley of the Kings, we saw its most famous resident, King Tut, whose mummified remains were on display in his tomb (they've since been moved to the new Grand Egyptian Museum). With all of the meticulously preserved monuments, temples, and tombs, it is no wonder that Luxor is often considered the world's largest open-air museum. The expansive beauty of the temple ruins at Karnak left me in awe. It made me realize how small I am and how extensive time is.

We visited in December and spent long, hot days touring the monuments—emphasis on *hot*. To cool down, we took a sunset cruise on a felucca, a traditional Egyptian boat. On the banks of the Nile, you will see dozens of feluccas whose operators will jump at the opportunity to take you for a cruise. After a little price negotiation, we boarded our vessel and enjoyed the slow pace and cool breeze as the sun turned the sky orange before disappearing below the horizon.

My visit to Egypt in 2009 was as magical as you can imagine. While some things never change (like the pyramids), I think a lot has changed culturally throughout Egypt since I first saw it. I visited pre–Arab Spring, and as I reflect on the trip now, I realize we only interacted with one woman—our guide in Luxor—during our six days in the country. Though I never felt uncomfortable traveling as a woman in Egypt, it was just the first of many places where I had to be comfortable being one of the few.

Two years after completing my journey, I continued to wonder how Egypt had changed since I first saw it. In December 2021, I got the opportunity to visit Egypt again. Two years after completing my journey around the world, this was a real vacation. In fact, it was the most relaxing trip I've had in my life. In part, I could thank the relief of the stress I had often felt to make it onto the next country and meet my goal. But through my years of travel I also learned a valuable lesson: You don't have to see and do everything while you're in a new place. You can always go back. You can try again.

For example, my friends and I landed in Cairo and I opted out of a tour of the pyramids. I was exhausted, and I chose to skip the pyramids for the sake of rest, for the health of my mind and body.

From Cairo, we flew to Luxor and boarded a small luxury cruise ship—no more grad student budget for me—for a trip along the Nile. I feel deeply connected to the Nile—its source is in Uganda and I have seen its waters in all the countries that it runs through, except for Ethiopia. Along the cruise we stopped at various monuments and ruins. Again, I opted to join or skip based on what my body needed. And just like that first trip to Egypt, as I stood among these centuries-old structures, I found it incomprehensible how people could build such impressive and perfect buildings without modern technology. I was overwhelmed by the sheer genius of the Egyptian people. I don't think I will ever not be awed by the wonders of Egypt, no matter how many times I visit.

In Luxor, we saw hundreds of feluccas, traditional wooden sailing boats, along the shores and in the Nile.

croatia

CROATIA WAS THE 22ND COUNTRY I traveled to but my first in the Balkans. As a grad school student with little disposable income, I chose to maximize my dollars and booked a ticket on a low-cost European airline, tolerating the cattle herd–like boarding, limited luggage options, and bombarding advertisements over the PA system. I didn't get so much as a free cup of water. I arrived in Split to beautiful summer weather

EUROPE

with my then boyfriend—I'll call him the Italian—whom I'd met in my master's program in London. We went on to explore 12 countries together.

Split is a beautiful city on the coast of the Adriatic Sea that is buzzing with life in the summer. It is home to one of the most impressive Roman monuments in the world, Diocletian's Palace. We spent time ambling along the atmospheric old walls of the city and gazing out at the islands just offshore. We decided to visit one of those islands—Brač, less than an hour away by ferry—for a night. The Italian, *of course,* wanted to rent a scooter to see as much of the island as possible. Though the third largest island in the Adriatic Sea, Brač has a quaint, small-town feel. The locals welcomed us at every turn. The mussels were always fresh and the wine always chilled.

Back in Split, we rented a car, which is the best and easiest way to explore Croatia and its neighboring countries. A three-and-a-half-hour drive southeast of Split lies Dubrovnik, which is one of Europe's most stunning cities. The idyllic, walled metropolis on the Adriatic Sea boasts beautiful alleyways, scrumptious seafood, and the backdrop to *Game of Thrones* (more on that in just a bit).

It's worth noting that if you visit you should be prepared for a workout. The city is hilly. Later, on my second visit to Dubrovnik, I am *pretty* sure we climbed 25,000 stairs to get back to our rental home.

In Dubrovnik, even the most touristy parts of the city offer fresh seafood. But once you start climbing the stairs and visiting smaller,

somewhat hidden restaurants, you'll find the really good stuff. One such restaurant was LAJK, a family-owned operation named after the first letter of each family member's name—Luka, Alan, Jasmina, and Karlo. We were so thrilled by the food at lunch, a perfectly seared tuna and asparagus risotto, that we accepted Alan's invitation for dinner the following day.

After that first, quiet visit to Dubrovnik, it was shocking when I visited again in 2017. The city was very crowded thanks to a boom in tourism. But crowds and all, my second visit was epic, mostly because of a *Game of Thrones* tour. If you have not watched *GOT,* as it is lovingly known, skip this paragraph, stop reading this book, and dedicate 67 hours of your life to the first seven seasons of the greatest television show ever made. Because I love you: Do not watch the eighth and final season, better known as the biggest letdown in television history.

Dubrovnik is the set of the show's fictional city, King's Landing. The two-hour walking tour took us to each of the 16 set locations. My favorite moment was walking the steps Cersei Lannister descended during her infamous walk of shame: "Shame, shame, shame."

The popularity of *GOT* is one of the many reasons Croatia has become a tourism hot spot. It has become such a popular destination that the country has even retired its famous slogan, "The Mediterranean as it once was." Even still, strolling through its cobblestone streets, you can't help but feel transported to a different, more peaceful time.

The iconic city of Dubrovnik is the setting of King's Landing in the television show *Game of Thrones*.

montenegro

WHEN WE ARRIVED IN THE Adriatic beach town of Budva, I quickly learned that Montenegro is the holiday destination for Serbians and Russians. Being only the second country I had visited in eastern Europe, I was completely shocked by how I was received. As soon as the Italian and I dropped our bags at our hotel, we eagerly made our way to the small rocky beach just in front of Budva's Old Town.

EUROPE

I hadn't seen another Black person in Montenegro, though that wasn't uncommon during my travels. But on the beach, I became acutely aware of my Blackness. As I removed my cover-up and revealed my very dark skin and my lime green swimsuit, I felt like everyone on the beach was staring at me. This was only country 23 of 195, and I was not yet used to being gawked at incessantly during my travels. Since visiting Montenegro I have been stared at more times than I can count. But this time was jarring, perhaps more so because I was in a swimsuit.

A young girl approached me and began talking in English. Sensing my obvious displeasure, she quipped, "I just want to practice my English." When I stood up to take pictures of the Italian, a woman put her baby in my arms and her husband sidled up next to me. Before I could even react, she took a picture. Somewhere in the world is a photo of me holding a white baby with a look of pure shock on my face.

Even though the stares seemed more out of curiosity than malice or racism, I asked the Italian if we could leave after about 20 minutes. We exchanged our beach day for a day of exploring the Old Town. But the following day, I decided to ignore the staring and enjoy the beach. It was an early travel lesson that I still carry with me: I chose to be comfortable in my own skin and wouldn't let anyone take that away from me. Stares be damned.

Our days in Budva were relaxed. We strolled the cobblestone streets and wandered among the stone buildings of Old Town, enjoyed the cool waters of the Adriatic Sea, and dined on deliciously fresh seafood dinners. I am a lover of fish and will typically choose it over meat, but

I am a little particular. At one spot, as a full menu of fish lay before me, I watched the Italian hilariously explain to the waiter that I did not want "fishy fish" for dinner. Considering the language barrier, I was happily surprised when my beautiful, whole fresh fish arrived and was not fishy but perfectly seasoned and grilled.

There's fresh seafood, and then there's *fresh* seafood. After an afternoon boat trip to explore the caves and rock formations just off the coast, the Italian noticed sea urchins on the walls close to the dock. He hopped in the water and scraped off a couple, handing them to me one by one. Horrified and tickled, having never seen one in person, I placed the black spiny creatures carefully on the ground. The Italian cracked one open and ate the bloodred, fleshy meat inside as I tried to keep from vomiting. I like fresh seafood, but I decided to pass on the just-out-of-the-water urchin.

I found myself back in the tiny Balkan country eight years later on a short visit, during which we stopped for lunch at a random roadside restaurant, Troja. If you visit, you must try the fish and meat platter, and most important, the house-made red wine—full-bodied and delicious. Tell them I sent you—maybe they will remember me!

Though my first experience in Montenegro was one of my earliest racialized vacation memories, the country still retains a sweet spot in my heart. The kindness of the people, freshness of the seafood, and beauty of the coast outweighed the stares.

UNEXPECTED LESSONS

You never know what lessons you'll learn while traveling, and shortly after crossing from Croatia into Montenegro, I had a surprising revelation. My period made a guest appearance that led the Italian and I to the nearest pharmacy. To my surprise, none of the tampons had applicators. That first experience with an applicator-free tampon ended up changing a lifelong habit, reducing the amount of waste I produce every month. Ultimately, it led me one step closer to ridding my life of single-use plastics, an effort I am incredibly passionate about after seeing firsthand the damage plastic has done to our planet.

On the border of Albania and Montenegro lies the gorgeously lush Lake Skadar, the largest lake in southern Europe.

benin

BENIN IS ONE OF THOSE COUNTRIES that many people have never heard of. I lived there for six months. Though I typically spend three months a year between the 54 countries in Africa, this was the only time I have ever lived on the African continent. Benin is so unknown that I find it easier to say, "I lived in West Africa," rather than call it by name. A narrow strip of land wedged between Togo and its more popular

neighbor, Nigeria, Benin was once a powerful kingdom in the region. Vodou (derived from the Fon word for "God," transliterated to "voo-doo" in English) originated here.

So, of all the countries in Africa, how did I end up in Benin? Throughout the school year at the London School of Economics I had applied to nearly 40 jobs, but I found myself with no offers and no plans after submitting my dissertation. Then, while we were on vacation in Croatia, the Italian asked me to join him in rural Benin, where he had been offered an internship with an Italian nongovern-mental organization (NGO). Side note: I remember exactly where we were on this vacation so clearly because it is where I saw the Italian cry (yes, shed actual tears) while watching Italy lose in the World Cup. (As an American, I am not sure I will ever understand the global emotional attachment to soccer.) Being offered the role at the NGO, and inviting me to join him, was a real win for him after such a heartbreaking loss. With nothing to do and nowhere to go, I said yes. Though the details were sketchy at best, the organization offered me an internship as well.

We arrived in Cotonou to oppressive heat in November 2010. While Cotonou is not the capital—that is Porto-Novo—it is the seat of govern-ment, economic center, and most populated city in Benin. The plan was to travel around the country with a group—eight Italians and me—until we landed in Dassa-Zoumé, our home for the next few months.

AFRICA

A young boy steers his boat around Ganvie, a village in Lake Nokoué, near Cotonou. The vil-lage of more than 30,000 resi-dents is built entirely on stilts.

Driving through the streets of Cotonou brought back nostalgic memories of Uganda. Out the window, we watched the hustle and bustle of Beninese life. But I was quickly confronted with the realities of being in an African country with non-Africans. I cringed as some of our companions took pictures and squealed with delight as they watched ladies walk down the streets with large, heavy baskets on their heads and babies on their backs. For days they kept up their pointing and shooting, treating people like objects of amusement and tourism. Though I wasn't the subject of their lens, these were my people, and they were being treated as if they were in a zoo. I couldn't help but smile when a group of fishermen angrily protested having their picture taken.

At one of our dinners, an Italian priest who lived in Cotonou said to my boyfriend, with a nudge of his arm, "I see you already found one." Knowing he was talking about me, the Italian promptly replied, "She's American." The shameless priest didn't even apologize.

We spent hours and hours playing with kids at a huge orphanage supported by the NGO we would be working for, and in the small town of Lokossa, we visited a rehabilitation center for children who had corrective surgery for ill-developed limbs. Although both experiences were eye-opening and no doubt had an impact on the children, I didn't continue to do this in future travels. Because I believe in travel equality, it didn't feel right visiting orphanages around the continent of Africa when I don't do the same in the United States, Europe, or Asia.

Our home base was Dassa-Zoumé, a small town roughly 125 miles (200 km) north of Cotonou. It is a journey that can take between three and a half to six hours, depending on the mode of transportation and hazards on the road.

Dassa is known for the pilgrimage site Grotte Notre-Dame d'Arigbo, where the Virgin Mary is said to have appeared. We lived in a small lodge managed by nuns from a nearby convent. We had no hot water, but we did have running water and electricity, which was five-star living in that part of the country. Life in Dassa took some getting used to. We barely had internet, and when we did it was impossibly slow. Before dinner, we would open 10 *New York Times* pages and a Napoli football club video on YouTube in hopes that they would be loaded by the time we

I met this little girl on my third day living in Benin, and every time I look at this image, the joy in her face radiates in my soul.

finished cooking. I was trying to keep up with my blog, The Catch Me If You Can, but couldn't add images to my blog posts because the connection was so bad.

For five months I lived the mundaneness of life in rural Benin. We studied French and read a lot. We watched, and rewatched, the first few seasons of *Modern Family,* which had been (thankfully) loaded to my hard drive by a friend. We hand-washed our clothes (only months later did we learn the nuns had a washing machine); ate baguettes and La Vache qui rit—the Laughing Cow—cheese for breakfast; and six days a week we ate the same lunch, prepared by the same woman, at Maquis La Marmite Africaine—*poulet bicyclette* (local "bicycle" chicken) and *riz blanc avec sauce de tomate* (white rice with tomato sauce). It was always a treat when she had *alloco* (fried plantains).

Adjusting to life in Dassa also meant dealing with the constant presence of bugs. I used to throw away food that had a single ant or fly on it. Since living in Dassa, I just pick out stray bugs and keep eating.

Zims (motorcycle taxis) were the best way to travel, though navigating around potholes and riding on dusty roads made the experience quite different from leisurely rides on the back of a scooter in the streets of Rome. Blackouts occurred every single day. The

In rural Benin, I lived in a small guesthouse (seen on the right side of this image) that was run by nuns.

cold showers were the hardest to adjust to—I'm used to taking showers so hot that others can't tolerate the temperature.

The repetitiveness of life in Benin was interrupted only by major events, like the time the oven used to make baguettes broke down. Baguettes were a staple in Dassa—a colonial leftover from France's invasion of Dahomey—and an important factor in many household incomes. Roughly 30 percent of food sold in the market was the perfectly crafted mix of a crusty exterior and soft interior. On the day the oven broke down, a few entrepreneurial young men took zims to a baguette producer a few towns north. The price of baguettes was inflated for a week.

Baguette crisis aside, I found myself missing comforts of home. I wrote a blog post listing the things I missed most: manicures and pedicures, hot showers, cooler temperatures (meaning something below 90°F/32°C), and various foods. But most of all I missed a social life. While I enjoyed my time with the Italian living and working together, I am a social butterfly. Benin made me aware of how much I missed my community, my friends, and family.

My work at the NGO was interesting. Here I was, a recent graduate of the London School of Economics, with a social science degree, auditing three different projects. I uncovered that an unexplained 10,000 euros had been spent in only two months and that nearly 3,000 euros were missing. It was clear that the person leading the project was mismanaging funds.

I was tasked with creating a new budget and new accounting system, implementing new projects, and fixing the old ones. That December, we could only pay the staff their salaries, nothing more. That meant some children who were expecting money to buy breakfast wouldn't receive it. Many nights I questioned how I got myself into this situation. But just as many nights I was thankful for a firsthand look at why development in Africa is so stagnant.

Outside of work, I found that being an expat in a country of all Black people is complicated. On the one hand, I can move about undetected, without people constantly asking for money as they do with white people. In Benin, I was regularly spoken to in Fon, the local language. Sometimes locals did double takes, realizing something about me was off but unable to put their finger on it. Although I loved being left alone, I was often annoyed by the lack of respect I received and the elevated status of white people, called *yavou* in Fon.

I was often in situations where I was completely ignored while the white people around me were greeted with slight curtsies and

THE MATCHSTICK TRICK

Whenever we had the luxury of vegetables in Dassa-Zoumé, we added onions or tomatoes to our daily pasta. One day while I was cutting onions, my eyes teared up from the sting. Before I knew what was happening, one of the nuns stuffed a matchstick in my mouth. She explained that it helps when cutting onions. I thought it was ridiculous, but I respect my elders and kept the matchstick in place. Of course, she was right. It worked. Amazingly well. Now every time I cut an onion, I put a matchstick between my lips, with the firemaking side on the outside of course.

My Beninese colleagues and I hiked to the top of a small mountain to enjoy the views of the valley.

handshakes. Once, after crossing the Beninese land border following a trip to Accra, the Italian needed to use the bathroom. The border guards pointed him to the public restroom—a tree across the road. When he didn't go, they offered him the private bathroom in their office. When the Italian tried to show me where it was, the border officers refused to let me use the bathroom. I was in such shock that I held my bladder for the three hours to Cotonou. I couldn't believe that I was being treated so poorly in a country full of people that look like me.

I have never been very attached to my American identity, but I sometimes found myself wanting to scream "I am *American!*" just to gain an ounce of respect. One time we did tell a taxi driver that I was American. He asked if my father is white. Though my dark skin is evident of no racial mixing, many locals had never met a Black American before, so they couldn't make sense of me.

Of course, there were other memorable parts of my time in Benin. I'll never forget seeing gasoline, smuggled from neighboring Nigeria, sold in old liquor bottles on the side of the road. Or a miscommunication that led to purple twists in my hair. Or the time four of us squeezed into the front seat of a standard sedan taxi. Or the time I listened as a few men tied five shrieking pigs to the roof of a taxi bus. Or the fear I felt as I rode on the back of zims along dirt roads, the wheels slipping and sliding, my face and clothes stained by red earth.

When we managed to be tourists in Benin, I loved visiting the Grand Marché, the largest open-air market in West Africa; Ganvie, a lake village, where the only means to and around are traditional wooden boats; and La Porte du Non-retour (The Door of No Return), a memorial arch that marks one of the many places in West Africa from where Africans began their trek across the Atlantic Ocean prior to enslavement.

On the flip side of things, Dassa also afforded me the opportunity to learn from people living in extreme poverty. I was living in one of the poorest areas in the world, where most people lived on less than a dollar a day. Those stats you read in campaigns to end global poverty, I looked them in the face nearly every day. It was a very humbling experience that often resulted in a heavy heart and feeling that I would never be able to help improve the lives of the people there.

I will not soon forget how some children rarely smiled, hunger zapping their glee; watching a boy with very long legs lap his entire class while running barefoot outside and knowing the right training could make him an Olympian, an opportunity that would likely not find him there; seeing hungry schoolchildren beg their classmates for a little bit of food.

La Porte du Non-retour (The Door of No Return) on the shores of the Atlantic Ocean memorializes the Africans who were stolen from their land.

I was face-to-face with the disparity between my privileged life in the West and rural life in one of the poorest countries in the world. Benin changed me—and the way I travel—forever.

At the end of our time in Dassa, I had to make a tough decision. The president of our NGO asked me to stay. The Italian was packing for a six-month assignment in Kenya. I didn't know what my next move should be. I decided to stay in Dassa for an extra month to earn more money while I figured things out. I couldn't stay in Benin longer than that. It was time for me to find a new direction and purpose.

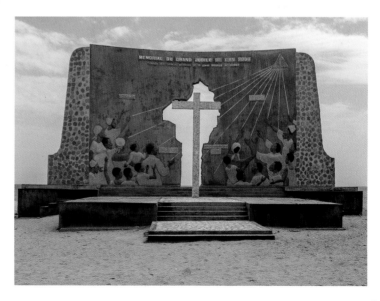

italy

I RECENTLY FOUND a 15-year-old bucket list I had written on a scrap of paper. The second item listed was "Spend at least one month in Italy." I scratched that off the list, and then some. I first visited Italy in June 2010, a few months before moving to Benin. That trip was all about the tourist spots the guidebooks recommended. Then, in April 2011, I got a chance to fully immerse myself in Italian culture.

After 39 job applications, 15 interviews, 1 medical deferral, and nearly 17 months since graduating from the London School of Economics, I secured a consultancy with the United Nations Food and Agriculture Organization at its headquarters in the Eternal City. From my first office, I had a view of Circo Massimo and the Vatican. The roof of our building offered the best view in Rome, overlooking the Colosseum, Palatine Hill, Vittoriano, and nearly the entire city center.

In total, I spent nearly three years living in Rome. I changed apartments too often. I lived in the neighborhoods of San Giovanni, Testaccio, and Colosseo. I explored the city through the eyes of my Roman friends, Grace and Pomicino leading the way.

It only took three weeks of living in Rome for me to fall in love with the dolce vita lifestyle that was made up of scooters, pizza, tiramisu, gelato, espresso (which put a little hair on my chest), wine at lunch without awkward stares, and limoncello. But after a few months, the charms of the city wore off. I began to realize how difficult simple things, like getting internet in your house, felt. And then there was worse. As I wrote on my blog on June 6, 2011:

I don't feel comfortable in Rome. I think it is largely because I am Black. I would say that 90 percent of the time that I am out, I am being stared at. Sometimes it is in a good way, like when I go to the market near Vittorio Emanuele with my flatmate and receive plenty of compliments from the men working at the stalls. But when I am on the metro or

EUROPE

In Venice, oftentimes the only way to reach your destination is by boat. I was obsessed with the beauty of the city and the chic water taxis.

walking down the street, I often get stares that make me feel uncomfortable, and worse, unwanted. Many people refer to Rome as an international city, but once you step outside of the three Rome-based United Nations buildings, many of the non-Italians are undocumented immigrants, making for a tense dynamic between Romans and non.

Living in Rome as an African woman presented many challenges. Though there are some Black people in Rome, most are not integrated into Roman society. For many Romans, seeing a Black woman walking down the street is like a unicorn sighting. Seeing me, dressed for my job at the UN, was likely very strange to people who often view Black women as sex workers.

During my 10-minute walk to the train, people stared at me. Old women looked uncomfortable. Lecherous men gave me hypersexualized stares. I was often mistaken for a prostitute. Once, while walking to work, a man on a scooter asked, *"Facciamo sesso?—We have sex?"* I replied, *"Vaffanculo"*—I'll leave you to Google the translation—and kept walking.

Aroma, a Michelin-starred restaurant in Palazzo Manfredi, overlooking the Colosseum, serves up a perfect carbonara, a quintessential Roman dish.

I did not take the bus at night because I was afraid that no one would care if something were to happen to me. I took taxis exclusively, which in Rome are incredibly expensive. That is until a taxi driver tried to kiss me on my mouth. I didn't go out in the evenings for a while after that.

Still, the pleasure and beauty of Rome always kept me coming back. I found joy in *aperitivi* at Yellow Bar, just across from the office; dinner parties at home, feasting on spectacular cooking from my Italian flatmate turned friend, Lucia; and long dinners with friends at some of Rome's best restaurants. I ran my first 10K after training along the Tiber River, only to learn that the race route was full of hills. I drank too much red wine and enjoyed laughs with friends who turned into family. A month after moving to Italy, my relationship with the Italian ended, mostly due to long distance. While I was living in his home country, he had taken a job in Kenya. My life was quickly changing.

Rome wasn't always perfect, but I would not trade the memories I created and the friendships I built for the world.

Everything the guidebooks tell you about Rome is true: You must go to the Colosseum, visit the Vatican, throw

a coin in the Trevi Fountain, and people-watch while sitting on the Spanish Steps. But after living in Rome for so long, I found other favorites throughout the city.

Rome has more than 900 churches. You can find countless lists of the best ones to visit, but Chiesa del Gesù, which dates back to 1580, never seems to make the cut. It's my little secret. On a summer afternoon, I was strolling around the city when I saw the church was open and walked in. It is stunning. The ceiling is the church's most striking feature. When you look up, it almost feels like the painting "Triumph of the Name of Jesus" is rendered in 3D. A magnifying mirror on the ground allows you to see the most intricate details of the rays of light, clouds, and figures painted amid a gilded ceiling in the nave.

The Italians taught me to savor the beauty of a moment and to prioritize living over anything else. Though this is apparent in the way they live everyday life, the philosophy of la dolce vita was most evident when my friends from home came to visit. On one such occasion, my Roman friend Marco was acting as tour guide. One of my American friends kept shrieking, literally shrieking, with delight at the beauty that popped up around every corner of every alley. At the Pantheon, she exclaimed, "What the f*** is this s***?!" Don't worry, she meant it in a positive way. Mouth agape, she started snapping pictures of the impressive, ancient building. Marco grabbed her phone

A staple in Italian architecture is the presence of large windows on residential buildings, which allow the light to spill in.

and gently covered her mouth with his hand. "Just enjoy it," he said. That, my friends, is the Italian way of life. Be it eating, sightseeing, or drinking a glass of wine, they know how to appreciate a moment.

In every city I visit, I seek out a speakeasy to be transported in time via craft cocktails, low lights, and beautiful decor. Rome's Jerry Thomas sits on a narrow street in the historic center of the city. If you aren't looking for it, you would never find it. At the door, you give a password to enter. Once inside, you are taken back to the 1930s. Not only is the decor reminiscent of the decade, but the entire staff is dressed in period clothing. As far as speakeasies go, this is definitely on my short list of favorites in the world.

Then there is the fact that Italy completely changed my palate. Before living in Rome, I rarely ate tomatoes. In Italy, the tomatoes come in all shapes and sizes and are magically delicious. They're so good, I still don't often eat tomatoes outside of the country. Sure, I enjoyed bruschetta (pronounced bru-SHE-ta in American English) from my local Italian restaurant in the U.S., but in Italy, not only did I learn to pronounce the word correctly (bru-SKE-ta), I also learned to make it myself. The fresh Italian ingredients are key! Also, Italy turned me into a wine snob—now I can taste the nuances in wines and can perfectly pair them with my meals.

There are constant debates about the best pizzeria in Rome. After much digestive research, I crowned Pizzeria Da Remo my favorite. (Side note: The first photo I ever posted on Instagram was taken on February 4, 2012, at Da Remo.) On summer evenings, throngs of people wait in line to experience the frenetic atmosphere of flirtatious waiters and chefs cracking jokes and yelling across the room. The basic margarita pie is sublime, and the staff is sure to give you an authentic and classic Roman experience.

The city's three staple dishes are *carbonara, Amatriciana,* and *cacio e pepe.* Cacio e pepe, a simple dish of pecorino Romano cheese, black pepper, and pasta, can be found everywhere, but not all cacio e pepe is created equal. (Tip: If people are asking you to come into the restaurant, do not enter!) For authentically delicious cacio e pepe, head to Felice (Romans actually eat here). It also happens to be in one of the best neighborhoods in Rome, Testaccio, known for its restaurants, nightlife, archaeology, and being authentically Roman.

With Rome as my home base, I could explore a lot of Italy. The big cities of Tuscany are worth visiting, especially Florence, which is one of my favorite cities in all of Europe. Siena, with its fan-shaped central square and medieval brick buildings, is one of the most unique places

In August 2021, Venice's Piazza San Marco, the city's iconic and typically bustling square, had just a fraction of its usual visitors.

MY ITALIAN FAVORITES

1. Eat *Amatriciana* at Da Bucatino in Rome.
2. Stay at the Four Seasons Firenze.
3. Shop and save on luxury Italian brands, namely Gucci and Prada.
4. Visit Nuovo Mercato Esquilino near Piazza Vittorio Emanuele in Rome.
5. Have a cocktail at Jerry Thomas in Rome.
6. Visit Lago di Como.
7. Eat pecorino with honey in Pienza.
8. Rent a car and visit the vineyards in Sicily.
9. Give the pilot a round of applause when landing in Italy.
10. Eat dinner at Sciué Sciué Cucina in Rome.

Though I used to live right next to the Colosseum, I am still in awe of its beauty and grandeur every time I visit.

I've ever visited. But the small towns of Tuscany are the most charming. It's best to explore by car, stopping to eat as much food as you physically can.

Once, I went to the countryside of Tuscany to visit a friend at his family home. We arrived at the house in the pitch-black. Without streetlights, all I could see was a large gate that we drove through into the driveway. We walked through a massive doorway into a home that felt ancient, almost medieval. Because it was late, I was shown to my room without a tour.

The following morning, on the way to showing me the bathroom, my friend told me to look up. What I saw was a *torretta*—castle tower. It hit me: I was inside a medieval castle. We climbed to the top of the tower and my friend pulled a *Lion King* move, pointing out all the land and groves of olive trees that belonged to his family. It was equal parts absurd and exciting—a truly Italian experience.

Another time, to escape the madness of Easter tourism in Rome, my friend Julio and I rented a car and drove south. (To understand what it's like to drive in Italy, I have to tell you about how small this car was. When I say tiny, I mean *tiny*. I was skeptical it would even get us to our final destination. It took more than a while to get to normal speeds, and I found it weird that I could reach into the trunk from the front seat. But it did its job.) We visited Sassi di Matera, a complex of cave dwellings in an ancient river canyon that has been continuously inhabited since 10,000 B.C. Many may remember the city as a backdrop of scenes in 2004's *The Passion of the Christ*.

From Matera, we headed to Positano, without a doubt the most beautiful part of the Amalfi Coast. Still, I strongly suggest you drive along the entire coast. Tackle it before mid-May or after mid-September, when the crowds are fewer. On our beautiful and relaxing drive, we even caught the sunset with a view of Mount Vesuvius.

Though I lived in Rome for three years, it took me seven years after I left Italy to finally make it to Venice. I had never visited the Floating City because I didn't want to deal with the hordes of crowds I'd often heard about. But Venice in 2021, due to the coronavirus pandemic, was virtually empty. When I wasn't walking along the beautiful streets lining the canals, I was taking a water taxi from one spot to another. And without all the crowds, locals were happier and the waters were clearer.

Italy had a profound impact on my life. I entered the working world again after a bit of a hiatus. I left and returned to my job at the UN, exploring new countries in between. I made lifelong friends, the continuation of a global network of people I relied on during my journey to every country in the world. But most significantly, I finally gave up my typical, type-A American attitude. I arrived in Rome trying to be as efficient as possible at work and running from one thing to the next. Slowly but surely, Italian culture seeped into my life. I learned to savor the beautiful moments and to prioritize living over anything else. I learned the art of la dolce vita! Now my only goal is to live my best day, every day. I thank Italy for that.

I like to think Italy and I have a love-hate relationship, but really I just love it. While I can see myself spending long periods of time there annually, I will likely never live there full time again. Still, I cannot help but visit every year. The food, the language, the history, the architecture—all of it brings me back to Italy again and again. It's one of my favorite places to be, and I discover more she has to offer every time I step foot back on her land.

I love road trips in the Italian countryside, and I particularly love the rolling hills and vineyards of Tuscany.

vatican city

MY MOTHER'S ENTIRE FAMILY is very religious. One of my first cousins even became a nun—Sister Beatrice Namusoke. While spending Christmas in my mother's village in Uganda, we walked to Mass with my grandmother. We celebrated at Kitasa Parish, where my mother was baptized, went to elementary school, and had her first Communion. The parish is still active to this day. On the other side of the Atlantic,

EUROPE

I was raised in the Catholic Church. We attended a weekly Sunday Mass at Saint Mary of Redford. My favorite part of the Sunday ritual was going to the penny candy store just a short walk away after services. The Easter egg hunts at church were a close second. From preschool through sixth grade, Sunday Mass was coupled with my Catholic elementary school's Wednesday Mass. I attended a Catholic university, St. John's, which helped convince my parents to let me go to school in New York City. I have completed four of the seven sacraments: baptism, first Communion, confession, and confirmation. I hardly consider myself a religious person—though I always travel with a rosary my mother gave me—but visiting the Vatican was a pretty big deal for me.

Whether you are a devout Catholic, Muslim, Jew, Buddhist, atheist, or agnostic, a visit to the Vatican Museums and St. Peter's Basilica is a necessary part of any trip to Rome. Plus, you get two countries for the price of one! The Holy See is the formal sovereign city-state of which Vatican City is the capital. Completely surrounded by Rome, the independent territory is one of the two nonmember observer states of the United Nations, Palestine being the other.

Vatican City makes it on those "must-visit" lists time and time again. And this one, I can say, deserves the attention it gets. Glimpses of St. Peter's Basilica's iconic blue dome can be seen from a number of places throughout Rome, but I had the most unique sighting during my first visit to the Eternal City in 2010. At the Giardino degli Aranci, my Roman friend Daniele led us to a large wooden door beneath an

I, along with more than 800,000 people, watched the historic canonization of Popes John XXIII and John Paul II in Rome.

The iconic blue dome of St. Peter's Basilica can be seen throughout Rome, the city that completely encompasses Vatican City.

intricate archway and told us to look through the small metal keyhole. I was completely stunned: Through this tiny keyhole in a random park on Aventine Hill was a perfectly framed view of the dome of the basilica. I returned to that little keyhole twice while living in Rome, once to see it again in the daylight and then once more to see it at night. While the daytime view is spectacular, the evening scene is something else entirely. To see one of Italy's most iconic buildings and the glowing city surrounding it from that perspective is another type of beauty. Later, my office at the UN overlooked the Vatican, but the view from the building's rooftop where we often took lunch or coffee was even better.

St. Peter's Basilica, fashioned in Renaissance architecture, was designed by artists Michelangelo, Gian Lorenzo Bernini, Donato Bramante, and Carlo Maderno. The massive church is the largest in the world, based on interior measurement. During the three years I lived in Rome, I regularly walked the 45 minutes from my apartment in the Colosseo neighborhood to Vatican City just to marvel at the beauty of the nearly 400-year-old building.

Pope John Paul II was at the helm of the Catholic Church the majority of my life. It therefore felt very meaningful that he was beatified, a measure taken right before sainthood, two weeks after I first moved to Rome. (Three years later, John Paul II was canonized, along with John XXIII.) With two living popes in attendance, the beatification was a historic event. Many camped out for multiple nights to attend the ceremony at the Vatican, but I—along with thousands of others—watched from screens set up along Via dei Fori Imperiali, a road that runs through the center of Rome.

Nearly 1,700 buses came from John Paul II's home country of Poland, and Polish flags flew everywhere. But the Mass attracted all walks of life, from all over the world. Nuns gathered in the streets. I saw worshippers from India, from parts of Africa, and from America. I even had a fateful encounter with my hometown. While I was standing among the crowds, I overheard a conversation about Grand Rapids, Michigan. I tapped the shoulder of the man who was speaking and came face-to-face with one of the most famous news anchors in Detroit, Devin Scillian. We chatted, and he ended up interviewing me for TV. Back at home, my mom saw me broadcast on the news. Her only comment: "Where are your earrings? You're naked!" Even in this most humble and sacred moment, I was experiencing the random joy and surprises that would continue to unfold throughout my journey. To be on TV in Detroit where my friends and family could see me while I was living in Rome felt so random and so serendipitous. I loved every second of it.

Following the Mass in Italian was easy given my years in the church. When it came time to say "Peace be with you," I exchanged the greeting with several Polish people standing nearby. Though estimates say 500,000 people were in the vicinity of St. Peter's and an additional 300,000 were spread out over the city's piazzas, the feeling in the air was very calm, peaceful, and spiritual. It almost turned me into a faithful follower.

More than a year after leaving Rome—in the fall of 2015—I first visited the Vatican Museums, finally building up the courage to brave the crowds. The ornate complex is home to more than 70,000 works of art, though only a mere 20,000 are on display. Walking through its halls, one is regaled by gold fixtures and centuries-old Renaissance and baroque paintings and sculptures. As I made my way through the 54 rooms, I got a crick in my neck from looking up for several hours at ceilings that are covered with immaculately preserved artwork. The last room is home to the Sistine Chapel and its ever so famous ceiling painting, "The Creation of Adam," painted by Michelangelo over a period of four years.

I often find my way back to the Vatican, and I look forward to the day when I can take my devout Catholic mother to experience it for the first time.

ghana

GHANA. GHANA. GHANA. I love this country so much. It's one that has produced some of my favorite people. It's a place where, upon landing, I always feel welcome. It's where I joke with immigration officers as I move across the border. Ghana has my heart. I first visited Ghana while living and working in Benin. Nothing is easy about traveling to or from Benin, and the result was a less than stellar first experience

AFRICA

getting to Ghana. Luckily I do not let travel woes color my experience of a country. If I did, I would've never returned to Ghana and fallen in love with the country.

The Italian and I (still together at that time) originally planned to visit my family in Uganda for Christmas, but exorbitant flight prices changed our plans. Instead, we decided to meet up with friends in Accra, Ghana's capital, for New Year's Eve.

Obtaining visas for Ghana was an *ordeal.* We struggled to prove our address in Dassa-Zoumé, Benin, was valid to a less than helpful civil servant. Once we did, we were told our visas likely wouldn't be ready until two hours *after* our bus was scheduled to leave. But we were learning a thing or two about getting around the continent of Africa. Not to be deterred, we called a day early to double-check and our visas were, in fact, ready. Bureaucracy be damned.

Early on the morning of December 30, we found a *zim* (motorcycle taxi) driver who, after some negotiation, took us to the bus station. But when we arrived at the station, we found out our bus had broken down and would not be leaving that day. It looked like we might be spending our New Year's Eve in transit. We went back the following day and were grateful to see the bus was there. We finally left for Ghana at 12 p.m. on New Year's Eve.

The drive to Accra is about 217 miles (350 km). On fully paved roads, the trip should take no more than four hours. It took us *11!* As I watched each hour pass, I felt sadder and sadder, the possibility of

Headquartered in Accra, Studio 189 is one of my favorite luxury African brands. Their stores in Osu and Kempinski are bursting with color.

a New Year's Eve celebration slipping away, thanks to four border stops and roads riddled with potholes.

One of the first tips I give to people who are new to traveling to the continent of Africa is to be willing to sacrifice comfort for the experience. I wouldn't go as far as to say that this bus ride was a worthwhile experience, but I was hoping the destination at the end would be worth the pain. Of course, you can travel to many African countries and have a stellar five-star experience—if that's what you're looking for. But I encourage you to step out of your comfort zone. Bathing in cold water never killed anyone, nor did going without electricity for a night or two. In many African countries, you need to be comfortable eating with your hands—and trying things you cannot recognize (it might turn out to be the best thing you've ever tasted). Just because things are different, just because a bus ride takes longer than you expect, doesn't mean it's not worth the time or effort. Now back to making our way to a Ghanaian New Year's Eve . . .

Once we made it to the Ghanaian border, we were greeted by more women who were clearly unhappy with their jobs. After lots of teeth sucking and slow stamping on their part, we were finally off to Accra.

Midnight hit while we were in a taxi heading from dinner to a club. We tried to go out, but we were so tired from traveling that we didn't have the energy. That New Year's Eve, like most years, was a bit of a letdown.

We spent the next several days with my friend Frema and her family, who were incredibly generous and made sure we maximized our stay in the country. We visited Cape Coast and St. George's Castle in the town of Elmina, which is where Africans captured in the interior of the continent were housed before being put on slave ships heading for the Americas. Our knowledgeable guide revealed the extent of the horrific acts committed by the Dutch, Portuguese, and British traders. The castle stands as a marker of the gruesome inhumanity of the transatlantic slave trade that changed the world as we know it.

In the evenings, we hung out with Frema and her friends, getting to know Accra nightlife firsthand. It was a preview for subsequent visits during which Accra quickly became one of my favorite party cities. We ate good food (my favorite being fried whole fish) and spent time on the shores of the Atlantic. While our visit was short and got off to a rocky start, our experience left me wanting more.

I love Ghana because I love Ghanaians. Whether at home or in the diaspora, Ghanaian people have a warm and fun energy. In September 2019, a dear friend, Nana Konamah, invited me to celebrate the Odwira

A young participant in a dance competition during the Odwira Festival in Akropong stole the show.

AKAN NAMING
TRADITIONS

If you have ever met someone named Akosua or Kwesi, you've met a Ghanaian. These names reflect the day of the week they were born. Akosua and Kwesi are traditional Akan female and male names, respectively, for people born on a Sunday. Day names in the Akan tradition are important because children are not officially given a name until one week after birth. Each day name represents an eponymous Akan deity. A girl born on a Thursday is named Yaa after the deity Asase Yaa (earth goddess). Legend holds that each female name represents a goddess and that the accompanying male name represents a steward of the goddess. For example, Akwasi refers to a servant of Akosua.

Festival in Akropong. During Odwira, the Akuapem people return to their hometowns to commemorate past military victories, celebrate a new harvest, remember the departed, pay homage to their gods, and revere their ancestors.

The streets of Akropong were filled with people—including beautiful Ghanaian men. It is almost unfair how effortless their attractiveness is. The buildings were covered in colorful murals painted by local artists (one even allowed me to add on to his artwork). As music blasted and the pungent whiffs of local foods tickled my nose, I soaked up the celebration. I watched a traditional dancing competition with proper judging panelists who, even when the crowd got excited, held straight faces. Each dancer was clothed in traditional garb, and their powerful movements were in sync with the drums, swift and coordinated. What looked to me like random movements were actually intricate moves that, for those who understood, held much deeper meanings. The dancers used their bodies to tell a story.

Ghanaians know how to party. Eight years after my first trip to Ghana, I returned to celebrate New Year's Eve and they affirmed their prowess. Ghana's president, Nana Akufo-Addo, declared the "Year of Return, Ghana 2019," marking 400 years since the arrival of the first recorded enslaved Africans in the state of Virginia and encouraging Africans in the diaspora to return to the continent. The president even granted citizenship to some of the diaspora community, confirming that Ghana was their home. The celebration was successful: Ghana's Ministry of Tourism, Arts, and Culture estimates that about 1.1 million people arrived in Ghana for the Year of Return. The year 2019 was full of events, and December was the culmination. It felt like the entire world was in Ghana.

What ensued was a plethora of concerts, festivals, parties, and cultural events. I am sorry if you had to witness it from afar. I spent an amazing 10 days celebrating and rang in 2020 on the beach with several close friends, my dress ruined from running into the salty and brisk waters of the Atlantic. It wasn't until around 10 a.m. that we finally made it home and I peeled that dress off my body. Considering all the fun we had, it may have been us that broke the planet. The

I spotted these three Ghanian men at the Odwira Festival.

memories of that time sustained me during the first few months of lockdown during the COVID-19 pandemic.

Accra is one of my favorite cities in Africa, thanks to a brand-new, ultramodern airport, an immigration process that is very efficient, a huge creative scene, and a lot of cool people. And we can't talk about Ghana without mentioning its amazing food. One of my favorite meals is at Chez Clarisse in Osu. My go-to order at the no-frills establishment is the whole fried fish, smothered in onions and peppers and served with plantains and jollof rice. Please note: My mention of jollof here is not a total endorsement of Ghanaian jollof. For those of you who don't know, there has been a decades-long feud among West Africans over who makes the best jollof, a traditional West African dish of rice, tomatoes, onions, and spices that is also regionally diverse. The loudest competitors are always the Nigerians and Ghanaians, but I think they should really watch out for the Liberians and Sierra Leoneans.

I stay connected to Africa through that small tattoo I got with keondra before leaving for Japan. Never having imagined this path when I boarded that plane to travel across the world, the Adinkra symbol is both a nod to my love for this country and the amazing journey I've been on.

Nana Konamah and I take selfies in front of one of the murals painted during the Odwira Festival.

MY ACCRA MUST-DOS

1. Visit during the Festive Season.
2. Have drinks at Republic.
3. Shop at Studio 189.
4. Shop in the Accra Arts Center.
5. Attend a cultural festival.
6. Hang out at Front/Back club.
7. Party at Polo Beach Club.
8. Visit the Nubuke Foundation art gallery.
9. Get a custom outfit from Chocolate by Kwaku Bediako.

uruguay

IN DECEMBER 2012, I decided to leave my job at the UN. I was ready for my next adventure. I wanted to travel more, continue to blog on The Catch Me If You Can, and see what other opportunities awaited. I flew home to Detroit on Christmas Eve and a few weeks later found myself in Buenos Aires for a six-week-long hiatus in South America. It was my first time on the continent. I planned a weekend getaway

to Uruguay because Colonia del Sacramento, the port city in Uruguay, is a short 75-minute ferry ride across the murky brown Rio de la Plata from Buenos Aires. Having never contemplated visiting Uruguay, I did not know much about what to see and do, so my friends and I just decided to go with the flow. After landing in Colonia del Sacramento, we took a two-hour bus ride to the capital, Montevideo, where we spent the night. The next morning in Montevideo, my friend Ricardo, his then girlfriend Vanessa, and I found a small—emphasis on small—rental car to explore as much of the Uruguayan coast as possible.

Our first stop was Punta del Este, the famed resort town perched on the Atlantic coast. Punta del Este is to Porteños what the Hamptons are to New Yorkers. Many Argentinians have homes here to escape to in the summer months. The coastal town left much to be desired, but the docked yachts and high prices at the seafood restaurants made it clear that this town caters to South America's elite.

Anxious to get to the smaller beach towns farther north before nightfall, we didn't spend much time in town. Still, we saw the iconic Mano de Punta del Este, located on Brava Beach. The sculpture, completed in 1982, features five fingers partially emerging from the sand and is one of Uruguay's most recognizable landmarks. The sculpture represents the human connection to nature. Replications have cropped up around the world, including in Madrid, the Atacama Desert, and Venice.

Uruguay's coast is dotted with quaint beach towns where the speed of life moves at a snail's pace, the seafood is plentiful, and

SOUTH AMERICA

The lighthouse in the remote village of Cabo Polonio is a UNESCO World Heritage site that sits just next to a large sea lion colony.

local beer is always available. As we drove between three different beach towns, we passed lush green plains dotted with cattle. Fun fact: Uruguay is one of the top producers of beef in the world—with beef products making up 25 percent of the country's exports. As a result, Uruguayans love their beef and rank second worldwide in average beef consumption per person at 114 pounds (52 kg) each year. That is a lot of beef!

We planned to slowly make our way along the coast back to Montevideo, so our next stop was Punta del Diablo, the northernmost town that we wanted to visit. Between the scent of marijuana, the dreadlocked men clad in colorful pants, and the carefree energy, Punta del Diablo felt like a hippie's paradise. One couple we met ran a sandwich shop and lived in a mind-bogglingly small van. They worked in Sweden part of the year to save money, then came back to Uruguay to live an easy life. The weather was surprisingly chilly in Punta del Diablo, but we sat on the beach and enjoyed the sunset and stargazing.

The following day we headed to Barra de Valizas, and, lucky for us, the weather warmed up. We had a delicious seafood lunch paired with cold beers and sangria, then walked around to see the craftspeople selling their wares on the small street in front of the restaurant. One vendor asked my friend for some of his beer. I thought it was an odd request, but after spending a few hours in this small town, I realized that it was not out of the ordinary. Most people here do not have a lot of money, and everyone shares what they have.

We digested our lunch lying under the afternoon sun. The Atlantic Ocean here is framed by sand dunes so immense (some are more than 130 feet [40 m] high) that people "surf" them. A man with a boat and sandboards took us across the small river between the beach and the large golden dunes. Not into the idea of bodily harm, I was a bit scared. But after watching my friends go, I mustered up the courage, hopped on a board, and surfed the sand waves. It was so much fun—and the sand offered a soft landing.

Our final day in Uruguay was spent in Cabo Polonio, my favorite little town—or perhaps village is more appropriate—of those we visited. The village is well maintained, largely because no roads lead to it. In fact, it's a little more than four miles (6 km) from the nearest road. We had to take a jeep across the small sand dunes and then walk the rest of the way into town. Cabo Polonio has a population of 95, no running water, no electricity (save for a few generators that power stores), and no cell service or internet. At one home, we saw the

owner lying on a couch fashioned from an old wooden boat, his horses tied in the back. We talked to a few residents, who all enjoyed their very simple life.

Though it lacks modern conveniences, Cabo Polonio offers expansive beaches and awe-inspiring views of the Atlantic Ocean. The highest point in the village, the lighthouse, is one of the few sites to see. On the rocks below, sea lions—part of the second largest sea lion colony in Uruguay—work on their tans.

We ate lunch at a quaint restaurant called Inn Mariemar, a staple in Cabo Polonio. Located in a beachfront two-story building, the guesthouse and restaurant have been operating for 45 years. With unobstructed views of the ocean, delicious paella, and ice-cold Cokes, it is a favorite of locals and visitors alike. We unfortunately only spent a few hours in this quiet haven, but I'd return for at least one night. In so few places in the world can you truly unplug, and this is one of them.

All in all, there was something peaceful and magical about the small towns that we visited during our weekend in Uruguay. None of them were very fancy, but they all felt very authentic, and the people were kind. It has been almost a decade since I visited Uruguay, and I cannot wait to return to see if I feel the same way I did the first time.

Cabo Polonio is a small coastal village with no running water or electricity and roughly 100 residents.

brazil

WHEN I PLANNED **MY TRIP** to South America, I didn't know I'd be in Rio de Janeiro at the exact time of Carnival. When I realized the coincidence, I felt like a giddy college student anticipating her first spring break in Cancun. But my lax planning actually backfired. I thought I would get my visa from the Brazilian Embassy in Buenos Aires, but they did not have a single appointment during the 10 days leading up to my trip.

SOUTH
AMERICA

The Pelourinho neighborhood of Salvador de Bahia, one of my favorite cities in the world, is full of character.

I needed to pivot, something I've become very good at, traveling all these years.

To get a Brazilian visa in time, I had to go to Puerto Iguazú, the border town known for its famed, eponymous waterfalls. There they issue Brazilian visas within 24 hours. Iguazú is a 17-hour bus ride from Buenos Aires. Then I had to take another 30-hour bus ride to get to Rio. Fortunately, buses in South America are really nice and incredibly comfortable. The funniest part of all this is that I had already booked a flight from Rio to Iguazú to see the falls on my return trip. I could not afford to change the flight, so I had to take that 17-hour bus ride *again* to get back to Buenos Aires.

Always relying on the travel network I had started to build in London, I reached out to my Brazilian friend Julio, who connected me with friends in Rio. I stayed at their house and we had a huge barbeque and too many caipirinhas—Brazil's national drink made with sugar, lime, and cachaça (a liquor made from sugarcane juice). We gathered at *blocos* (street parties) in celebration of Carnival. In those pre-COVID days, I was surprised to learn that people kiss strangers in the streets during Carnival, no doubt fueled by the energy of the parties and a seemingly endless flow of alcohol. If you have ever planned to go to Carnival, do it sooner rather than later. It is a young person's game that requires serious endurance. I was knackered!

People talk a lot about the dangers of Rio, but I often traveled around the city alone. One night, after two too many passion fruit caipirinhas on Ipanema Beach, I took the local bus. As I stumbled

aboard, armed with my elementary Portuguese, the driver allowed me to sit in the front, no doubt recognizing how drunk I was. When we reached my stop, he helped me secure a taxi for the rest of the way home. I made it home safely despite my poor choices. I have always found beautiful, helpful people everywhere in the world. I was lucky to find one that day.

Brazilians—a mixed bunch with African, Indigenous, German, and Portuguese heritage—are welcoming and very open. Between the beautiful people on the beach, the caipirinhas, the fresh juice bars on nearly every corner, the coconut water straight from the source, nonstop partying (it almost killed me), and the breathtaking views from the mountain on which Christ the Redeemer sits, my first trip to Rio was worth every second of the 64 hours spent on those buses.

I got an ankle bracelet near that bus stop in Iguazú. It finally broke off in February 2021, but it served as an eight-year reminder of a time period that once again changed my life.

Three years and one flight deal later, I found myself—along with 18 friends—back in Brazil. In 2015, I started traveling pretty regularly with a mix of friends from Detroit and friends of friends. The group includes a stylist, photographer, yoga teacher, filmmaker, and other creatives. When we get together, our time is beautiful, joyful, and effortless.

By the time our Brazil trip came around, I had quit my last full-time job and was running my boutique travel agency, Jet Black (more on that later). I had been growing a steady following on my blog, and Instagram was taking over as the social media outlet of choice. As a result, our group trips became well known for our coordinating fashion, photography, and *wildly* good looks.

In Rio, we slayed a photo shoot that we fed out to our individual feeds and caused a significant dent in the internet. We only spent three days in the city, but we managed to see all the major spots. My favorite was Parque Lage, where, all dressed in florals, we posed for the camera. After an impromptu party on Copacabana Beach—videos of which I hope never surface—we woke up and headed to the airport for Salvador.

Brazil has the second largest number of Black people in the world, second only to Nigeria. With more than 108 million Black people, this large African diaspora, a result of the transatlantic slave trade, is a marker of the country's culture. Afro-Brazilians are mostly concentrated in the northeast, which includes the magically beautiful state of Bahia. The capital, Salvador, offers pristine beaches where you can hang out with locals, devour delicious and unique food, learn the

Frequented by locals in Salvador, Praia da Gamboa is a laid-back beach that's perfect for an afternoon dip.

history of the slave rebellion, and dance to music in the streets. We did all of it!

My favorite memories in Salvador were in Pelourinho. By day, its cobblestone streets, colorful buildings, and welcoming residents offered fun surprises, like playing with a group of children and witnessing impromptu capoeira (Brazilian martial arts) demonstrations. At night, the main square filled with stalls where we bought food and—you guessed it—caipirinhas. With music blasting, locals poured into the streets and danced the night away. The people of Salvador exude a freedom and joy in the simplicity of life that continues to bring me back. The energy reminds me of Havana, Cuba, in the most beautiful way. Something about the African spirit has stood the test of time and continues to permeate the cultures of my favorite places around the world.

I also quickly became obsessed with *moqueca* while I was in Salvador. The Brazilian seafood stew is a staple throughout the country. It's typically made with fish or shrimp, stewed with onion, tomato, coriander, garlic, and lime. The Bahian version adds coconut milk and palm oil to the mix, which is a reflection of the Portuguese and African influences in the region. The stew is served with rice and *farofa,* a toasted cassava flour. All moqueca is not made equal. The best I had was on a small island called Ilha de Maré, which is accessed by boat from São Tomé de Paripe beach. But I can't tell you the particular restaurant I went to: There are several right on the beach with, I am sure, a Brazilian grandmother in every kitchen. So just try your luck.

A small group of us continued on to the tiny island of Boipeba, which required two different boats to reach. On the car-free island, a man with a wheelbarrow helped move our things to a tractor-pulled bus, which got us closer to our rental home.

Over the next few days we laughed, had philosophical discussions, played in the warm waters of the Atlantic Ocean, and watched a local beachside football (soccer) match while eating fresh seafood. We walked on the beach in a torrential downpour and saw wild horses running along the shore. If all of that was not enough, our friend Chef Roblé managed to cook one of the most amazing meals I've ever had. From a ragtag group of ingredients he picked up in a very small and ill-equipped market, he served a very elevated version of rice, beans, and sausage to my taste buds' delight.

My last trip to Brazil started with a FaceTime call at 10 a.m. on a Monday in January 2021. My friend Sam was lying on a rooftop in Salvador, drinking fresh coconut water and a caipirinha. I was in a

very cold Detroit, working. Three and a half hours later, I was at the airport making a beeline for Salvador. I managed to grab a same-day flight for $550. After stops in Atlanta and São Paulo, I too would be sipping caipirinhas again. Long flights and connections have never stopped me from a good time. And, luckily, Brazil had lifted visa requirements for Americans.

I value my freedom and that I am able to travel at the drop of a hat. I am grateful for this immense privilege, that I have the money to buy a plane ticket, and for devices that allow me to work from anywhere in the world. I literally designed the life of my dreams. My biggest piece of advice: Figure out exactly what you want and fill your days with it.

Just over 24 hours after that call, I landed in Salvador and was picked up by my friend David, who permanently moved from Brooklyn to Salvador and always serves as the best guide in the city. The next five days were what Brazilian dreams are made of—and exactly what was needed after the dumpster fire that was 2020. We woke up early in the morning and walked to Porto da Barra Beach, where life was just beginning. We drank fresh coconut water and floated in the salty sea. We paddleboarded, daydreamed, and enjoyed the cool breeze as the morning sun beat down on us.

Scattered around Salvador are fruit carts filled with delicious papayas, bananas, mangoes, pineapples, and so much more.

ethiopia

WHEN I LEFT MY JOB at the   UN in December 2012, my team asked if I would stay on board, and though I agreed to continue with the team, I was adamant about not wanting to live in Rome. So I worked remotely for eight months—I was a digital nomad before it was even a thing—allowing me to travel and earn money at the same time. During this period, I visited Ethiopia for the first time. I had been in Uganda

AFRICA

for a month with my mother when I decided to hop over to Addis Ababa and visit my friend John, who was working at the capital city's UN offices. My own agency, FAO, had subregional offices headquartered in Addis, so I tacked on work plans for an in-person training and meeting a few colleagues, too.

Addis Ababa is often referred to as the political capital of Africa. The Organisation of African Unity (OAU) was founded there in 1963 by Ghana's Kwame Nkrumah and Ethiopia's Haile Selassie. The OAU was replaced in 2002 by the African Union, which is still headquartered in Addis. The city is also home to a number of international organizations, including the UN Economic Commission for Africa.

On arrival, I was surprised to find myself—a pretty active person— winded as I made my way up a few flights of stairs at the airport. Turns out, Addis Ababa sits at an elevation of 7,726 feet (2,355 m), making it the fifth highest capital city in the world, and the highest in Africa. Unprepared, I was feeling the altitude.

John, our friend Antoine, and I made our way to a typical, though touristy, Ethiopian restaurant, zigzagging past Soviet-era taxis, the beeping blue hunks of metal that are a staple in the city. The restaurant was packed with tourists, expats, and locals alike, and the food was accompanied by lively traditional singing and dancing.

Ethiopian cuisine is one of my favorites. Traditionally, the meal is served on a large round communal platter with a base of injera, a sour fermented flatbread with a spongy texture. The injera serves as a sort of plate beneath the other food and is also set in small rolls on the side

In Ethiopia, the agricultural sector accounts for 80 percent of employment, mostly on a subsistence basis.

Under the afternoon sun, two women in Debre Birhan sort through barley, preparing it for market.

to be used in place of a fork. Atop the injera can be any number of Ethiopian salads and stews, including vegan options such as lentils and vegetables; *doro wat* (one of my favorites, a chicken curry of sorts); *tibs* (grilled beef); and *shiro* (a stew of chickpeas).

Dinner was punctuated by a small cup of traditional coffee, served in a *jebena,* a special spouted pot in which it is also brewed. Coffee is incredibly important to the Ethiopian economy—60 percent of foreign income comes from coffee sales. No surprise, as *Coffee arabica,* the coffee plant, originated in Ethiopia. Its discovery is said to date back to the ninth century.

The rest of my time in Addis was spent sightseeing and partying. We went to the National Museum, which houses a replica of Lucy, the 3.2-million-year-old woman thought to be the earliest known human ancestor. We went for a long drive to Mount Entoto, where Emperor Menelik II resided, ruling over the country from 1889 until 1913. The colorful octagonal Entoto Maryam Church sits atop the hill, as does the modest former palace of the emperor. From that vantage point, you can see expansive views of the city below.

The parties in Addis back in 2013 were lit, as the kids say. The locals and the huge African-expat community *did not disappoint* when it came to clubbing. One club was so packed I found myself memorizing the locations of the exits in case of emergency. But with the liquor flowing freely, I soon forgot.

Less than two years later, I found myself on a nonstop flight from Washington, D.C., to Addis on a work assignment with the United States Agency for International Development (USAID). I was sent to meet with farmers in the highlands of Amhara as part of a natural resource management project. We visited the city Debre Birhan, where I met with farmers and heard how formalized land rights improved their lives, particularly for women, as land was a leverageable asset. In this rural part of Ethiopia, smallholder farmers do not have much besides the land they tend. Many do not have running water or electricity, but they make the most of their circumstances. In one of the several homes I visited, a woman had lined the walls with newspaper, giving the otherwise drab home a pop of color.

The men I was working with wanted to go to a local drinking house. This is traditionally an activity reserved for men, but I convinced our local consultant to let me go along. The location was inconspicuous, a very simple single-story building with wooden and metal benches along the walls. In front of one wall was the "bar," a slightly elevated, narrow wooden table with five bottles on top. The "bartender," if we want to give him a formal title, was pouring a liquid from a rather sketchy-looking plastic bottle—the type typically used for antifreeze—into a slightly used Johnnie Walker Red Label bottle.

We tasted several different local liquors (read: made in someone's backyard). One tasted like garlic; the others were so strong that I could only register the burning sensation of alcohol. As the only woman in the bar, I sipped slowly to keep my wits about me. Still, I held my own. Before leaving, I asked to purchase an entire bottle of the house liquor. Though I knew I wouldn't drink it, I wanted it to join the ranks of other spirits that I brought home from my travels—a collection on my bar at my apartment that I first began in 2012.

My last trip to Addis was on New Year's Eve in 2018. On a forced layover between Burundi and South Sudan, I found myself dancing the night away with champagne and fireworks as I watched Tanzanian music group Navy Kenzo put on a live show as we ushered in the new year.

While I have fond memories of Ethiopia, there is so much I have not yet seen. I long to travel to Lalibela to see the rock-cut monolithic churches. I want to visit the Hamar tribe in the southwest and learn about their cultural practices. I want to stand on the banks of the Blue Nile, one of the few parts of the Nile I haven't seen yet. Like in so many countries in the world, I have so much more to see.

Newspaper was used to decorate this home, and the wooden shelf made a beautiful addition to the decor.

kenya

THE WHEELS ON THE PLANE touched down at Rome's Fiumicino International Airport on my return from a whirlwind week back in the U.S. After collecting my bags and finding my driver, we made our way into the city. I was heading straight to the office when my phone rang. On the other end was the Italian, his voice panicked and full of pain. In Nairobi, Kenya, for the last two days—and what continued for two more—

the popular Westgate Mall was under siege by terrorists. In total, nearly 70 people were murdered, one of whom was the Italian's best friend. I was shocked and tried my best to comfort him. To top it off, I was scheduled to travel to Kenya for the first time in just over a month.

Because my sisters and I were born in the U.S., our parents decided to conform to American traditions and gave us our dad's surname, Nabongo. The name Nabongo traces back to a great Kenyan king named Nabongo Mumia, a member of the Wanga Kingdom and direct descendant of the Buganda Kingdom, the tribe I belong to. Upon reading or hearing my surname, most Kenyans assume that I too am Kenyan. I gently correct them. But the truth is, Kenyan and Ugandan identities are relatively recent—the two are singularly tied to the colonization by and subsequent independence from the British.

I grew up around many Kenyans in Detroit. My parents met the Nzoma family a few years after permanently settling in the city, well before any of their eight combined children came along. The Nzomas' twins, Mercy and Isaac, and I were the last born, arriving less than three weeks apart. Our Detroit family also included the Massasabi, Ngare, and Alighali families, as well as Kumuyu, Ginny, and Kiamba. In fact, our life was so intertwined with Kenyan immigrants that at the time of my father's death in 2003, he was vice president of the Association of Kenya Students and Nationals. Our participation solidified that the lyrics of the Kenyan hit pop song "Jambo Bwana" would be stuck in my head forever: *"Jambo, Jambo Bwana,*

AFRICA

Standing on a dhow, a traditional boat, at sunset on the Indian Ocean off the coast of Lamu, my favorite city on the Kenyan coast

habari gani, mzuri sana, wageni, mwakaribishwa, Kenya yetu, hakuna matata." But even I have to Google the translation: "Hello, hello, sir. How are you? I am fine. Visitors, you're welcome. Our (country) Kenya, there are no worries."

In September 2013, four gunmen entered the Westgate shopping mall in Nairobi and opened fire. What followed was a four-day siege. On news networks around the world, you could watch as military surrounded the building and smoke billowed into the sky. There were gun battles between the military and the attackers, who were armed with machine guns and explosives. More than 1,000 people were safely evacuated, but too many lives were unnecessarily lost. When I got the call from the Italian that his friend was one of the 63 victims, my heart broke—for him, for the other casualties, for Nairobi.

Despite the terrorist attack in Nairobi, my work mission with the UN went ahead as planned. Having grown up with so many Kenyans in Detroit, I felt like I would be visiting a place I already knew. Nairobi, the capital, had long captured my fascination. It attracted me as a global and cosmopolitan city, and I often dreamed of living there. What I did not imagine was that I would be so incredibly busy with work that I would not get to enjoy much of what the city had to offer.

The trip started with a reality check: To reach my hotel, we drove past the Westgate Mall; the bullet holes in the building were still fresh and a gate surrounded the massive crime scene. The heavy energy in the air was palpable. I offered up a quick prayer as we passed by.

After an energy shift and wardrobe change at the hotel, I headed to a house party at my friend Jabari's, who I had met when I was living in Japan. After spending two months in Nairobi, Jabari decided to stay for two years. From his house we went to Casablanca, a really nice hookah bar. When I pulled up to my hotel at about 3:30 a.m., I had nothing but great things to say about my first night in Nairobi.

Though time was limited, I arranged to go on a safari the next morning. It required a 6:30 a.m. departure from the hotel, but it was more than worth it. Lake Nakuru National Park is about 125 miles

When we spotted this tree in the middle of a safari in the Masai Mara National Reserve, I decided to climb up to see farther out into the Kenyan plains.

(200 km) from Nairobi—far enough to sleep on the way. More important, to catch long glimpses of the famed Great Rift Valley, a massive and lush intracontinental ridge system.

In Nakuru, we saw zebras, buffalo, flamingos, impalas, rhinoceroses, a leopard, which required patience and quiet, and the king himself, a lion resting under a tree. Oddly enough, what amazed me most was Lake Nakuru. On our visit, the lake was serenely still and reflected the sky above. Flamingos rested on its shores. Here, contemplating her beauty, I proclaimed, "Africa is perfect."

I already loved Kenyan crafts and jewelry, so being introduced to the Maasai Market the following day was like taking a kid to a candy shop. The market, which changes locations most days of the week, was filled with brightly colored bags and baskets, a plethora of brass jewelry, statues made of ebony, and bowls and plates made of olive wood. I saw dresses made from traditional African fabrics and stalls selling textiles that you could take to a tailor to design your own outfit. There were Maasai blankets, wooden board games, and children's toys. In 2020, I designed rings for my jewelry line with The Catch that are handcrafted by artisans in Kenya, inspired by multiple visits to this very market.

The market has plenty of vendors vying for your attention. That first visit was a bit overwhelming, but now I am a pro. I have returned

You never forget your first kiss at Nairobi's Giraffe Centre. A giraffe's saliva is antiseptic—don't be scared!

Lake Nakuru National Park in the Rift Valley is beautiful and peaceful; it is also home to a huge flamingo population.

to the Maasai Market on every visit to Nairobi. I thoroughly enjoy perusing the stalls and taking part in my favorite Olympic sport: negotiating. During my last trip to Nairobi, in November 2019, a few months before the global lockdown, I met a kind vendor named Arthur. After some bartering and a sale, he said, "You're very kind and you listen to people. I can tell you can fit in anywhere you go." It is funny how sometimes strangers see you more clearly than people you've known for decades.

I have returned to Kenya more than five times (the number at which I stop counting my visits to countries). Now, Nairobi feels like home. I have fallen in love with kissing giraffes at the Giraffe Centre and watching baby elephants roll around in mud after being fed milk from impossibly huge baby bottles at the Sheldrick Wildlife Trust Elephant Orphanage. I have created memories with expats and locals. I've explored a tea plantation, partied at a Damian Marley concert, and even brought a group of 10 clients to the country through my travel agency, Jet Black.

During that trip, I took my clients on safari and visited the Masai Mara for the first time. From Nairobi, you can fly to the Masai Mara or drive six to eight hours to reach the park. We took the latter option and arrived in the late afternoon at Basecamp Masai Mara, where a former U.S. senator who went on to be president once stayed. The Masai Mara, commonly thought to be a national park, is actually a national reserve that belongs to the Maasai people.

One of Africa's most recognizable tribes, Maasai are known for their height, beadwork, and traditional jumping dance known as *adumu*. In the movie *Black Panther,* the costumes of the Dora Milaje, the elite troupe of female bodyguards and special forces, were 80 percent based on the Maasai people, according to Anthony Francisco, the senior visual development illustrator at Marvel Studios Visual.

We spent time in a Maasai village, which was truly a highlight. Julius, the chief of the village, welcomed us with open arms and told us about Maasai culture, including adumu. According to Julius, part of the reason the dancers engage in jumping is to attract women—a motivation that clearly transcends cultures. The higher a man jumps, the more likely a woman is to approach him. At the end of the ceremony, the women all take a stick and put it in front of the man they choose. It's worth noting Maasai also practice polygamy.

I have been on safaris in more than 10 countries, and Kenya's Masai Mara is tied with Tanzania's Serengeti for first place. During our game drives, we saw herds of elephants and antelopes, prides of lions, a dazzle of zebras, a bloat of hippopotamuses, a tower of

Julius, the chief of his village, welcomed us with open arms and told us about Maasaï culture.

giraffes, and, most exciting, we watched a cheetah kill its prey. Our guide spotted the cheetah atop a hill. Other safari jeeps moved on, but we stayed. Before I realized what was going on, we started driving along the dirt road at high speed, chasing the cheetah as he pursued his prey, a rabbit who zigzagged his way across the plains, hoping to outsmart the world's fastest land animal. The rabbit's pattern threw the cheetah off for a bit, but inevitably only added mere seconds to his life. (*Game of Thrones* spoiler alert: I still do not understand why Rickon Stark did not zigzag when running from Ramsay's arrow.) The rabbit ran into a hole that was tragically too shallow, and the cheetah swiftly pulled the rabbit out in his mouth. It all happened so fast that not a single one of us got footage of the chase and kill. Our guide, who had been working in the park for more than two decades, said it was the first time he had ever seen a cheetah kill.

The Jet Black trip ended on Lamu Island, in the Indian Ocean off the coast of Kenya. One note: Don't go to Lamu in June, better known as "fly season." There's an extreme increase in flies due to the great migration, during which millions of wildebeests, zebras, and other animals move between the Masai Mara and Serengeti. The flies were nauseatingly annoying. They were on our food, bags—everything—and we could do very little about it. Consider this a warning.

Having been continuously inhabited for more than 700 years, unpretentious Lamu is one of the best preserved Swahili settlements in the region. There are no cars in Lamu's Old Town. Given the narrow streets, only donkeys that transport goods and, occasionally, people, are used. The mash-up of Swahili and Arab architecture is reflected in the arches of the beautiful white buildings, each constructed from coral limestone, and in the large hand-carved wooden doorways that adorn the ancient homes. Lamu's beaches might not be the best you will ever see, but the vibe and energy can't be beat.

We took in a gorgeous sunset aboard a dhow—a traditional sailing vessel—cruising on the Indian Ocean. Watching the skipper manually hoist the sail was mesmerizing. I watched the skipper's taut muscles at work as he skillfully moved to the sail to catch the next gust of wind. I thought to myself just how much we have lost the art of manual labor in the West. We really could save a lot on gym memberships if we all worked like this.

The food in Lamu is good. I mean *really* good. Aboard the dhow, our captain cooked a fish curry in a questionable steel drum. It was the best curry I've ever had. We all fought over the remnants with pieces of bread.

My food, growing up, included Indian flavors, a vestige of the British bringing Indians to East Africa. So I have been eating samosas since I was a child. Knowing my love for the dish, someone told me to ask for a fellow named Captain on Lamu. I was assured he would bring me some of the best samosas I've ever had. I can confidently report that he did. Though my mom's samosas are my favorite, Captain's fish samosas were so good that I called to tell her of this culinary discovery.

Kenya has solidified itself on my list of favorite countries. Nairobi should be on the list of top cities in the world, right up there with Rome, Paris, and New York. Outside of the city, there is so much on offer, from the Masai Mara to the national parks. The coastline along the Indian Ocean offers beautiful beaches and towns like Diani and Lamu. You can hike Mount Kenya, a UNESCO World Heritage site. What more can a place have to offer? How is this not topping everyone's bucket lists?

Fried whole fish is a staple in Kenya. My favorite can be found at Mama Oliech Restaurant in Nairobi.

iceland

JUST BEFORE I HAD MOVED BACK to Rome, I received an email from my dear friend keondra with the subject line "Thanksgiving in Iceland?" In the body of the email was a link to a travel deal from Icelandair, followed by, "I'm so serious." I immediately responded, "That sounds perfect to me." And just that easily, our trip to Iceland was born. One of the things I hate most about America's corporate workforce is that people never

EUROPE

use their time off. In 2018, 768 million vacation days went unused in the United States. Even before I traveled full time, I made sure to use every single vacation day that I had. When I had none, I took unpaid time off to explore. I made seeing the world, not my office, my priority. And the best trick I learned along the way was to pair paid vacation days with holidays and weekends to get through your bucket list.

Because of its location, the days in Reykjavik, the capital, are incredibly short in winter. I landed at 3:30 p.m. to a twilight sky. Our first dinner was at Snaps, where we dined on beefsteak, lamb, and the fish of the day. The prices gave us a bit of sticker shock. Iceland is an expensive country, but at least the food was delicious.

Following dinner, we went to a bar called Dolly and quickly made friends with the bartender, who let us taste the wide variety of Icelandic alcohol. Several of them are made from the same ingredients as bitter and salty Icelandic licorice (not my favorite), and the vodka tasted like gin. After a bit, keondra and I popped over to the beloved hot dog stand Baejarins Beztu Pylsur for a delicious snack.

The following day, we joined a glacier walk and northern lights tour. It was scheduled to be an intimidating 12-hour day, but it was worth every minute. Our guide shared the history of Iceland and several cultural traditions as we explored the surreal icy landscape. As we walked across the frozen mountain and ducked to make our way through tunnels made of ice, I realized this was one of the coolest things that I had ever done.

We made our way back down the glacier and took off our crampons—a new word in my vocabulary—cleaning off the dirt in a nearby lake. As she was cleaning her crampons, keondra slipped into the glacial lake. I spotted her, one leg submerged in the water. Not knowing how deep the lake was or if she was going to disappear into the icy depths before my eyes, I screamed at the top of my lungs, signaling our guide and another man to run over and pull her out. Always the trooper, she shook it off, while I remained slightly traumatized. On our way back to the city we stopped to see the Seljalandsfoss waterfall, one of the country's 10,000-plus waterfalls. In fact, 73 percent of the country's energy comes from hydropower. The waterfall was a wonderful site to see, dropping 200 feet (60 m) from an ice-covered cliff with sweeping landscapes in the distance. The falls slightly made up for missing the northern lights due to heavy cloud coverage.

The following day, alicia (keondra's then girlfriend, now wife) and I woke up early and headed to the Blue Lagoon, a geothermal spa of sorts. The lagoon was unlike anything I had ever seen. Still blue waters stretched for more than two acres (0.8 ha) with steam rising up as the heat of the water hit the cold air. The water was surrounded by black rock formations and wooden decks.

Iceland offers many options for the adventurous traveler looking to explore nature. Hiking a glacier was my favorite.

The experience at the lagoon was, at times, uncomfortable. Imagine standing in your swimsuit in freezing temperatures. I think I got frostbite on the bottom of my feet in the five seconds it took for me to run from where I hung my robe into the lagoon. Once you hop into the 85°F (29°C) water, you regain feeling in all parts of your body. Being in the water was very relaxing, but because it is only about two and a half feet (0.7 m) deep, you have to duckwalk to avoid exposing your body to the freezing temps. Your face is unguarded from the harsh winds, but the free silica mud masks offered some protection.

On my last afternoon in Reykjavik, I walked around the city and went to the flea market in search of an Icelandic wool sweater that wouldn't set me back $200. I found a gorgeous gray sweater with white accents that I still wear every winter. I finished the night at Icelandic Fish and Chips near the harbor, dining on fried pollack, garlic-topped potatoes, and a local beer, the perfect ending to my Icelandic adventures.

That visit to Iceland made me fall in love with winter in Scandinavia and started a new tradition. I've visited each Scandinavian country except Sweden during the Thanksgiving holiday.

senegal

I TAKE CELEBRATING MY BIRTHDAY, life achievements, and milestones incredibly seriously. So it came as no surprise to the more than 80 people that have traveled with me for one of my celebrations that I planned "30 days of 30," a multicity, multicountry, multicontinent 30th birthday celebration. My contract with the UN was coming to an end in May 2014, so I asked my supervisor for two months off to celebrate

AFRICA

my birthday. He countered with two weeks. I took the two weeks, then called to say I wasn't coming back. Once again I was out of a full-time job, but I was making travel my priority more and more. And I was being financially savvy about it, too. Having travel goals, I spent less money on clothes and shoes. I maximized the number of stops on a single trip and took advantage of airline and credit card rewards. I started a 52-week savings plan for my personal travel fund. So while I was without a job, I was not without means to get where I wanted to go.

Senegal was the first stop of seven countries on that 30-for-30 birthday trip, and that's exactly when my love affair with the country began.

For that first trip, I visited the Italian (though we were broken up, we were still close friends), who was living in Dakar. The bustling capital city is perched on the coast of the North Atlantic Ocean in western Africa and is the westernmost point of the continent's mainland. On the back of the Italian's scooter (of course), we rode around the city, visited markets, and ate good food. As we explored daily life in Dakar, I discovered a remarkable fitness culture. Just before sunset on the beach along the corniche was a fantastical sight: hundreds of people working out side by side. Nowhere in the world have I experienced such a display. At other famous beach destinations, you will see a few people using outdoor gym equipment, but nothing compares to this. In Dakar, men played soccer barefoot in the sand; women speed-walked with friends; others did

Senegal has a great local surf culture, and Paje, a Senegalese surfer, was the first African surfer I ever met.

pull-ups, dips, sit-ups, and jumping jacks. It is a big and beautifully uncoordinated workout.

Dakar is also known for its surf culture. My first full day in the city, we had lunch across the street from a surf shop. I watched as one surfer came out of the water. I was struck by his dark skin. I had never seen a Black surfer, let alone an African one. I used my French to ask for his name—Paje—and for a picture. I was starting to hone my photography skills at this point and found the most joy in capturing portraits of the people I encountered on my adventures. He thought I wanted a picture with his surfboard. When I corrected him, he seemed delighted.

The waves in Dakar are great for beginners and experts alike, so during two subsequent visits, I took surf lessons. Though I was not super successful, I did enjoy lying on my surfboard on the beach, watching the men catch waves. (On Yoff and Ngor beaches, you'll see plenty of dark-skinned, tall, and muscular surfers.)

There is something ethereal about Dakar. While you'll find the same hustle and bustle of the vast majority of the continent, the Islamic influence brings a sense of peace over the country, a calm energy. Every time I go, I fall in love all over again.

With 331 miles (533 km) of coastline, Senegal has plenty of beaches to choose from, and many locals and tourists escape the city for the slower-paced life of the beach towns south of Dakar. Little more than an hour's drive from the capital is the idyllic Toubab Dialaw. This little-known hideaway is often overshadowed by the much more popular Saly, which I also love and where I have spent many lazy days during subsequent trips. I fell in love with Toubab Dialaw because of the uncrowded beaches, the locals who were not working in the tourism industry, and the delicious food.

The beach was full of characters. A playful group of young boys, noticing my camera in hand, took turns jumping in front of my lens, inviting me to capture their bountiful joy and energy. There was Mohammed from Conakry, who I could tell was rapping, even from a distance, by the notebook in one hand and gesturing with the other. From my terrace, I watched another Mohammed swimming and wondered if the water was not cold on his skin. I decided to take a walk and met him on my way. After chatting for a while, he asked me to meet him later. He showed me a bag with a strange substance inside and all I could understand from his attempts at English was the word "gritty." I left, thinking he had offered me drugs. Later, after being invited to tea by Conakry's Mohammed, I realized this other Mohammed was trying to say "green tea." Talk about lost in translation. I met him later for tea and it was lovely.

On the shores of Lac Rose, artisans sell crafts next to the salt that is harvested from the bottom of the lake.

African countries are never a part of the conversation when talking about the world's best cuisines. Too many global food experts have barely scratched the surface of the African continent, only elevating the cuisines of North America, Europe, and Asia. A notable exception was Anthony Bourdain, who filmed episodes in 10 African countries; the final season of his television show *Parts Unknown* opened in Kenya.

The truth of the matter is traveling throughout the countries of Africa is an amazing culinary adventure for those willing to step outside of their comfort zone. Africa's food is as diverse as its people. And Senegal is at the top of my list for African fare. If you love food, go to Senegal.

As the westernmost point on the African continent, Senegal has seafood that is plentiful and fresh. Pointe des Almadies, a neighborhood on the western end of Dakar, offers expansive views of the Atlantic and several waterfront restaurants serving up fresh mussels, clams, and prawns. My favorite fish is the local *thiof,* a large, white grouper that is typically served whole and smothered in a chimichurri of sorts, or as part of a dish called *yassa poisson,* covered in lemon, garlic, mustard, and onions. *Yassa poulet,* made with chicken, is much easier to find.

You can find artisans selling beautiful home goods at Dakar's bustling Marché Kermel, my favorite market in the country.

Senegal is also home to *thieboudienne,* what many would consider the national dish. Prepared with fish, tomato sauce, rice, and vegetables, it is the original jollof rice, which has now been exported and adapted across West Africa. The word "jollof" is an alternate name of the Wolof people, a tribe that dates back to A.D. 300. The tribe dominates the Senegambia region.

Senegal also offers endless opportunities for adventure and culture seekers. The markets of Dakar are among my favorite places to buy home goods like baskets and plates made of teakwood. You can take an ATV from the city of Saly through the countryside to a baobab forest. The forest leads to a beach in Samone, where you are rewarded with delicious fresh seafood. You can also check out Lac Rose, a naturally pink lake where local people harvest salt; Dak'Art, the biennial art show; and amazing fashion brands like Tongoro Studio and Diarra Blu. And you can see the African Renaissance Monu-

ment, which at 171 feet (52 m) is the tallest statue in Africa, designed by a Senegalese architect and built by a North Korean company.

A 20-minute ferry ride from Dakar is Île de Gorée, a small island that played a role in the transatlantic slave trade. I recommend everyone visit its shores to understand firsthand the pure horror and inhumanity of slavery. This is not only African history and American history; this is European history, global history.

On my third visit to Île de Gorée in 2019—two months after making it to country 195—I thought long and hard about those who came before and those who will come after. I thought about the immense symbolism of my journey to every country in the world as a Black woman, an African woman, without the major sponsorship of some other country counters. I thought about my parents and the sacrifices they made to move to America. I thought about all the global forces set against me and people that look like me. My journey was long, arduous, lonely, exciting, fun, exhilarating, eye-opening, and life changing. The goal belonged to my community and the sacrifices of our ancestors as much as it belonged to me. My journey helps to normalize Blackness in traditionally white spaces. To normalize the female voice in male spaces. I increased visibility for Ugandans, Africans, Black people, and women. I am indeed my ancestors' wildest dream.

This energetic group of boys jumped in front of my lens while I was walking on the beach and taking pictures in Toubab Dialaw.

colombia

THOUGH I HATE TO ADMIT IT, I wasn't always the open-minded traveler that I am today. It took years of experience to get there. Need an example? In 2009, Spirit Airlines had a flight deal to both Colombia and Honduras. Elton asked which I wanted to go to. "Honduras," I quipped. "I want to come home with all of my organs." Back then, the stigma of a long-standing civil war and violence perpetrated by the Revolutionary

Armed Forces of Colombia (FARC) left an indelible mark on the country. That mark left many, including 24-year-old me, afraid to visit.

Five years later, a musician flew me to Medellín to see his show. In a city famed for its perfect weather, my 36 hours there were met with low-hanging gray clouds and light rain. Although I did not fall in love with Colombia on my 2014 whirlwind visit, my second trip secured the country's place in my heart.

In 2015, I was living and working in Washington, D.C. In a taxi home, I asked my driver where he was from, as I always do when I hear a foreign accent. I assumed he was from an African country. I was surprised when he told me that he was from San Andres, an island of Colombia. I immediately pulled out my phone and did a quick Google search. What I found was an island 93 miles (150 km) off the coast of Nicaragua and 497 miles (800 km) from the Colombian mainland. I had known there were Afro-Colombians, but I don't think I ever pictured them looking exactly like me. This is the interaction that led me to San Andres.

That September, after 12 hours of travel, my friend Kerrie and I arrived on the island, exhausted but overjoyed to see people who looked like us at the immigration station. San Andres is full of beautiful Afro-Colombians, and we immediately connected with them. Though the island lacks tourism infrastructure, we managed to get around using my Italo-Sprench—a beautiful and useful blend of Italian, Spanish, and French. We ate sublime shrimp ceviche and perfectly crispy french fries, washed down with *tinto de verano,* what I describe as a Colombian

SOUTH AMERICA

On my first trip to Cartagena, the colorful city on Colombia's Caribbean coast, I immediately fell in love with its energy.

Getsemani, a neighborhood in Cartagena's walled city, is great for people-watching and delicious food.

sangria. For Kerrie's birthday, we went to La Regatta, considered the best restaurant in San Andres. It was colorful and had lots of art, most of it made from recycled bottles. We were served breadfruit as an appetizer, something I had never heard of before. The "fruit" part is a misnomer. Breadfruit isn't sweet, but starchy like cassava or potato. I've since had it on many Caribbean islands. We feasted on lobster, fish, shrimp, and calamari, paired with the best piña coladas on the island.

For our last full day in San Andres, we made our way to Rocky Cay beach. Before lying under the Colombian sun, we had a beachfront lunch at The Grog. The no-frills spot served up big flavors on plastic tables and chairs on the beach. I had a whole red snapper with coconut rice that was so damn good! The staff, like the people everywhere on the island, were kind, funny, and welcoming.

San Andres is politically part of Colombia, but culturally very Caribbean. We met two fishermen on the beach and learned that the inhabitants of San Andres don't consider themselves Colombian; they think of themselves as islanders. One went so far as to say that he didn't like that Colombians were coming to the island and taking their jobs.

Though I enjoyed my time in San Andres, it was Cartagena that made me fall in love with Colombia. I am relatively easy to please when it comes to cities. Give me colorful buildings, beautiful architecture, lively and happy people, delicious food, and I am all yours. Cartagena is a city that sucks you in as soon as you arrive. More than anything, the energy of the city stole my heart.

Cartagena's architecture is sublime. Getsemani, the old, colonial walled city and fortress, is designated a UNESCO World Heritage site. Behind many of its beautiful doors are wonderful courtyards boasting an abundance of light, plants, and color. The building exteriors are an array of oranges, reds, and yellows, all punctuated by white trim. And if you look down, you will see that Cartagena has some of the most beautiful tiled floors in the world.

In the historic old town, you come across Palenqueras, Black women clad in colorful dresses, often seen with bowls of fruit atop their heads. The word originates from San Basilio de Palenque, a small village of formerly enslaved people who managed to escape to outside of Cartagena. In 1691, the town became independent and was effectively the first free African town in the Americas. Historically, the women took their fruit to Cartagena to earn an income for their families. While they make more money taking pictures with tourists today, their significance and quintessential position in the city cannot be ignored.

**MUST-EAT:
LA COCINA DE
PEPINA**

I am not sure how I stumbled upon this small restaurant on a small street in Getsemani. One fateful day, I walked in and my life was changed. La Cocina is a warm and homey spot for Colombian food influenced by the culinary tradition of Córdoba, a region on the Caribbean coast. The dishes are inspired by Pepina, aunt of the owner, Christian. On my first visit, he recommended I try *sopa Caribe*, a stew made with fresh fish—it blew me away. I've since been back countless times. With its rotating menu, you may not get the same thing twice, but no matter what is on your plate, you will not be disappointed.

Iconic Palenqueras are seen carrying their bowls throughout Cartagena—and these bowls are heavier than they look!

And the food . . . I have never had a bad meal in Cartagena. You have typical food like arepas, which are almost like a pita but made of ground maize and stuffed with eggs, meat, or cheese. At a small shop, Quero Arepa, I had a vegetable arepa, washed down with a fresh strawberry and mint juice. Dinner at Demente Tapas Bar is always on repeat when I visit the city. The langoustines in tamarind sauce are definitely my favorite; the beef tenderloin a close second.

During that first trip to Cartagena, we were unable to experience the city's nightlife because it was a dry weekend. Yes, during certain weekends that precede elections, the entire country restricts alcohol! A little bit of charm helped convince an older man running a liquor store to follow me into the back and stuff a bottle of rum into my purse. We entertained ourselves by people-watching in Plaza de la Trinidad, walking the walls of the fort, and dancing salsa with some locals.

You can take great day trips from Cartagena, like a *very* choppy speed-boat ride to Islas del Rosario, which offers great snorkeling or lazy days on the shores of Playa Blanca. The islands off the coast all offer more delicious seafood. With a front-row view of the Caribbean Sea, you can dine on fresh lobster and oysters shucked in front of you while you sip rum punch from a pineapple.

At El Totumo Mud Volcano, after a walk up some shady-looking wooden stairs, I reached a 50-foot-tall (15 m) mud bath, where I spent 10 minutes floating, and for a little extra, got a massage. After the soak, I moved on to the nearby lagoon, where a local woman washed me down, making sure no crevice on my body—none of them—had any remnants of mud. My skin felt like a newborn's booty.

During two trips with Jet Black, I took clients to Cali for a deeper dive into Afro-Colombian culture. On one trip, we had the pleasure of meeting the women of Asociación Lila Mujer, an organization that supports Afro-Colombian women living with HIV. They provide housing and access to health care, lawyers, and job opportunities. Janeth, the founder, is a bright light changing the lives of many in her community.

We also explored Galería Alameda, a must-visit food market with tasty local eats. Our trip would not have been complete without our stay at the Nomada, a spectacular home in the mountains that offers a respite from the city. The French host, Candice, and her Colombian husband truly made the stay in Cali one of my favorite city escapes. The high-energy salsa classes they organized in the massive living room were the icing on the cake.

My fifth trip was also my first visit to Bogotá, the capital. Did you know that Bogotá is the world's fourth highest capital city? Yeah, I didn't either. That 8,612-foot (2,525 m) altitude hit me like a ton of bricks. With only two days in the city, I wanted to see what I could, so I took the funicular up to Monserrate, roughly another 1,000 feet (300 m) above sea level. I had a quiet solo dinner overlooking the city. Then, on my walk back to the funicular, I felt dizzy and began to fall over. Lucky for me, an older security guard caught me and held my hand for 10 minutes as they called a nurse. I am always finding the kind people the world has to offer—even when I have to faint to do so. I took it easy for the rest of my time in the city. The staff of the Four Seasons kept the coca tea flowing and even gifted me with a dozen roses after my little fainting spell. Service at its finest.

Colombia has shaken the violent image that kept so many from visiting. Now it can proudly boast all it has to offer: Beautiful weather year-round; booming cities like Medellín, Bogotá, and Cartagena; great art, food, culture, and beautiful boutique hotels will bring me back again and again.

In Cali, I met Janeth, who founded Asociación Lila Mujer to support Afro-Colombian women living with HIV in the city.

denmark

MY VISIT TO DENMARK CAME EXACTLY when I needed it. In 2014, after a seven-year hiatus from the United States, I moved to Washington, D.C., to work for a consulting firm and to be closer to friends and family. After just two months in the nation's capital, the reverse culture shock was real. I couldn't get over the fact that the first thing a person asked upon intro-duction was, "What do you do for a living?" Or that people worked well

EUROPE

past 6 p.m. Or that getting fresh food could sometimes be a daunting task. So much for la dolce vita! To top it off, the nation was having a burgeoning overt racism reckoning. I was not enjoying my long-awaited return to my home country.

The night before I left for Denmark, I sat on my couch with my roommate, Anthony, and watched the announcement that the Ferguson grand jury would not bring charges in the shooting death of Michael Brown, Jr. Both of us cried and struggled to process another disappointment from the American criminal justice system. I woke up in tears the next morning at 6 a.m. My only comfort came from my perfectly timed vacation: I could escape 5,000 miles (8,050 km) from the reality of the country I lived in.

During my layover in the lounge in Amsterdam's Schiphol airport, numerous newspapers displayed the Ferguson decision on the front page. Headlines were in English, Spanish, French, Dutch, and German. Michael Brown, Jr., will never see Paris, but his story made it to the front page of *Le Monde*.

Copenhagen is a very homogeneous city full of wonderfully kind peo-ple. Unlike back home, I was not once made to feel aware of my race. Not once did someone default to English without me speaking it first. And to add icing to the metaphorical cake, I had a great conversation about race with a Danish bartender, who, blessed with an admirable ignorance, could not wrap his mind around racism in America.

The November weather was chilly, but I managed with a knee-length down jacket; a bright orange, chunky hand-knit scarf; and a vintage wool hat. Even with the threat of icy wind on your face, biking is by far the best way to see the city. Being that I'm always drawn to color, my favorite area was Nyhavn, a 17th-century waterfront spot where red, blue, and yellow buildings reflect on the water just below. It has been reimagined since its days as an active port and is filled with restaurants and shops.

Copenhagen has an extensive culinary scene, which should come as no surprise as it's home to the world's best restaurant, Noma. On my budget, I didn't make it to Noma, but I did find some gems. A recommendation led me to DØP's organic hot dog stand in the city center. Not only was it delicious, it was probably the cheapest treat in the otherwise pricey Nordic city. I spent about $6.50 on the Grillmedister, a pork sausage seasoned with wild garlic.

I looked up the top happy hours in the city, which led my friends and I to Kassen in the Nørrebrogade neighborhood. On the divier side of things, the bar's two-for-one drinks made it stand out over the other contenders. And the surplus of beautiful men more than made up for the lack of frills. I made it a point to mingle with some of the locals. As the bar filled up, the ratio of men to women was in my favor.

My friend made reservations for us at Oysters and Grill, a bustling restaurant where we shared tasty razor clams, scallops, tiger prawns, and fried soft-shell crab. The mahi mahi was perfectly seasoned—and as a bit of a french fry snob, I must say, their fries are divine!

I was dead set on getting to one of the city's best cocktail bars, even if that meant biking alone in temperatures below freezing. The Barking Dog did not disappoint. The ambience is exactly what you would expect in this pseudo-speakeasy. The interior is dark and moody, giving a mid-century feel. The cute and kind bartender suggested a Penicillin Highball—scotch and honey-ginger syrup. What's not to love?

Denmark is a cold country full of warm people. The five days of great food and handsome men were the welcome respite I needed from a harsh reality at home in America. In fact, Denmark was one of the friendliest countries I have ever visited—I am sure that is somehow related to the fact that it is considered one of the happiest countries in the world.

Nyhavn, once a bustling port in the 1600s, has been reimagined and is now filled with restaurants and shops.

haiti

HAITI IS A COMPLEX COUNTRY that has had to overcome many challenges. And it does not seem to be getting easier. At the time of writing, Haiti's president has just been assassinated in his home in the dark of night, an event that is sure to send this already fragile country into a spiral. As if that weren't enough, in August 2021 the country suffered a devastating magnitude 7.2 earthquake that left more than 650,000

people in need of humanitarian assistance—11 years after a horrific earthquake from which the country was still struggling to rebound.

But unlike most, I did not go to Haiti on a "mission" or for work. I went to Haiti for vacation, and it was better than I ever imagined. May my words be a love letter to a country that is etched on my heart.

Haiti is the most populated country in the Caribbean, and the poorest in the Western Hemisphere, despite sharing an island with the Dominican Republic, the most visited country in the Caribbean. Much of this poverty can be traced back to January 1, 1804, when Haiti gained independence from France in a successful slave rebellion following the defeat of Napoleon's army. This act made Haiti the first independent nation in Latin America and the Caribbean, and the second republic in the Americas, after the United States. But France, suffering a huge loss of their "property," demanded reparations be repaid for more than a century. Then, in the early 1900s, the U.S. invaded the country, leading to more political and economic instability.

Fast-forward to more recent years, and Haiti can't catch a break. The country has struggled to find its footing ever since a devastating earthquake in 2010. To make matters worse, a cholera outbreak, linked to UN peacekeepers, killed nearly 10,000 Haitians and sickened another 800,000. It was another dagger in the country's back.

I first visited Haiti in March 2015, as a spring break of sorts while living and working in Washington, D.C. Since living abroad, my wanderlust hadn't abated, and I was taking every opportunity I had to

NORTH AMERICA

People do not often think of Haiti as a tourist destination, but the island boasts beautiful beaches with turquoise waters.

The streets of Port-au-Prince are buzzing with energy, people, and life despite Haiti's hardships.

travel. Though I hadn't officially declared a goal of seeing every country in the world, I had generally hoped to by the time I was 50. At this point, I managed to continue adding countries to my count while still working a nine-to-five.

I wish I could say I was taken aback by the reactions people had when I said I was visiting Haiti for vacation—but I wasn't. I was met with shock, awe, and outright disbelief. I found it particularly funny when these reactions came from people who had more than happily vacationed in the Dominican Republic. I wondered if they knew the two countries sit on the same piece of land.

I was eager to shake off the chill of the East Coast, and the Caribbean island was the perfect salve. Haiti immediately felt like home once I exited customs. The buzz of taxi drivers trying to secure their next fare reminded me of Uganda. In a sea of Black faces, I spotted a man holding up a misspelled version of my last name; his beauty had me thinking about relocation.

As we rode through the streets of the capital, I could see clear damage from the 2010 earthquake. But more important, I saw resilience: A man sold fresh sugarcane on the side of the road. I watched hawkers selling cell phone chargers and chewing gum in traffic, people joyfully yelling to one another across the street, and the telltale hustle of people who often do not have enough. From my perspective, Haiti is Africa.

Following a three-hour drive through the mountainous Haitian countryside, we arrived in Jacmel, a coastal town in the south of the country. At a boutique hotel, Villa Nicole, owned by brothers Yves-Nick and Stephane, my friends and I spent days lazing under the Haitian sun and being serenaded on the beach by a gentleman named Jameson who sang "African Queen" to our delight. Late nights were spent around the pool, drinking whiskey and champagne and listening to waves crash on the beach. I have never eaten so much lobster, which I ordered at every meal. The garlic butter sauce was made fresh every time we ordered it—and we ordered it a lot. Seven years later, it is still the best lobster I have ever eaten.

We rode about 45 minutes in the back of a pickup truck to get to Bassin Bleu, a series of pools and waterfalls. A short hike and a climb down a small cliff led to a serene cove with a beautiful little cascade. You could dive into the cobalt pools below from several levels. While some people climbed to the top, fear got the best of me. But I managed to jump from two of the three levels.

That first trip to Haiti confirmed what I already knew: Haitians are incredibly welcoming and proud of their country and history. There are beautiful beaches to see, delicious foods to eat, and adventures to be had.

Always one to go for the shot, I posed on the bow of the ship, lost my footing, and fell into the waters below.

In July 2015, I founded my boutique travel agency, Jet Black. The idea came to me after helping a friend organize his honeymoon. I wanted to curate trips, with the focus of "changing the narrative," as our tagline said. I was still working full time, but this side hustle took me one step closer to making travel the sole focus of my career. I used my job income to print business cards and create a website. That first trip to Haiti sparked an idea to go beyond working only with private clients and to also lead group trips, which I dubbed Jet Black Jaunts.

The inaugural Jet Black Jaunt to Haiti was in November 2015. Eight intrepid travelers joined me to learn about Haiti's culture, taste its food, and explore its beaches. I couldn't have asked for a better or more dynamic group of clients for that first Jet Black trip. They were adventurous, open-minded, and ready to take Haiti on. We explored Port-au-Prince, stopping first at the Cathedral of Our Lady of Assumption, once the largest church in the Caribbean. The church was destroyed in the 2010 earthquake, and its beauty remains a shell of its former self. Remnants of the stained glass windows are evidence of its former elegance. We went to the Iron Market, the largest in the city. One side is dedicated to food and home goods, the other to souvenirs, leather goods, and paintings from local artists. There, a seller asked how I was so good at bargaining. I simply replied, "This is what I do," our exchange in French.

We dove further into Haiti's complex story at the National Museum. It was an emotional experience delving into colonialism, slavery, triumph, and other moments of the beautiful nation's complex history.

We also went on a challenging hike in the mountains to the village of Kay Piat. None of us was prepared for the difficult path in the brutal early morning Haitian sun. Though locals sometimes walk this route three times a day, we struggled in our single attempt. But our efforts were rewarded with a dip in the cool waters of a watercress pool and fresh coconut water to drink. The rest of the trip was full of jokes, photo shoots, cultural experiences, rum punches, intense games of Connect 4, and lobster after lobster.

My third trip to Haiti was to celebrate the two-year anniversary of Jet Black's group trips. On our last full day, we turned our urban holiday into a beach vacation, enjoying the warm waters of the Caribbean at la Côte des Arcadins. We boated to the strikingly clear, azure water in front of la Gonave island, where we disembarked to snorkel, float in the sea, and speak with merchants who paddled up to our boat to sell paintings, freshly cooked lobster (best decision ever), and small sculptures.

That afternoon, Ms. Helen, a Taiwanese American grandmother and the mother of another guest, Stacey, played bartender. She refilled everyone's glass with the deceptively potent rum punch that our boat host had prepared. What we didn't know was that Ms. Helen was filling her own glass every time she filled ours! By the end of the ride, she was passed out at the front of the boat. We applied sunscreen and covered her with a towel so she wouldn't wake up sunburned. I may or may not have passed out next to Ms. Helen, having washed my rum punches down with a celebratory bottle of champagne. I also may or may not have also fallen off the front of the boat during an attempt to get an epic Instagram photo.

Haiti is a true example of a place that changes depending on the lens through which you view it. Many think Haiti is a place of poverty and suffering, one that they would only visit for volunteer work. But Haiti stole my heart. It is a beautiful Caribbean island with a lot to offer tourists. Its history makes it one of the most fascinating countries in the Caribbean. And though turmoil continues to embroil the country, tourism will only help to increase the livelihoods of these people.

To the people of Haiti, my love has always been and always will be with you. Your strength and resilience is a testament to the human spirit and community. May you continue to survive, continue to live, continue to love.

laos

IN AUGUST 2015, I left my last full-time job. My first experience working in an American office, at a consulting firm near Washington, D.C., was also my last. I left the toxic work environment for better mental health. And though I didn't have a clear plan, I knew that travel was still a top priority. Jet Black, though not yet financially viable, was getting there and needed more of my attention. And I had enough savings to

ASIA

hold me over for a bit. I knew things would work themselves out. Without regrets, I walked out of those office doors, put my belongings in storage, and began my next chapter.

To celebrate my new, freer life, I planned a solo trip through five countries in Southeast Asia. Laos was not on my original itinerary, but a Thai friend from grad school, Prat, suggested I visit Luang Prabang.

A short and ridiculously picturesque flight from Chiang Mai, Luang Prabang is what dreams are made of: As we dropped below the clouds, I could see the lush green mountains, pierced by the majestic Mekong River—a source of life in Thailand, Laos, Cambodia, and Vietnam.

Home to hundreds of monks, Luang Prabang's energy brought me an unshakable peace in a way that very few places have. I had traded my gray cubicle for this. No regrets to be had here.

I began my adventure at a quaint two-story hotel north of the city on the banks of the Nam Ou River. I was the only guest and was grateful for the remote setting. From an infinity pool overlooking the mountains, I enjoyed the slow pace of life.

I took a cruise up the Nam Ou and Mekong Rivers on a traditional boat. As the boat made its way through the murky waters, we were surrounded by mountains with jagged cliffs, covered in bright green trees. Our first stop was in a small village, where two kind and curious villagers offered us cold beer, a welcome relief from the heat.

Our journey continued up the river to the Pak Ou Caves, which were filled with hundreds of wood and metal Buddha statues. From the lower cave, Tham Ting, we climbed what felt like a million stairs to Tham Theung. It was worth the sweat to see the 16th-century temple.

On the advice of a local, I biked to Mount Phousi to catch the sunset. But on arrival, I met a daunting 328 steps to the summit. What is it with Buddhists and all of these steps? My efforts were rewarded with 360-degree views of Luang Prabang from Wat Chom Si, the temple at the peak. At the end of the rainy season, the dense green landscape was only interrupted by the tops of gilded temples and slanted roofs. With the Mekong River in full view, mountains in the background, and cumulus clouds hugging the blue skies, the sun said its goodbye, leaving a trail of pink across the horizon.

I was not going to skip out on Luang Prabang's famous bustling night market, where I purchased rice wine with a snake in it. Seven years and counting, that bottle still sits with the collection on my bar, untouched. Now I'm just scared to open it.

As an early riser, I was rewarded by witnessing *tak bat*—almsgiving— where people line the streets just after sunrise to offer food to hundreds of monks. You see the joy on the faces of the givers as they place a handful of rice into the bowls of barefoot monks—still one of the most beautiful displays of humanity I have witnessed.

Tak bat—almsgiving—begins just after sunrise, when people in town line the streets to offer food to hundreds of monks.

SNAPSHOT FROM INDONESIA: The stunning landscape of the Tegalalang Rice Terrace north of Ubud is quintessentially Balinese.

finland

IN 2014, I SPENT THANKSGIVING in Denmark. In 2015, I continued my Scandinavian tradition by visiting Finland with my friend Veronica from Detroit. My Finnish grad school friend, Suvi, played host to us in Helsinki. Our first night, she took us to Cafe Talo, which was part dive bar, part pub. I ordered the organic lamb neck, served with root vegetables, mashed potatoes, and a perfect red wine sauce. At 18 euros, it was a

EUROPE

well-priced Scandinavian meal and one of the best I had in the country. The bartender gave me the history of various traditional drinks, and I ultimately chose to go with glogg, a hot mulled wine, sans the usual raisins and almonds. We also had cocktails at a packed bar called Why Join the Navy When You Can Be a Pirate. Yes, that is the actual name.

But this trip wasn't about Helsinki. Because I was unable to see the northern lights in Iceland, this was my second attempt to see the aurora borealis. To stack the odds in our favor, we wanted to be as close to the North Pole as possible. So we ended up in Lapland, an area of Finland in the Arctic Circle.

I usually do not get overly excited about trips; as a seasoned traveler I'm typically even-keeled and allow the experiences to unfold in real time. My trip to Lapland was different. The buildup was insane. I was like a child anticipating Christmas. The flight from Helsinki was only an hour, but the landscape outside "Santa's Hometown Airport" was completely changed. We swapped the cold urban center for vast stretches of woods, even colder temperatures, and snow!

Our first stop was the famed Santa Claus Village, which was incredibly exciting for my inner child. The way they go all out for Christmas, with a giant decorated tree and bright lights strung throughout Santa Claus Village, made me pretend, if only for an hour, that I still believed in Santa Claus. Santa himself—a multilingual but slightly creepy man, like all mall Santas—wasn't the thrill. But within Santa Claus Village was the marker of the Arctic Circle line of latitude. We were at the southernmost point of the Arctic Circle! Can you tell that I am a geography geek?

An hour's drive south was Ranua, a small town where we spent our two nights in Lapland. In the evening, we went snowshoeing; it was much more difficult and much less fun than we had imagined. Luckily for us, the Finns have got the whole surviving-the-cold thing down pat. They provided us with super warm boots, snowsuits, and mittens that were much warmer than the gear we brought. We lasted about 30 minutes snowshoeing through the dark woods, though I have a feeling if Veronica and I had complained a bit less, it would've been much longer.

After the trek, we returned to a "Lotte house," a small wooden shelter built by the government. They are built throughout rural parts of the country to ensure that passersby can build a fire and take a break from the freezing temps. Our guides heated berry juice, and over a fire we roasted marshmallows that Veronica had brought from Paris. We used the Finns' chocolate and gingerbread cookies to complete our s'mores.

My first visit to the Arctic Circle was to Finnish Lapland. Rovaniemi, the capital, is Santa's hometown.

If you are in Finland, you must go dogsledding! Because we were in Lapland during low season, we were the only ride of the day. As we approached the tour facility, we saw the owner's daughter anxiously waiting for us—and the 80 dogs they owned were quite anxious, too. As soon as we got out of the car, we could hear them yelping with excitement.

Our team of eight dogs whisked us through the wooded, snowy landscape, leaving our exposed cheeks frozen. And while our guide led the way on his own sled in front of us—effectively regulating the speed—I took liberties to speed up when I had the chance, removing my foot slightly from the brake as often as I could. Even though it was blisteringly cold, that dogsled ride is truly one of my most memorable vacation experiences.

By our last evening, it was clear the northern lights had eluded us, thanks again to heavy cloud coverage (I still have yet to see them). But we still decided to hop in the car and drive around at 2 a.m. We were rewarded with an arctic fox spotting and the silence and solace of Lapland. We parked the car on the side of the road, turned off the lights, lowered the windows, and simply enjoyed the peace.

Peru

ONE OF MY TRAVEL MOTTOES IS "Chase the deal, not the destination." When you get stuck on visiting a specific destination at a specific time, you're at the mercy of available flight offerings and ticket prices. If, however, you just want to travel, let the flight deal lead the way. This practice has taken me all over the world on a budget. So when I saw a $295.50 flight deal from Washington, D.C., to Lima, Peru, it was a

SOUTH AMERICA

no-brainer. I invited Elton and his then boyfriend, Jeff, along. (Note: I really like traveling with friends, but be wary of traveling with couples. You will undoubtedly get the short end of the stick. In the case of Peru, this meant sleeping on a rollaway bed in the middle of a kitchen.)

We touched down in Lima and immediately caught a domestic flight to Cusco. The southeastern city is the gateway to Machu Picchu, one of the Seven Wonders of the Modern World. As we approached, the snowcapped Andes came into view, cutting through the clouds. Cusco, the former Inca capital, sits at an elevation of 11,200 feet (3,400 m). As had happened in Addis and Bogotá, I could feel every inch of that high elevation. High altitude and I are not friends. Walking around, I felt like a baby elephant was sitting on my chest. Knowing how drastic the effect is on tourists, some of the taxi stands offer coca leaves—a remedy for altitude sickness.

Our hotel, four flights of stairs above the street, offered a firsthand understanding of how elevation affects the human body. We dreaded the walk up. One night, I asked Elton for a piggyback ride. I am not sure what superhuman strength he activated, but he *ran* up those stairs with me on his back.

Snuggled in a valley of the Andes Mountains, Cusco is picturesque, with a clear architectural nod to its Spanish colonizers. The reddish roofs sit in beautiful contrast to the brown mountains and bright blue skies. The energy of the city is calm, genuine, and kind.

Just outside the city lies the Sacred Valley of the Inca, also known as the Urubamba Valley, home to Machu Picchu. It is worth exploring the valley outside of the famed monument. The easiest way to do so is to

This gorgeous 80-year-old grandmother focuses intently on spinning her wool in Peru's Sacred Valley of the Inca.

The Sacred Valley of the Inca, home of Machu Picchu, is best visited with a private driver for fun stops along the way.

hire a driver. Ours, William, made suggestions along the way and would stop at a moment's notice when we wanted to take in the scenery.

At Tika Huerta, a small textile production center run by women, the kind and energetic crafters took their time to explain every bit of the process of creating the beautiful handwoven alpaca and sheep's wool pieces that they, of course, tried to sell us. Since 2500 B.C., weaving has been an important part of Peruvian culture. It sits at the very core of Quechua culture, shaping personal and regional identities and acting as a form of interregional communication, the intricate patterns carrying very specific meanings. We learned how to clean the wool, dye it using natural products, and weave it. I even got a chance to try spinning wool myself. These women don't miss a beat and proudly showcased their expertise. The star of the show was an 80-year-old grandmother who paid us little mind, intent on spinning her wool.

After a few hours in the car, we arrived in Ollantaytambo, a very quiet and quaint town with a name that took me several attempts to pronounce correctly. Like many places in the Sacred Valley, there are Inca ruins throughout. Ollantaytambo, once a retreat for Inca royalty and nobility, is where the Inca fought some of their last battles, resisting Spanish conquest from the still intact fortress and staggered terraces rising up around the town. The top of the ceremonial center is the perfect place for panoramic views of the Sacred Valley.

If you make it to Ollantaytambo, have a meal at Uchucuta. The rolled chicken with mushrooms was amazing. The restaurant served hands down the best pisco (grape brandy) sour of the entire trip. We stayed at La Casa del Abuelo Riverside, a very simple, cheap, and clean hotel with comfortable beds and a very good breakfast. They even packed us breakfast to go when we took an early train to Machu Picchu.

To get the best experience at Machu Picchu (read: how to avoid tourists), we went during low season. Though there are still a lot of people, it does not compare to the high season (July and August). At the end of April, the weather was warm and our pictures weren't littered with crowds.

We took PeruRail from Ollantaytambo to the base of Machu Picchu in Aguas Calientes. We chose the early train, or the expedition service, which is the lowest-priced option.

Machu Picchu is a testament to the intellectual prowess of the Inca. Built into the mountains over a span of 60 years during the 15th century, it was abandoned when word came that the Spanish killed the king in the north. The ancient city was left largely untouched.

While the beauty of the landscape and the archaeological site are not lost on me, I have to admit, it was all quite anticlimactic. I had been inundated with so many images of Machu Picchu that it didn't feel new. Unpopular opinion, but Machu Picchu looks just like the pictures and it just isn't that exciting.

The following day, we explored more of the Sacred Valley. At a pit stop on the roadside in Lomay, our driver insisted we try what looked like rat kebabs. The animal in question was actually *cuy,* better known as guinea pig, a local delicacy. In Lomay, cuy is roasted on a stick, a particular preparation in this city. It really does look like a rat, with its little paws intact. I tried a tiny piece. Unable to get the rat on a stick out of my head, I threw up a little in my mouth when the tiny morsel hit the back of my throat. Elton and Jeff were much more adventurous.

Back in Cusco, we had a much more palatable dinner at Chicha, a restaurant by world-famous Peruvian chef Gaston Acurio. From the carpaccio to the *lomo saltado* (sirloin stir-fry) to the pisco sours the meal was the best we had in Peru.

Peru makes the top of many people's bucket lists, and for good reason. Though most only go for Machu Picchu, this South American gem has so much to explore. I found more joy in exploring the Sacred Valley, seeing artisans at work, and learning more about Andean culture than I did standing in view of the world-famous ruins.

Abandoned in 1572 during the Spanish conquest of the Inca Empire, Machu Picchu, an Inca citadel, has been restored to its former glory.

cuba

IN 1961, THE UNITED STATES SEVERED its diplomatic ties with Cuba during the Cold War. Although the Cold War ended in 1991, diplomatic relations weren't restored until 2015 (with financial, commercial, and economic embargoes still in place, which continue to suppress the Cuban economy). In January 2021, the outgoing U.S. presidential administration placed Cuba on the list of state sponsors of terrorism.

American tourism is still banned, and the U.S. government only allows its citizens to visit the country for one of 12 reasons (the list ranges from work-related activities such as journalism and research to religious trips and visiting family).

For most Americans, Cuba is uncharted territory, but I visited four times in an 18-month period. (My travel media platform allowed me to enter Cuba for journalistic reasons.) I made my first trip to the Caribbean's largest island with 18 of my friends (many of whom I traveled with to Brazil) to celebrate my 32nd birthday. We were picked up from the airport in vintage American cars, a reflection of the U.S. trade embargo and Cuban ingenuity. We were immediately introduced to the warmth of the Cuban people at our rental house in the Miramar neighborhood, once home to Havana's elites. The house staff made us feel like family, even though they did not speak much English and we, not much Spanish.

We spent five days eating fresh fruit, visiting Viñales to see how the world-famous cigars are made (and smoking a few), dancing in the streets, watching sunsets on the Malecón (a five-mile [8 km] stretch of waterfront that starts in Old Havana and ends in Vedado), drinking more mojitos than I can count, and making an entire music video in the pool at the house (without internet, you find ways to entertain yourself).

Cuba has a magnetic energy. It is the beauty of the Cuban spirit, the dilapidated though beautiful buildings that line the streets of Havana,

NORTH AMERICA

The faded yet colorful buildings lining Havana's streets tell its storied history, a reflection of Spanish colonization, yet uniquely Cuban.

Walking down the streets of Havana, I met this beautiful woman who invited me to share a cigar.

the joy and community among people who have so little. That energy is what brought me back to Cuba three subsequent times with Jet Black clients, who I hoped would fall in love with the country just as I did. Spoiler alert: Everyone loved it!

I could write a whole book on what to see and do in Cuba. To start, a visit to the Viñales Valley is imperative to understand the history and process of one of Cuba's most famous products, cigars. Surrounded by mountains, Viñales is a small and sleepy town in the Pinar del Rio Province of Cuba's countryside. Here, the best tobacco is harvested. The famed Cuban cigars take around nine months to produce, from seed to cigar.

Cigarmaking is one of the primary livelihoods for families living in Pinar del Rio. The same families have owned many of the farms for generations. (For example, we visited a small family farm and met Dagoberto, a farmer and expert who has been hand-rolling cigars nearly his whole life.) Despite the farmers' hard work, every year the government takes 90 percent of the harvest to make official Cuban-branded cigars. The farmers are allowed to do what they want with their 10 percent share of tobacco, but they can only sell their cigars in Pinar del Rio. On the farms, cigars are much cheaper than those you find in Havana.

Back in Havana, I always leave time to wander the streets. Habana Vieja, or Old Havana, is as enchanting in person as it is in pictures. I am transported back to the golden days when the now tattered buildings were newly built and Nat King Cole enjoyed mojitos at La Bodeguita del Medio. Surrounded by beautiful architecture, bright colors, and lively people, Havana abounds in good vibes.

The sense of time traveling is bolstered by riding along the Malecón in a 1950s Chevy. This should come as no surprise. In almost every picture of Cuba you will see old American cars lining the streets. It is easy to get a ride in a classic car, whether you are doing an official city tour or flagging down a taxi for a quick ride to dinner. I felt like I was on a movie set the afternoon we rode around in a convertible with salsa music blaring from the speakers, waving at people in the street as we drove by. Warning: Many of these old-school cars don't have air-conditioning. Be prepared for a hot ride!

For a must-do experience in Old Havana, I highly recommend a visit to La Guarida. The restaurant is nestled on the third floor of a beautifully aged multifamily building. The food is exquisite, but the best way to experience it is at their rooftop bar during sunset. With a cocktail in hand, you can look over the entire city coming to life at night as you dine on tuna tartare and beef tenderloin.

WHERE TO EAT IN HAVANA

Navigating the food scene in Cuba can be tough thanks to U.S. sanctions that affect food imports and access to ingredients. In my experience, Cuba is not the kind of place where you just stumble into a delicious restaurant. After four visits I have fine-tuned a list of restaurants that I always go back to:

1. El Chanchullero, Habana Vieja—cheap delicious eats
2. El del Frente, Habana Vieja—great food, rooftop, and staff
3. El Litoral, Malecón—great for sunset
4. El Cocinero, Vedado—relaxed rooftop vibes
5. San Cristóbal, Centro Habana—where Obama ate
6. La Guarida, Centro Habana—requires reservations
7. La Bodeguita del Medio, Habana Vieja—where Nat King Cole was a regular
8. Nao Bar Paladar, Habana Vieja—great traditional Cuban food
9. Flor de Loto, Centro Habana—Chinese food and a local favorite

When I encountered these men playing dominoes in Havana and asked if I could join, they let me in on the fun!

Cuba, first and foremost, is a Caribbean island. That means tons of beautiful white sand beaches jut out into the warm waters of the Caribbean Sea. The pristine beaches of Varadero are reserved largely for tourists. I prefer Playa Santa Maria, a beach just 30 minutes outside of Havana. The crystal coastline is filled with local people enjoying fresh seafood, good rum, and lots of music. The few times I visited, we were the only tourists, and the locals made us feel like friends.

Havana boasts the largest population of Afro-Cubans in the country. The ties to Africa can still be felt in many ways, including in the practice of Santería—a local religion derived from the Yoruba religion of West Africa—and in Cuban salsa dancing, which has African roots.

Salsa originated in Cuba in the early 1900s. The iconic Latin American music that we hear today evolved from a blend of African drums and Spanish guitars. And a trip to Cuba is not complete without learning the dance for yourself. At La Casa del Son, located in the heart of Old Havana, you can do just that. The dancers teach you traditional Cuban dances, in addition to salsa. The teachers are full of energy and the class feels like one big party.

My Spanish is far from perfect, but native speakers applaud my rolling r's, which I perfected after nearly three years of living in Italy. With the little Spanish I could muster, along with my French and

Italian, I was able to unlock Cuba in a way that made it a bit more special. My mash-up of languages allowed me to speak easily with locals and make authentic connections. Walking down the streets of Central Havana, a beautiful Black woman who was sitting on the curb in a bright blue Playboy Bunny tank top, smoking a cigar, called me over. When I told her I was from East Africa, she got excited and said that we are family. Her people are from Mozambique. I was filled with so much joy as she introduced me to the rest of her family and we shared her cigar. Later, another woman walking by with her two sons pushed the older one into a picture with me. Though he barely reached my waist, he had a smile that lit up the world. With his dark skin, he looked like he could be mine.

The Cuban people are full of joy and a rare kindness. Despite tough economic circumstances, Cubans have a zest for life that is infectious. Cuba's history is, of course, fascinating, but it's the people's joie de vivre that makes the place. It's beautiful to witness and worth the effort of getting to the hard-to-access country. It's the people who continue to draw me back to the island. Cuba is easily in my top 10 favorite countries. It is often harder for me to write about the places I love so much, so I will leave you with this love letter to her:

I miss your colors and your energy. I miss the vibe when I step out of the airport, the feeling that I have arrived in another world. I miss the green lands and rolling hills of Viñales. The care with which cigar rollers twirl the delicate paper. I miss your smells—fresh fruit in the market, the salt water of the Caribbean at Playa Santa Maria. I miss the sounds, feet dancing salsa on wooden floors in the studio, the yelling of young men playing football in the streets, blaring music on street corners. I miss your people—your beautiful Black people who I feel a kinship with—who welcomed me with open arms. Who, with my broken Spanish, I connected with, heart to heart, in the absence of tongues. I miss your rum, the mojitos, and the sweet sips of a seven-year añejo. I miss your food, ropa vieja, arroz y frijoles negros, and maduros. I miss your sun rays on my skin and the joys of dancing in your streets. I miss the detail of your architecture, colorful and faded, showing your storied history, colonial yet uniquely Cuban. Cuba, I miss you. When you allow me, I will run into your arms, and I know you will hug me back!

Most of the cars on the island—including this 1950s Chevy—pre-date the U.S. embargo, which began in 1962.

ireland

JUST OVER A YEAR INTO full-time entrepreneurship, I was doing well with Jet Black. I was living the life of a digital nomad, bouncing between L.A., New York, and Detroit, sleeping on the couches of friends and family who would have me, and traveling internationally when the right flight deals came about. Even after spending four years living in Europe, I never had a strong desire to visit Ireland. Enter a flight deal. While in

EUROPE

Oakland, California, with my friends Ashley and Rosie, I saw flights from San Francisco to Dublin for around $350. I am very good at convincing my friends to take international trips with me (of the 195 countries, I explored 126 with friends). Within 30 minutes, we had booked our flights and began planning an epic road trip.

I have road-tripped across 25 different countries. Driving offers the freedom to go exactly where you want and the opportunity to stop on the roadside or meander into off-the-beaten-path places. Though there are some challenges: I am still mastering driving on the left side of the road and have bumped into a curb or two.

Our route began in Dublin. Though we managed to avoid any pubs—none of us are avid beer drinkers—we did come upon a low-key spot called the Vintage Cocktail Club. The dimly lit speakeasy instantly transported us back in time. Our waiter, who looked like he had been spit out of a Lower Manhattan vintage store, delivered cocktails and food so exquisite that we went back the following evening.

From Dublin, we drove south. The beautiful rolling green hills were dotted with sheep outnumbering the citizenry. We drove from Cork south to Killarney, a cute town with lots of shops, restaurants, and sights, including Aunt Nellie's Sweet Shop, where we stocked up on treats for the rest of our trip.

The next stop was the Cliffs of Moher, one of Ireland's most visited sites. The jagged brown cliffs, topped with bright green grass, stand high above the Atlantic as its waters crash on the shores below.

After a few hours at the cliffs, we headed to Doolin Sea Salt Décor for a delicious lunch of perfectly fried cod and chips. After receiving our check, we were told that it was a cash-only establishment. Not one of us had cash on hand. The nearest working cash machine was approximately 40 minutes away. The manager told us we could wash dishes in lieu of paying—as if we were in a movie.

Suddenly I blurted out, "I have cash!" When I travel, my mother gives me cash that I stash in my travel wallet. She insists I take it, just in case. Until that moment, I had forgotten that a crisp $100 bill was sitting in the wallet. I let out a "Thanks, Mommy" and have never refused her money since.

Back on the road, we made our way through the beautiful seaside town of Galway before we landed at Dromoland Castle. The imposing castle, which sits on meticulously manicured grounds with a small lake, dates back to the 16th century and currently operates as a luxury hotel.

While on the property, we entertained ourselves with "gentlemanly" activities. Having not done archery since summer camp when I was 12, I was thrilled at the chance. I proved I still had a few skills. Falconry, on the other hand, made me nervous; I was sure that the bird would gouge out my eyes. We finished with clay pigeon shooting. The day was punctuated by a glass of whiskey in the parlor.

Ireland is one of the reasons I've stuck to my flight deal motto—had I not been open-minded, I would never have had this experience.

Atop the famous Cliffs of Moher sits O'Brien's Tower, marking the highest point of the cliffs.

indonesia

INDONESIA IS A VAST COUNTRY, with a land area of more than 735,000 square miles (1,903,500 km²). It is home to more than 270 million people, making it the fourth most populated country in the world. I was hesitant to include it in this book, because I have only visited one of its 17,508 islands. But Bali holds such a special place in my heart. It is where my official journey to 195 began. In 2017, I was using L.A. as a home base,

running Jet Black with no permanent address. Business was going well—Jet Black boasted more than 100 clients and accounted for 85 percent of my income—and I enjoyed running the travel company, but I wasn't incredibly passionate about it. If I am honest, I was mentally checked out, a bit depressed, and unsure about my path forward. So when a flight deal to Bali popped up, I booked a two-week trip to give myself some time to figure things out. I mean, who didn't read *Eat, Pray, Love*?! I knew Bali was a place where people had spiritual journeys and awakenings. Maybe I could find peace and clarity.

Bali is far. Incredibly far. From L.A., I took a 15-hour flight to Sydney, Australia, had a two-hour layover, and then a six-and-a-half-hour flight to Denpasar, the provincial capital. Then, I had a one-hour ride to my hotel in Ubud, Bali's spiritual center. I was more than grateful to check into my beautiful hotel room, designed in quintessential Balinese style with rich dark wood floors, mixed use of indoor and outdoor spaces, and a stone bathtub just in front of an outdoor space filled with green plants. A peace came over me, and the stress of more than 25 hours of travel melted away.

My days and movements were dictated by suggestions from friends and the wind blowing me in the right direction. In Ubud, a friend and I went on long walks in the oppressive heat and humidity of the rainy season. Sweat ran down our bodies as we discovered delicious restaurants and small shops around every corner.

Over a meal of succulent pork ribs and a ginger martini, we had a conversation that ultimately changed my life. I went back over my

ASIA

Green Bowl Beach on Bali's southern tip is a relaxed and uncrowded beach, perfect for enjoying the afternoon sun.

résumé. Most would say I was successful. I earned two university degrees with honors; had a great, even if short-lived, corporate career; worked for the United Nations; and was having a cocktail in country 60. But I was unfulfilled. I wanted more.

Me: I want Oprah to interview me.
My friend: Why would she interview you?
Me: I don't know, I will figure something out.

I had recently read about Cassie De Pecol, who at that time had visited every country in the world in the fastest time. Her story sent me down the rabbit hole that is competitive travel. It turns out there is a whole community of "country counters," a community I belonged to but didn't know existed. They range from those, like Cassie, who focus on speed to those who are the "firsts"—first female, first person under 30, you get the idea. As of this writing, fewer than 250 people on record have visited every country in the world.

I emerged with a new goal: to be the first Black woman to travel to every country in the world. (Note: Slawek Muturi, who is half Kenyan and half Polish, was the first Black person to travel to every country in the world, and he has done it twice.)

I had always wanted to visit every country in the world by the time I was 40 or 50, but it was just an idea in my head. Now, I was making this a real goal, and I was moving up the deadline. I would visit all 193 UN member countries and two nonmember observing states by the time I hit my 35th birthday. That gave me roughly two and a half years to make it to another 135 countries. Easy, right?

I didn't create a plan immediately. A lot of times people get paralyzed in the planning process. I just wanted to get started. I'd figure out the details along the way. But one thing I knew for sure: I wanted to have real experiences in every place I visited. I knew I wouldn't be able to spend an exhaustive amount of time in each destination—sometimes I'd have three or four days, sometimes even less—but I wanted every country to truly count.

Some people can spend an entire week in a location and never chat with a local person or really experience the place. I felt no point in going to a country just to take pictures at the biggest tourist site and leave. I knew I could be in a country for 48 hours or less and have more authentic experiences. After all, I had been doing just that for years already.

Dressed in jewel tones in Ubud's lush rice paddies, my friends and I were caught in a torrential downpour just after this was snapped.

I ultimately overshot my deadline by almost five months. But, spoiler alert, I did it. And though I am still waiting for that Oprah interview, I am confident it will happen.

New goal established, the rest of my trip to Bali was a joyful and healing experience. Elton eventually met me in Bali, too. We traipsed through glorious green rice paddies, getting our feet muddy, to get unique and beautiful pictures. I even climbed a tree in a white dress. We visited the Tegenungan Waterfall, whose cool waters were a reprieve from the blazing sun.

We tasted the world's most expensive coffee, made from beans found in the feces of the palm civet, a small cat-size mammal. I am no coffee connoisseur, but I did not taste what all the hype was about. We went to Uluwatu, where there were fewer tourists and more surfers. Elton drove a scooter, and I held on as we made our way to Green Bowl Beach, a somewhat hidden and magical spot reached only by descending what feels like hundreds of steps, past more than a few aggressive monkeys. But the white sands, turquoise waters, and lack of people made the trek worth it and make it my favorite beach in Bali.

Bali was transformative. The energy of the island is aligned with my soul. It feels like love to me. But most significant, Bali is where my adventure around the world truly began, an adventure that would change my life.

The most notable feature of Pura Taman Saraswati, a Balinese Hindu temple, is the gorgeous lotus pond.

morocco

THOUGH I HAD SET A GOAL to visit every country in the world by 35, I didn't make a road map to accomplish the task. When I got back to L.A. after Bali, I created a list of the remaining countries I needed to visit. I downloaded a country-tracking app, and I continued to look for flight deals, knowing this new venture would cost a lot of money. Thankfully, the freelance writing I had taken up, UN consulting, and Jet Black

AFRICA

Perched on the shores of the Atlantic, Casablanca's Hassan II Mosque is the world's seventh largest, hosting up to 105,000 worshippers.

were continuing to turn a profit. Things felt more or less the same at first. At this point in my journey, I wasn't on a plane every other day or dealing with the complications of getting a visa for one country while being a tourist in another. It was easy-breezy in the beginning. And a group vacation to Morocco for Elton's birthday—thanks to a flight deal—felt like just the right way to really kick things off.

With bustling souks (marketplaces), camels in the desert, colorful madrassas, the golden sands of the Sahara, and labyrinth-like streets that snake through walled cities, Morocco is a photographer's dream.

The second most visited country in Africa (after Egypt), Morocco is a shining star of tourism, from the souks of Marrakech to the alleyways of Fez to the blue walls of Chefchaouen.

We started our adventures in Marrakech, a welcomed jolt to the senses. On every corner there are beautiful bright colors, varying textures, and gorgeous buildings begging to be photographed.

We stayed in a *riad,* a traditional Moroccan house, that boasted an interior tiled courtyard, cerulean blue walls, black-and-white floor tiles, intricately designed archways, and uniquely designed bedrooms that made us feel like we were sleeping in eight different hotels.

The souks of Marrakech are some of my favorite markets because of the glory that is Moroccan interior design. You can buy beautiful poufs that can be used as ottomans, uniquely colorful rugs, pillows, and bedding. My senses were on overdrive from the spices, fabrics, and colors. (I was so inspired by Morocco's colors, my home in Detroit now has a blue wall with yellow accessories that is influenced by the

After a day of exploring Berber villages, we took a camel ride in the Sahara desert at sunset.

colors and design of Jardin Majorelle at the Marrakech home of Yves Saint Laurent.)

As you navigate through the stall-flanked alleyways, keep your wits about you. Stop to gauge prices before you commit to one store and start negotiating. In Morocco, the first price is never the last price. Everything is negotiable. Practice your skills and go low!

I must say, Marrakech is the scammiest place I have ever been. Is that a word? No, but it describes my feelings. For example, a man approached us at Jardin Majorelle and encouraged us to go see the leather tannery (leather is one of Morocco's main exports). I was skeptical, but we obliged and were taken on a tour where we were shown how they use traditional practices to transform hides into more manageable materials using pigeon feces, urine, lime, salt, and water—and it smells like it.

Following the tour, we were taken to a shop where we spread out among three floors and began selecting from leather shoes, duffel bags, poufs, rugs, and more. Most of us left with something. Then, as we walked around the souk, we were shocked to find that the prices at the tannery were 10 times what they were in the market. They got us. We did go back to the tannery, and some money was recovered, but please don't make the same mistake we did.

Not to let a little extortion get in the way of our enjoyment, we continued on to the Ben Youssef Madrasa. The college, with its colorful tiled walls and beautiful arches, was one of my favorite places in the city.

From Marrakech, we moved on to the desert. We stopped at a Berber village where we learned about their simple way of life. Berbers use tea to welcome guests into their homes. We were offered green tea and told the higher the pour, the better the tea. We spent the night in the desert, rode camels, then made our way to the port city of Casablanca. My friend Hicham guided us to the magnificent Hassan II Mosque, the world's seventh largest mosque, perched on the shores of the Atlantic Ocean. It was a sight to behold.

Our next stop, by way of flight and bus, was Chefchaouen, lovingly known as the Blue City. It turned out to be my favorite of the four Moroccan cities we explored. Founded in 1471, the mountainous city is full of blue-washed buildings that serve as homes, hotels, hammams, and places of worship. The blue walls were accentuated by terra-cotta rooftops, colorful flowerpots, and cobblestone streets. As a lover of all things brightly colored, I fell in love with the city. We had to hike to our hotel, as many of the streets are pedestrian only, but the beauty of the architecture and the people and the delicious food more than made up for it.

Throughout our stay, we had more tagine, Morocco's national dish, than we cared to eat. But in Chefchaouen, I found my favorite variety of the slow-cooked meats and vegetables. The tagine there was made with lamb and vegetables, with the unexpected addition of apricot, which added a welcome sweetness to the savory dish.

On our way back to Marrakech to catch our flight home, we stopped in Fez, the country's second largest city. With its labyrinth of alleyways, the unique walled city offers beautiful surprises. We stumbled upon stalls selling handicrafts and home goods, massive walls that hide gorgeous riads, and delicious restaurants serving up traditional Moroccan dishes, such as couscous with vegetables (originated from the Berber people) and bastila, a sort of chicken pie. I try the street food in places I travel to for a deeper understanding of a place's culture. Morocco's was delicious—and cheap!

Similar to Cuba, Morocco is super Instagrammable, which has largely contributed to the rise in tourism in the past few years. But the country has so much more to offer beyond what you see on your feed. Visiting Morocco with friends was such a joy. To this day, we often find ourselves starting a conversation with, "Remember that one time in Marrakech?"

The souks of Marrakech are filled with colorful spices, handmade home goods, such as the iconic leather poufs and Berber rugs, and dried flowers (pictured here).

grenada

GRENADA WAS THE FIRST of my trips that truly felt random. I needed to move fast to reach 132 new countries in two and a half years, so I looked for one that I could fly to relatively cheaply before a Jet Black trip to Colombia. This quickly became my modus operandi: I squeezed in trips when I had short breaks. A word to the wise: Should you decide to visit every country in the world, go continent by continent.

NORTH
AMERICA

Finish each one before moving on to the next. It will be cheaper and save your body from the torture of extra intercontinental flights.

One of the things I treasure most about my journey is the community I have built both in person and online. Friends of friends often connect me with locals, and as I built a large Instagram following, along with readers of my blog and Jet Black patrons, I also began soliciting travel advice from my followers. Online friends later became tour guides when I visited their home countries. In Grenada, that was a woman named Kered, who I met via Instagram.

As the plane descended on my 63rd country, I watched the blue of the Caribbean disappear into tarmac, but I could still see the sparkling sea in the distance. As we drove through the densely populated and colorful capital, I realized that I could see water in every direction, a benefit of the country's size. Grenada is smaller than my hometown of Detroit.

Kered connected me with a guide who took me to a small beach in Dragon Bay so I could see the underwater sculpture park—the first of its kind in the world. The subaquatic exhibit features 75 sculptures and was first constructed in 2006. On the beach we found a man with a boat and headed into the water. Swimming below the surface, I saw "Vicissitudes," a sculpture of 26 Grenadian girls holding hands in a circle. Some believe the installation may be a memorial for the lives of the enslaved lost in these waters.

Grenada's main island has 45 beaches to choose from; moreover, the landscape of Grenada offers forests, mountains, rivers, and even rainforests, as well as 18 waterfalls.

I visited Adelphi, a cascade very far off the beaten path. To reach it, we had to navigate our way across rivers and streams populated with large rocks—one even had a rope to help you reach the other side. Every time we came to one of these crossings, I said a quick prayer, hoping I wouldn't slip and face-plant into a boulder. I managed to stay upright as we trekked through the muddy forest and was rewarded with a private viewing of the falls. I swam in the cool waters and washed off some of the mud and sweat.

Grenada is known as the "Spice Isle." Most notably, it is the home of nutmeg, which is its number one export and is featured on the national flag. During our trek, my guide showed me nutmeg in the wild. Grenadians use every part of the nutmeg fruit, making jams from the pod and using both the mace and nutmeg as spices.

Out of the wilderness, Kered took me to a vegan lunch (and organic rum tasting) at Mango Bay Cottage. Then she took me to a hidden black sand beach. The beautiful dark sand, flanked by large boulders, was the perfect setting for a picture. With my growing Instagram following, getting great content became a key part of my travels. I wanted to continue to grow my platform's audience to help spread my message of inclusive and ethical travel, and for the financial opportunities Instagram provided. As I balanced myself between two rocks, a wave almost took me out. Kered managed to snap that image, all the while laughing at my misfortune. Like the professional that I am, I managed to quickly recover, and Kered got the shot! All of that for 446 likes from my 10,000 followers, at the time.

This image was taken by another tourist who I met in the water. Never be afraid to ask a stranger to take your picture.

djibouti

MY FRIEND ASHLEY AND I landed in Djibouti on a blazing hot afternoon in April. While descending into the tiniest nation in the Horn of Africa—a nation largely known only as the butt of many jokes—we learned of its importance. Djibouti is perched on the Gulf of Aden, along one of the world's busiest shipping lanes. It is also home to the largest U.S. military base in Africa. As one of the least visited

AFRICA

countries in the world, immigration found it difficult to understand that we were only there for tourism. Multiple times, confused immigration officials asked if we worked for the United Nations or the military. My simple reply, "On est tourists seulement!" (French and Arabic are the country's two official languages), was met with confusion, though never suspicion. After an hour, the immigration hall was deserted, except for us. Finally, following several phone calls, including one to our tour guide, we were granted tourist visas and allowed to enter the country.

Djibouti does not have much tourism infrastructure. Our taxi from the airport, for example, was a run-down Soviet box car that looked as if it may or may not make the 20-minute drive to our hotel. It is also an expensive country; inflated prices are propped up by staycations for the in-country military personnel and the development industry. The best hotel (read: the *only* one I am willing to stand behind) is the Kempinski. Although it is beautiful, with the perfect infinity pool to balance the extreme heat of the desert, it is pricey. At the time, we paid $350 a night for a standard room.

Lake Assal, at more than 500 feet (150 m) below sea level, is the lowest point in Africa. It is also the most popular tourist destination in Djibouti. For our day trip, our local guide, Yassin, picked us up. On our way, we stopped at a bakery for croissants and pain au chocolat, pastries courtesy of the country's French colonial legacy.

On the two-hour drive to the lake we passed through a mostly dry and at times mountainous landscape. Out the window, we saw goats eating leaves on top of a bush. I was mesmerized by the goats' ability to easily hop on and off acacia trees, which were about four feet (1.2 m) off the ground.

At the lake, we saw an expansive salt bed that looked like snow. Only the 100°F (38°C) temps assured me it was not its frozen doppelgänger. Lake Assal has an average salt concentration of 34.8 percent, making it saltier than the Dead Sea. If you have ever struggled to float in water, visit Lake Assal. It is impossible to sink! But be careful not to get the water in your eyes. It *burns!* After prancing on salt beds, floating in the sea, and taking a Lake Assal shower (water poured from a jerrican by Yassin atop the SUV), we made our way back to town.

Given the close proximity to its neighbor on the Arabian Peninsula, Yemeni food is not hard to come by in Djibouti. And Yemeni-style fish is a must-eat. The small no-frills restaurant Saba served up the best meal we had in Djibouti. The uber-fresh fish was butterflied and topped with flavorful seasonings. Once that first bite hit my palate, I could care less what was in it; I just wanted seconds. Although I had eaten plenty of Yemeni food at home in Hamtramck, a small city inside of Detroit, this trip to Djibouti led to an addiction. When I visited Somalia (page 290), the best meal I had was at a roadside Yemeni restaurant. And, of course, the ultimate food experience was in Yemen, where I watched bread being freshly made and ate freshly caught fish (page 334).

Djibouti was a beautiful reminder that no matter where you go in the world, you can find something spectacular. I also realized that my extensive travels were making me a trusted expert, even if only to my friends. Ashley had never had an intention to visit Djibouti, but she joined me anyway. When I later asked her about our trip, she said, "I felt safe. I thought certain things, you know, pirates, but I'm with Jessica." I love that.

At Lake Assal, far from a tourist trap, I saw only this man and his son selling salt. The boy was so cute I had to buy a few packets.

Tanzania

TANZANIA, the largest country in the East African Community, is bordered by the Indian Ocean and eight countries. After gaining independence separately in the early 1960s, Tanganyika and Zanzibar merged in April 1964 to form the United Republic of Tanzania, as the country is known today. The nation is home to a population of more than 50 million and the highest mountain in Africa, Mount Kilimanjaro.

In May 2017, I was using Nairobi as a home base for a month. It was the location of a Jet Black trip I was hosting and a great jumping-off point to a couple new countries in the region. Having heard tales of the Serengeti for years and of the wonders of Zanzibar, I chose Tanzania to celebrate my 33rd birthday, with two friends. It would be my 65th country and 10th African country. With my growing social media following, presence in mainstream travel media, and a thriving travel business, I was starting to get comped hotel rooms in exchange for social posts and photos. For this trip, I reached out to the Four Seasons and shared my travel plans. I was hesitant at first, but then figured, What could I lose? The worst they could say was no. And given I already had an existing business relationship with them through Jet Black, this felt like a no-brainer. This was a perk I continued to use throughout my journey. Many other country counters rely on big-name sponsorships. I didn't have those. Exchanging Instagram posts for free or discounted rooms, along with other travel experiences, ultimately helped me maximize my budget and get me to every country in the world.

I went on my first safari at the age of six with my family in Queen Elizabeth National Park in Uganda. Thirty-two years later, the only thing I can remember are the baboons climbing all over the jeep. My second safari was in 2013, on a day trip in Lake Nakuru National Park while I was in Kenya for work. My 33rd birthday trip to Tanzania would mark my third safari, and it turned out to be the best of the bunch.

AFRICA

Nungwi was by far the most beautiful beach I visited in Zanzibar, making it into my list of top five beaches in the world.

Our journey to the Serengeti started in Nairobi, where we took a short flight to the Kilimanjaro airport. From the plane, I laid my eyes on the iconic peak for the first time. Kilimanjaro cut high above the clouds, wearing them like a crown. Next, we boarded a nine-seater plane that flew us across the grasslands. The name Serengeti is derived from the Maasai language, Maa: *Serengit* means "endless plains." The vast plains are home to 70 large mammal and 500 bird species. The national park shares a border with Kenya. The Kenyan side of this tract of land is the Masai Mara.

At the airport we met our guide, Kimambo, from the Four Seasons Safari Lodge Serengeti. Before heading to the lodge, Kimambo popped a bottle of champagne and we toasted to our impending three-day adventure. Though the ride to the Four Seasons from the airstrip is typically an hour and a half, Kimambo decided to take us on a slightly longer game drive, and we were instantly rewarded. Within 10 minutes we spotted a pride of lions, a rare experience (even Kimambo was clamoring to take pictures with his cell phone).

At the lodge, we were shown to our Water Hole View rooms. Through-out the day we could watch animals quenching their thirst while we quenched ours on our balconies. The lodge's infinity pool, below the restaurant, also sits in front of the watering hole; it is my favorite infinity pool in the entire world. While we were taking a dip to unwind from a half-day game drive and the African sun, elephants, zebras, and antelopes absolved themselves of thirst right in front of our eyes.

Lucky for us, my birthday falls around the time of the great migration—a phenomenon when millions of wildebeests, zebras, and other animals move between Kenya's Masai Mara and Tanzania's Serengeti.

During our half-day game drive we saw three of the Big Five—lions, elephants, and Cape buffalo. We watched hippopotamuses and crocodiles living in harmony. We spied on a cheetah as it plotted devouring a gazelle. We gawked at giraffes as they gracefully traipsed the plains. We bore witness to the early migration of elephants, wildebeests, and zebras, swatting away the flies that also swarm during the migration period.

I've gone on safari in more than 10 countries. The Serengeti remains my favorite of those experiences. In addition to the troves of animals, I love the breadth of the Serengeti's flat grasslands, the bright blue skies and picturesque clouds, and how quintessential acacia trees punctuate the landscape.

Set on the shores of the always warm and inviting Indian Ocean, Zanzibar boasts some of the world's most beautiful beaches. We spent our next four days in Tanzania on the largest of the islands, Unguja.

Beach holidays tend to be my favorite. Waking up to the sounds of the ocean outside your window, enjoying the water while bathing in the sun, and endless sunsets are something I never tire of. Though I have not been to every beach in the world, I've certainly visited a lot, and Zanzibar's are definitely in my top five. My favorite is Nungwi. To put into words the beauty of her crystal clear waters is difficult; a word to describe the color has yet to be invented.

And yet, Nungwi—or any of Zanzibar's beaches for that matter—almost never appears on lists or in travel publications. A conversation needs to be had about proclaiming "the world's bests" when most writers have barely scratched the surface of what the entire world has to offer, particularly within the African continent. Why not just say "the most beautiful beaches I have been to"? But I digress.

Offshore, you'll find amazing marine life. During a snorkeling trip I spotted bright red and cerulean starfish. On the beaches you will also often see Maasai people, many of whom work as security guards or sell wares or earn money by taking pictures with tourists. You will recognize them by their height and traditional Maasai clothing, *shuka,* which are typically red and blue and often have a plaid pattern.

It feels criminal that I have only been to Tanzania once, a class A felony to have visited Zanzibar's shores only a single time. In Tanzania, I have a long bucket list I still need to tackle that includes hiking Mount Kilimanjaro, visiting the Ngorongoro crater, eating and partying in Dar es Salaam, and diving off the coast of both Pemba and Mnemba Islands.

En route from the airstrip to the lodge, we saw three of Serengeti National Park's "Big Five" animals, including a pride of lions.

Tunisia

THE NORTHERNMOST COUNTRY IN AFRICA, Tunisia boasts a coastline that is 713 miles (1,147 km) long. Its Indigenous inhabitants were the Berbers, though the Phoenicians, Romans, Muslims, Ottomans, and French all had a hold on the territory at one point or another, until its independence in 1957. The remnants of these various influences can still be seen throughout the country. Today, Tunisia holds great significance

AFRICA

as the place where street vendor Mohamed Bouazizi set himself on fire in protest of police harassment, thus beginning the Arab Spring.

I first traveled to Tunisia in the blazing hot August of 2017 to visit my dear friend Faten, whom I met while working in Rome. My flight landed on what was the coldest day of my trip: 99°F (37°C), though the humidity made it feel firmly in the triple digits.

Perched on the Mediterranean Sea, Tunisia's capital, Tunis, gave me Greek island vibes. In Sidi Bou Said, a city close to Tunis, the cobblestone streets, blue-and-white houses, and impeccable sea views felt like Mykonos. On the streets, you can buy beautiful ceramics, eat delicious street food, and have tea.

The oldest part of Tunis is Medina, which was founded in A.D. 698. Full of palaces, mosques, and fountains, Medina is perfect to explore in the afternoon. But enjoying its treasures in August was tough. Nothing would stop the sweat from seeping from my pores. Despite the heat, I managed to enjoy the beautifully carved, brightly colored doors, eat delicious local food, and check out the wares of local artisans. In the Mekki Design store, the owner, Jamel, who designs handbags from old Berber rugs, was kind enough to take us to his rooftop terrace. The eclectically decorated space featured rugs, brightly colored tile, and ceramics that held cacti and other greenery. But the best part was the view overlooking all of Medina. The white buildings and lively rooftops gave the city a new dimension.

Always trying to be respectful of the customs in the countries I'm traveling in, I had asked Faten what I should pack before the trip. She

Jamel, the owner of Mekki Designs, took us to his rooftop terrace overlooking the entire Medina of Tunis, with phenomenal views of the city.

I was captivated by the doors in Tunis, drawn in by their bright colors and intricate designs.

MUST-DO:
HAMMAM AT THE FOUR SEASONS

The Four Seasons Tunis is a stunning beachfront resort with some of the best hotel food I have ever had. The restaurant, Creek, is not to be missed, whether or not you are staying at the hotel. The food is inventive, delicate, and delicious. But the highlight of my stay was the hotel's hammam. A hammam is a Turkish bath found throughout the Middle East, North Africa, and other nearby regions. Here, a very strong woman washed and exfoliated my entire body in a steam room. I was a little reluctant when I first laid down on the marble slab, but the hot water kept me from getting too cold and, afterward, my skin felt like silk. It was a unique experience and one that I can't wait to try again.

insisted I could wear anything that I wanted. Hesitant because it was a Muslim-majority country, I erred on the side of conservative. After our day in Medina, we spent the evening at one of the beachfront nightclubs, where I watched a 20-something in a crop top and mini-skirt pass by me. It was then that I understood how liberal Tunisia is compared to its neighbors. You really could wear whatever you want. I quickly regretted what was in my suitcase. I felt like the old lady who is slightly overdressed at the club. Still, my wardrobe didn't stop me from dancing the night away under the stars.

As an escape from the brutal heat of Tunis, we headed southeast to the beach resort town of Hammamet, about 40 miles (64 km) from the capital. It was the perfect escape to enjoy the sun as it should be, beachside and poolside.

On my second trip to Tunis—a forced overnight layover before my 2019 trip to Libya—my perspective of travel changed. At the airport, I was stopped by customs because of my drone. I always packed my drone in my carry-on—without the battery so I wouldn't raise flags in security—but this time it was flagged.

After finding the drone, a security officer began flipping through every page of my passport. I asked if there was a problem and he assured me it was nothing, but he picked up the phone to call over another officer.

They looked at my passport together and asked what I do for work. I replied, "I am a writer and a photographer."

"A journalist?"

"No, just a writer." Wrong answer, apparently.

By the time a fifth person, a woman who seemed to be the manager, asked me, I responded aggressively, *"Je ne suis pas une journaliste*—I'm not a journalist." She was taken aback, but it all ended simply enough: The airport would keep my drone, which was illegal in the country, and I would retrieve it upon exiting the country.

I returned to the airport early the following day to retrieve my drone. At customs I was told I had to check in to my flight first. Several more counters and offices later, I was getting frustrated. But I kept my cool because everyone was at least emanating warm energy. When I finally got the drone back, a bit of a disagreement ensued: They wanted me to put the drone in my carry-on, but I wanted it in my checked luggage to avoid the same ordeal in Libya. I was sent to the head of customs.

My handler explained the situation. The manager on duty took my passport and said, "Oh, you're American." What happened over the next 10 minutes was a welcome reprieve from the last hour of back-and-forth: lots of laughter, a marriage proposal, me getting to put my drone in my checked bag, and him slipping his number into my passport. Rather than being frustrated by the whole process, I walked away filled with joy!

Brightly colored artisan wares line the streets of Sidi Bou Said, my favorite town near Tunis.

Like many travelers, I am highly stressed when I travel. If you want to see the worst of me, find me in an airport. On top of check-ins, waiting in long security lines, being forced to remove shoes after placing a water bottle next to several others that likely will not be recycled properly, leaving a 10-year-old Movado watch in a bin never to be seen again (it happened in Slovakia, country 70), we're also forced to walk through a fluorescent-lit, sensory-assaulting space while being urged to buy perfume and makeup. When I finally reach my gate, it's a desperate search for a lounge and a gin and tonic to relax my nerves and aggravation from getting stuck behind a family of six that seemingly has never been inside an airport.

Until the incident in Tunisia, I never thought to seek joy in airports—and at the height of my travel, I visited 340 in a single year. I never thought about the joy in the mundane, in the needless smoke screen processes meant to make people feel at ease (though I still do not quite understand how forcing people to carry 10 100-milliliter bottles is better than a single liter bottle).

north macedonia

TRAVELING WILL TEACH YOU a lot about politics. Being completely unfamiliar with the history and political landscape of the Balkans, I was a faithful student. As my friends Ashley, Rosie, and I prepared for a road trip through six Balkan countries, we had to quickly get up to speed regarding the tensions surrounding North Macedonia. Our plan was to rent a car in Sofia, Bulgaria, then drive to Skopje, the capital of

E U R O P E

North Macedonia. Turns out, the rules of the road are never that easy. At the time of our trip, it was illegal to drive a car rented in Bulgaria (a political ally of Greece) into North Macedonia. We ended up having to hire a taxi to take us the nearly four-hour journey between the two capitals. On this ride our driver shared the lingering political tensions that had led to this travel hiccup.

Formerly known as Macedonia, North Macedonia—after gaining independence following the collapse of Yugoslavia in 1991—was forced to use "the Former Yugoslav Republic of Macedonia," so as not to be confused with the region in northern Greece of the same name. The Republic of North Macedonia officially changed its name in 2019, after a decades-long dispute with Greece. Now that the country officially goes by North Macedonia, Greece will no longer block the country from entry into NATO and, potentially, the European Union.

In North Macedonia we settled into our hotel in Skopje. Sightseeing the following day was made easy by our location right on Macedonia Square, Skopje's main square.

The square sits in the heart of the city, next to the stunning 702-foot-long (214 m) Stone Bridge, which was built in the mid-15th century and serves as a symbol of the capital. It even appears on the city's coat of arms and flag. From Macedonia Square, it is just a short walk to Skopje's major museums and historic sites, including the Mother Teresa Memorial House (the beloved humanitarian was born in Skopje).

After a brief tour of the city, we got our rental car in just enough time to reach Kosovo for lunch (since we were in the neighborhood, we

figured we might as well stop by) before making the three-and-a-half-hour drive to Lake Ohrid—back in North Macedonia—one of Europe's deepest and oldest lakes. We had to drive through the unlit mountainous region in the southwest of the country in the middle of the night to reach Ohrid and missed seeing the beauty of the lake on our way in.

We woke to expansive views. The idyllic lake is surrounded by the same mountains that tortured us the night before. A rocky beach enclosed the crystal clear waters, giving us an easy view of fish swimming just below the surface. As we sat on the beach, a man selling corn approached. He didn't speak English, and when we asked "How much?" he just shrugged his shoulders. Never one to let a language barrier get in the way, I put a few Macedonian denar coins in my hand and held my palm out to him so that he could pick out the correct amount.

In August, the height of European vacation time, few people were enjoying this little-known hideaway. We stayed at a small bed-and-breakfast in a little quiet town called Lagadin. Most of the residents did not speak English but were incredibly kind and helpful. In the morning we bought fruit from a cart, where I employed the same payment technique as I had on the beach. We ate fresh whole grilled trout caught in the lake, paired with fish soup and a Greek salad. Afternoons we spent lazing in the chilly calm waters and taking in the mountains and dense forest that surrounded us.

As we watched a gorgeous sunset from our balcony, I was filled with gratitude for a journey that led me to the countryside of North Macedonia, to a lake I may have otherwise never seen.

Lake Ohrid, one of the oldest in the world, offers a welcome respite from the North Macedonian sun.

bosnia and herzegovina

SINCE I WAS ON A MISSION to make it to every country in the world in a short amount of time, I had to be savvy about grouping countries together when I could. (Though throughout my journey I didn't always get to plan things to work out so easily.) Our Balkan road trip was the perfect opportunity to cross another four countries off my list. After North Macedonia, we stopped in Albania, then made our way to Bosnia

EUROPE

and Herzegovina. Like North Macedonia, Bosnia and Herzegovina has a charged political history. The Bosnian War, in the mid-1990s, rendered Bosnia one of the poorest countries in Europe. The primary victims were Bosnian Muslims, who today make up 50.1 percent of the population, the second largest Muslim population in Europe behind Albania. But Bosnians are a resilient people who welcomed us with open arms.

Bosnia sits on the Balkan Peninsula, part of the former Yugoslavian bloc. With a tiny coastline of only 12 miles (19 km) along the Adriatic Sea, the nation's beauty lies largely in its interior. And that beauty truly wowed me.

Entering the country just as the sun was painting the sky pink, we drove through the Dinaric Alps, the sunset disappearing behind the mountains and reappearing as we made our way along the winding roads.

At our destination, Mostar, we navigated the narrow cobblestone streets to our charming bed-and-breakfast, Pansion Villa Cardak. After sharing a number of options for traditional meals and activities throughout the city, our phenomenal host even offered to park our car (for a novice, the narrow, steep roads proved a bit scary).

Mostar, a medieval town founded in 1452, is Bosnia's fifth largest city and one of its most beautiful. A few minarets dot the skyline, reflective of the large Muslim population. The city's unique architecture is a mix of Austro-Hungarian and Ottoman, the latter being represented in the iconic Stari Most, a bridge dating back to the 16th century, from which the city gets its name. With towers on either side, the pedestrian-only bridge crosses the Neretva River, connecting the two parts of the city. Although Stari Most, or Old Bridge, is certainly the star, you can find many other bridges. My favorite was a small arched stone bridge nearly completely covered in ivy.

Mostar's cobblestone streets lead you to numerous restaurants offering traditional and filling food such as *dolma,* vegetables stuffed with ground meat and rice; *sarma,* stuffed cabbage leaves; and fresh-baked bread. The city's relaxed energy makes it easy to turn an afternoon of strolling around the town into an evening enjoying comfort food while sipping rakija, the national spirit of Bosnia, and listening to the soothing sounds of the river.

A 15-minute drive from Mostar is Blagaj Tekke, a picturesque Ottoman-era dervish monastery. The nearly 600-year-old monastery sits on the banks of a spring fed by the Buna River. The emerald green water, dotted with large stones and a small cascade, sits below the monastery. A sandstone cliff hovers above the white Ottoman-style buildings, which are covered in windows to give residents a glimpse of the gorgeous views. The scene felt like a page out of a fairy tale.

This bridge, one of several over the Neretva River, connects the two sides of the medieval town of Mostar.

guatemala

AFTER THE BALKANS, I planned a road trip in Central America to help me cross more countries off my list at a rapid pace. From Belize, country 82, I crossed into the north of Guatemala by car. I arrived in the city of Flores on a blistering hot day. The temperatures flirted with 90°F (32°C) and were paired with intense humidity. After a two-hour drive, I was delighted to arrive at the beautiful and secluded

NORTH AMERICA

Las Lagunas Boutique Hotel, which hosted my stay, nestled within a 300-acre (120 ha) private reserve of forest on Laguna Quixel.

A welcoming frozen hibiscus drink immediately freed me from the grip of the heat. I was then whisked off to my room, a spacious luxury wooden cabin situated directly on the lagoon. Huge windows offered views of the forest and lagoon, but most important, I could watch the pink glow over the still waters every morning as the sun ushered in the new day. The food was delicious local fare, including ceviche, tortilla soup, and *pescado blanco,* a local fish found only in Lake Peten Itza in Flores.

Approximately one hour's drive from my hotel lay Tikal, the ruins of an ancient Maya city and the main attraction in northern Guatemala. Dating back to the fourth century B.C., Tikal was the capital of one of the most powerful kingdoms of the ancient Maya. The ruins, located in a rainforest, have been relatively well preserved. Though only 20 percent of the site has been excavated, Tikal's magnitude can be clearly felt. (For *Star Wars* fans, Tikal served as the setting of the rebel base in *Star Wars: Episode IV—A New Hope.* If you hike to the top of Tower 4, you will see a view of Towers 1 and 2 as seen in the movie.)

I spent several hot and sweaty hours walking up and down the stairs of the massive complex of ruins learning more about the economic and political history of the kingdom and its military might. To see the magnificence the Maya built—palaces and towers flanked by dense lush forest—is truly awe-inspiring. I wish I could hop in a time machine to see how they built such a majestic and intricate city without modern equipment. I imagined what this part of the world would be like had the Spanish never colonized the region and destroyed its cultures and communities. Would the Maya kingdoms still exist today? Would they have eventually conquered what is now the United States?

After a one-hour flight to Guatemala City, I met my friend Ursula from the UN in Rome. We drove to Antigua, one of Guatemala's former capitals, known for its colonial legacy of Spanish baroque–influenced architecture. Color exploded from every corner, from the bright pastels in the wardrobes of the local people to the yellow, red, and orange buildings lining cobblestone streets. We wandered around and checked out cute shops and ruins of colonial churches. El Mercadito, just off Parque Central, is a massive indoor market with handwoven rugs, traditional woven bags, and everything else your heart may desire. The bright fabrics and wares draw you in, and the unique details keep you lingering in the different booths, trying to decide what to leave behind. Be careful: You are bound to spend money on all the beautiful handcrafted items and I will not be at fault. (I went home with a large rug and custom-made leather boots.)

Tikal, a complex of Maya ruins dating back to the fourth century B.C., is believed to be the remains of a powerful ancient empire's capital city.

With Ursula's friend Helen as our guide, we ate and drank our way through Antigua. Set in a maze of gardens, Saberico was a cute place for an outdoor lunch with the best kale chips. I generally do not like dive bars, but Café No Sé is a blend of dive bar meets speakeasy meets live music venue. We headed straight to the back to a doorway where anyone shorter than about four foot five (1.3 m) has to stoop to enter. A tucked-away bar is marked by a handwritten sign, "Mezcal Bar," and accordingly only serves mezcal and beer. As a mezcal lover, I was in heaven.

Another standout was XQ No? (Porque No?—Why Not?), a tiny restaurant that cooked up dishes like shrimp curry and chicken in a white wine sauce with big flavors. I wrote my name on a table there—try to find it!

sri lanka

I WAS QUICKLY MAKING MY WAY through countries by October 2017, having ticked off 26 in just eight months. I was consistently posting to my Instagram, and my profile as a travel expert was rising, particularly after Bloomberg named me a Distinguished Travel Hacker. Though it wasn't easy, I was getting into the pattern of this busy life on the road. ¶ Sri Lanka was my first stop in South Asia. At 3:30 a.m., Elton and I arrived

A S I A

in Colombo, one of the nation's two capitals, and made our way to our hotel before the city had a chance to wake up.

That day, I made one of many travel missteps that have happened over the years. We visited the Pinnawala Elephant Orphanage, where we watched two dozen elephants getting an afternoon sip of water around a small lake. Once we made our way closer to the elephants, we noticed something wasn't right. The elephants had chains on their ankles and were being beaten by the workers. There was one elephant using her trunk to tug at her chains; many of the elephants did not look very happy. I don't believe in inhumane animal practices. Had I known what it was like, I would have never visited that "orphanage."

The following day we made our way to the south of the country and stopped on a beach somewhere between Unawatuna and Weligama, where we found traditional fishermen on stilts. Since seeing Steve McCurry's iconic *National Geographic* image of these local fishermen I was determined to see them for myself. Just like the elephant orphanage, though, things were not as they seemed. Nowadays, you have to pay to take a picture of the fishermen, which I did not mind at all. What was a bit disappointing was that it seemed like most of the fishermen were no longer climbing on the cross-like structures to fish but instead to pose for those tourist pictures. I was, however, relieved when a local told me that it is still possible to see practicing fishermen early in the morning and late in the evening, when big fish are nearest the shore.

From the south of the country, we decided to take a train back to Colombo. First class was sold out, so we purchased second-class tickets for $1.17 each. We arrived late and saw second class was completely full. While we saw some foreigners sitting on the floor of first and second class, we decided to take our chances by grabbing actual seats in third class.

The lively ride featured a sword swallower; a man who fell asleep on me; someone playing traditional music loudly; and people selling everything from toys to food. It certainly wasn't the train ride I had expected, but it was nice to get a glimpse of Sri Lankan life.

I usually travel to countries at the end of the rainy season to save money and avoid large crowds. It had always worked in my favor up until this trip. But we didn't see a single blue sky the entire time we were in Sri Lanka. To top it all off, I was treated horribly in the country. Men outright ignored me, even when I was speaking. Our hotel bellman assisted Elton but didn't pay me any mind. On my return trip from Maldives through Sri Lanka, I was held up by immigration officials, despite the fact that I had already entered the country just days before with my Ugandan passport and a tourist visa. I pulled out my American passport, which made them relax and let me enter the country, even without the proper visa. The privilege of being able to pull out the American passport is not lost on me.

A stilt fisherman allowed me to sit on this platform and try my hand, and all I can say is they must have very strong core muscles.

maldives

LOOKING TO ESCAPE THE DREARY WEATHER in Sri Lanka, we decided to hop over to the relatively close neighbor Maldives for a few days. One last-minute purchase and a short hour and 30 minutes later, Elton and I landed in the sunny and—most important—dry paradise. When I first stepped out of Velana International Airport onto the North Male Atoll, I was stunned into silence. Like everything in Maldives, the

ASIA

airport sits on its own island. One step outside and you immediately understand why Maldives is an iconic destination. The aquamarine waters surrounding the airport are more beautiful than the waters of most of the other countries of the world. Sublime.

Though Maldives may feel a bit cliché, it is cliché for a reason. The collection of islands in the Indian Ocean makes up one of the world's most stunning countries. The archipelagic nation comprises nearly 1,200 islands—stretching across more than 500 miles (800 km)—of which nearly 200 are inhabited. And Maldives has one of the most unique tourism structures in the world: a one-island, one-resort policy. Every resort has its own island. Once only accessed by the world's wealthiest and most elite travelers, the country has opened new resorts to more tourists with a range of budgets—though vacationing here can still be pricey.

We were whisked from the airport in a small yacht to reach our resort, Velassaru. You read that right: not a little motorboat or a dinghy, but a yacht. Honey, I'm home! After a 25-minute ride, we arrived and I was again rendered speechless. Imagine the most beautiful waters and beaches in the world. This is better than that.

The resort (reminder: the only one on the island) is situated on the South Male Atoll, and the staff met us with drinks in hand and a warm welcome to their stunning beaches. You've seen the photos of bungalows and boardwalks hovering over the crystal blue waters of the

Indian Ocean. The architecture and integration between land and water is even more remarkable in person.

For two days on the atoll, we walked along powdery soft sand for sunset drinks, swam in the infinity pool, snorkeled, and relaxed. What else does one do in paradise?

But you can't talk about paradise without mentioning its possible demise. At least, I can't. I have seen firsthand the destruction climate change is making in the very places I have fallen in love with. With the privilege of this journey, I began using my platform to inform my audience about what was changing around the world—and how we as travelers can help protect these sacred places from off-setting the impact of air travel to avoiding plastics.

Higher temperatures and rising sea levels have hit this island nation hard, and many of their islands have already disappeared. Famously, in 2009, the president held an underwater cabinet meeting to bring attention to the rising sea levels. The 30-minute meeting was an SOS from Maldives to the rest of the world.

While it's still here—and hopefully changes are made before it's too late—the country's one-island, one-resort policy will leave you feeling like you have carved out your own personal space in paradise. What a shame if we let that disappear.

The gloriously blue waters of Maldives are best enjoyed in an overwater bungalow.

india

INDIA IS A VAST COUNTRY that requires a shrewd strategy and numerous visits to see and digest in its entirety (though that is probably impossible). For my first trip, we had four days to explore—just enough time to see some of India's most popular cities and sights. We landed in Delhi shortly after 4 a.m. on a relatively cool October morning and immediately departed on a four-hour drive to Agra, home of the Taj Mahal.

We struggled to get comfortable in the back of a small sedan, desperately trying to capture a few winks of sleep after our middle-of-the-night flight.

We arrived at the Taj Mahal, one of the Seven Wonders of the Modern World, early enough to beat the huge crowds. Completed in 1653, the white marble mausoleum took 22 years and 20,000 people to build. Its intricate tile work includes tiny handmade flowers, some of which, at little more than two inches (5 cm) in size, took two and a half days to create. Commissioned by Shah Jahan in honor of his favorite wife, Mumtaz Mahal, who died giving birth to their 14th child, the Taj Mahal is a superb example of both Mughal architecture and undying love.

But as we wandered the gardens around the Taj, I quickly became a spectacle. More than 30 people stopped to take pictures with me. I took selfies with women draped in saris and with schoolgirls in pleated skirts and plaid tops. One woman even told me how to pose as a line formed behind her. Some of these people had traveled seriously great lengths to see this magnificent world wonder and somehow began marveling at me.

Given all the commotion, Elton dubbed me the Taj Majessica. Although some people may be turned off by the attention—and sometimes I am—it is important to note that not every acknowledgment of your race is racism. I've realized while traveling that what could be perceived as racism is often actually fascination, curiosity, and admiration. That's what I felt in India, where everyone was polite and asked permission, which isn't always the case.

ASIA

I was traveling in Udaipur during Diwali, India's biggest holiday of the year, during which bright orange and yellow flowers adorn the streets.

The British brought Indians to East Africa to build the railway. The result, after a number of years, was a mash-up of cultures. In my Ugandan household, my mom often cooked dishes such as curry rice and chicken, paired with chapati and samosas. During trips to Uganda, we often ate at an Indian restaurant across from the National Theatre. When I lived in East London, I'd dine on some of the world's best Indian food. So it should surprise no one that on the road from Agra to Jaipur—another four-hour ride—I told my driver I wanted to eat lunch somewhere that he would eat, somewhere authentic, not super touristy. He said he knew the perfect place.

We arrived at a large restaurant and I immediately saw four tour buses outside with white tourists teeming inside. I am not sure if something was lost in translation, but this was obviously a restaurant where drivers eat free as an incentive for bringing guests. It was the worst Indian food I have ever eaten.

We continued our trip to Jaipur, the third and final city on the Golden Triangle circuit. Known as the Pink City due to the color of many of its buildings, Jaipur is the capital of the state of Rajasthan. The state is known for its palaces and *havelis,* traditional mansions, many of which have been converted into hotels.

Children sit on the steps of Jagdish Temple, a Hindu temple in Udaipur that has been in continuous use since 1651.

We visited the Sujan Rajmahal Palace for lunch and were stunned by the palace turned luxury hotel that dates back to 1729. Through the conversion, it retained the glamour and grandeur of its former royal residents, with brightly colored wallpaper and marble tiles. The chandeliers and crystal glassware made me feel like royalty—it's no wonder, as the palace previously hosted the Queen of England and Jackie Kennedy.

From Jaipur, we hopped a quick flight to Udaipur and arrived just in time to celebrate Diwali. India's biggest holiday and festival celebrates the triumph of light over darkness, knowledge over ignorance, and good over evil. In honor of Diwali, there were various artworks on the ground made from flower petals and the streets were filled with people. The energy was buzzing; yellow, orange, and green flowers were everywhere. We met and chatted with kind shop owners who were not pushy. I asked one for a good place to eat. When he warned me I might get sick, I said I wanted good food, "Delhi belly" be damned.

The shopkeeper put us in a *tuk tuk* (motorcycle taxi) and gave the driver directions. As we made our way through the narrow streets, with endless honking horns, motorcycles whizzed by carrying multiple passengers. A woman draped in a sari smiled at me with her bare belly hanging out. India feels

like the home of body positivity. No matter the body shape, many women wear waist-baring saris and walk with their heads held high.

We arrived at a very small, nondescript restaurant in the center of town where no one spoke English. Though I did not dare drink the water in the carafe on the table, I was game for the food. Devoid of English menus, we weren't entirely clear what we ordered but ended up with two delicious curries paired with naan. My taste buds did a dance. We went back to that restaurant one more time before we left.

Despite India's beauty and culture, I would be remiss if I did not talk about how uncomfortable I felt as a woman in Delhi. I've now been to Delhi with a man and solo—my discomfort was the same in both scenarios. Men openly gawked at me and got too close into my personal space. When I traveled with Elton, other men oftentimes ignored me, even when I was talking. They chose to direct their gaze at Elton and wait for him to speak. In a country where women are abused at astounding levels, including public gang-raping and having acid thrown on them, this behavior was unsurprising. I am not a fearful traveler or prone to thinking the worst of a place, but after several of my own experiences and talking with other women, I would not travel alone to India again. I would prefer to travel there with a man.

Even still, India is a country with an incredibly rich history and diversity of people, landscapes, and food that I look forward to exploring more.

The iconic Taj Mahal is a white marble mausoleum that took 22 years and 20,000 people to build.

nepal

TRAVELING TO EVERY COUNTRY in the world has taught me a few golden rules, one of which is to always travel with large, crisp U.S. bills. In many countries, you have to pay for a visa in cash. Large bills also come in handy for currency exchange; many countries offer a better rate for newer, bigger bills. I broke this golden rule when I traveled to Nepal, the second to last stop on my first trip to South Asia. On arrival in

ASIA

Kathmandu, Elton and I were told we could pay the $25 visa fee by credit card, but when we reached the front of the line, we were asked for cash. Leaving our passports at the desk, we were informed by the visa officer that we could exit the airport and return the following day for the visa if the airport's cash machines did not work. (Can you imagine the U.S. or any European country allowing someone to enter their country without a proper visa?!)

After two cash machine visits, we finally had Nepali rupees. Phew! We thought we were in the clear until we were told we could only pay with U.S. dollars, euros, pounds, yen, or one of five other currencies, of which Nepali rupees was not one. An hour and two currency-exchange counters later, we finally had the U.S. dollars to purchase our visa. It was time to head into the city for an overdue good night's sleep.

Our entry nightmare over, we explored Kathmandu, a densely populated and bustling capital of more than a million people. The city, which sits in a valley of the Himalaya mountain range, bore evidence of the devastating magnitude 7.8 earthquake that killed nearly 9,000 people and rendered 3.5 million homeless across the country in 2014. Though the epicenter was 48 miles (77 km) northwest of Kathmandu, more than 600,000 buildings were damaged or destroyed in the capital city and surrounding area. The damage was impossible to miss. With centuries-old buildings, many of which were designated UNESCO World Heritage sites, turned to large piles of rubble, I could not help but feel for a country that had lost so much.

Nepal was a spiritual experience. The energy of the country is peaceful, gentle, and kind, all feelings that washed over me.

As the sun began to set at Swayambhunath Stupa, also known as Monkey Temple, hundreds of monkeys came running out, ready for happy hour.

MUST-SEE:
HIMALAYA MOUNTAINS

The Himalaya mountain range contains the world's tallest peaks. One morning, I woke up before dawn and made my way to the Kathmandu airport for an aerial sightseeing tour. Given the petite size of the plane, the scale, typically reserved for luggage, was used to weigh each passenger. As we ascended high above the clouds, the snow-capped mountains came into view, the jagged tops revealing their majestic beauty. I saw the world's highest peak, Mount Everest, a mere 20 miles (32 km) from the window. With a map in hand and the pilot dishing all the details, I also learned about many of the other mountains in the chain. The tour was $200 and roughly an hour. It was worth every penny.

As I've seen time and time again, from Haiti to Bosnia to Nepal, people are resilient. Kathmandu was teeming with life. The city was filled with people buying fresh food from local farmers, some of whom were holding babies as they sold eggplants, tomatoes, and green beans. The narrow streets were colorful, punctuated by farmers' stalls of produce and buildings with painted doors. We even saw a bike doubling as a fruit stand, a clever way to transport goods to the market.

I had been in Asia for two weeks now and hadn't had a haircut. I decided now was as good a time as any. In a barbershop with large mirrors lining the walls, I was able to see every angle once the cut was in progress. My barber finished the simple cut with an *incredible* head massage. I have never had my head rubbed like that. I wonder if I could find that shop again if I return.

Later in the afternoon, we headed to Patan, a city close to Kathmandu. Patan had a slower pace and was much less crowded. Devastation from the earthquake was visible here as well, as was that same resilience. As we made our way through the narrow streets, dodging motorcycles and bicycles, people waved from windows and greeted us with "Namaste." When we asked for help, even those who struggled with English gladly pointed us in the right direction.

Nepal's greatest asset, by far, is its people. They are welcoming, kind, and community oriented. When my phone died, my Nepali friend Sneh, from grad school, told me to just ask people on the street to lend theirs. I didn't believe her, but later that day I asked my taxi driver, and, without hesitation, he handed over his phone.

Nepal is the birthplace of the Buddha, also known as Siddhartha Gautama, the philosopher who founded Buddhism. Although there are numerous Buddhist temples in the country, 80 percent of the population actually practices Hinduism.

We of course needed to explore the country's historic temples and religious icons. First we visited Boudhanath Stupa, one of the largest stupas (Buddhist shrines with a dome-shaped structure) in the world. The massive white structure can be seen from a window seat when descending into Kathmandu airport.

Our second stop was Pashupatinath Temple, a sacred Hindu temple complex on the banks of the Bagmati River. During our tour, we were shown buildings that dated back to the sixth century, complete with carvings from the Kama Sutra. Our guide explained how the ancient drawings were often used to show young people how to procreate. This complex is also where many Hindus cremate the bodies of their loved ones. The last temple we visited was the Swayambhunath Stupa. After climbing 365 stairs—because Buddhists love stairs (see Laos, page 140)—we came to understand why it is known as the Monkey Temple. As the sun began to set on 360-degree views of Kathmandu, hundreds of monkeys came running out as if a bell had rung to announce happy hour. The monkeys, who clearly were not afraid of people, walked around like they owned the place. Many carried babies on their backs.

Nepal turned out to be a spiritual experience. The energy of the country is so peaceful, and that feeling washed over me. The temples, no matter your religion, feel like holy places. At each, I spent a lot of time watching those who were there for prayer. As I observed their reverence, I wondered, Why not create our own religions? Each of the world's largest religions have so many great tenets—why not borrow ideas from different books and cultures to curate a spiritual ethos that works for you? Through my travels, I feel like I have done that in some way—picked up and kept the pieces of each culture that resonated with me the most.

We spend a lot of time criticizing and judging others for the ways they live their lives, often through a religious lens. If travel has taught me anything, it's to live and let live. To find peace and happiness within our own lives. May we wish this upon all those we love and upon our worst enemies.

I've had my hair cut in many countries, and Nepal was one of the best. My barber finished the simple cut with an incredible head massage.

south africa

SOUTH AFRICA IS THE MOST visited country in sub-Saharan Africa. It is many travelers' first foray into the massive continent. Some insiders call it "Africa lite." My trip to South Africa was my first and only country adventure that was fully sponsored. I was invited to explore the country as a guest of the South African Tourism Board. As my blog and social media had started to soar (I was nearing 20,000 followers at

this point), I was leveraging my social media presence to secure tours and hotel rooms in exchange for social posts. I knew I needed around $130,000 to get to the remaining countries, if hotels, flights, and tours weren't comped. Using my platform to secure some of my travel needs helped make my journey more feasible. Anna, a generous follower, reached out to me on Instagram and offered to help with my blog. Ultimately she ended up helping me plan travel to the last 75 countries. She and I spent countless hours sending pitches to hotels, brands, and tourism boards. Most of our emails went unanswered, but I am incredibly grateful to those who supported the journey.

My trip started in Johannesburg—aka Joburg or Jozi—an African megacity home to nearly six million people. I was floored by its modernity, skyscrapers and highways, massive malls, and countless hotels. I had never seen anywhere else on the continent quite like it.

Johannesburg feels alive. I've only visited in the summer, when warm temperatures give rise to rooftop parties, music festivals, and outdoor markets. Neighbourgoods, a Saturday market in Braamfontein, is my favorite. Not only can you find unique fashion pieces, but you can also eat delicious food, drink good wine, and hang out with fascinating people.

My favorite neighborhood in Johannesburg is Maboneng. The area draws the creative and hipster crowd. It is home to innovative restaurants (Little Addis and Living Room are faves), numerous bars, and a buzzing nightlife. Be sure to check out the Marabi Club.

AFRICA

Johannesburg's Apartheid Museum offers a detailed and emotional history of the dark stain on South Africa's past.

You cannot visit Johannesburg without visiting Soweto and learning the history of the storied township. SOuth-WEstern TOwnship was the site of student uprisings in the late 1970s, calling for a fair and decent education. Soweto is also where 90,000 men were placed in inadequate housing, away from women and children, because the government wanted them to focus on mining and to control population growth. It is where Nelson Mandela and Trevor Noah were raised and where Black South Africans organized to fight against apartheid. While on a Jet Black trip, we took a bike tour with Lebo's Soweto. Our guides, Lungile and Sfiso, were honest, open, and fun as they educated us on the history of the area. In Soweto you can see joy, freedom, frustration, oppression, community, and love.

Cape Town, South Africa's second largest city, is idyllic, with an expansive coastline along the Atlantic and the famed Table Mountain. Only two cities in the world have this same type of beauty, where the city meets the ocean and mountains serve as a backdrop: Cape Town and Brazil's Rio de Janeiro.

While most people flock to Table Mountain for a hike or to the Victoria and Alfred (V&A) Waterfront for a nice meal, my new friends Trevor and Gemaen took me to a party in Khayelitsha, South Africa's second largest township. Located in the parking lot of a former post office, Rands is an open-air club where the drinks were flowing, the *braai,* or local barbeque, was fresh, and the music was thumping. The experience was one of Black South Africa, something many do not encounter in Cape Town. Despite apartheid ending nearly 30 years ago, Cape Town still has a white-centered design. The majority of Black and Coloured South Africans (how the apartheid government defined anyone of mixed race or Asian descent) live on the outskirts of the city to this day, so the primary destinations for tourists are in predominantly white areas.

In Cape Town, I connected with Omphi, a bright and bubbly local. As a lover of colorful cities, I fell in love with the vibrant Bo-Kaap neighborhood. The Cape Malay people, whose ancestry can be traced back to enslaved people the Dutch brought from Indonesia, traditionally occupied Bo-Kaap. A man named Ismael gave us a brief history of his people and the gentrification in his beloved neighborhood.

I rode in a helicopter for the first time in Cape Town. Flying in such a small aircraft in the notoriously strong winds of the cape made me incredibly uncomfortable. The only thing that calmed my anxiety was the view. On the 15-minute ride, I was offered a panorama of the Atlantic Ocean, the peaks of the Twelve Apostles, part of Table Mountain overlooking the luxe Camps Bay neighborhood below, and Robben Island, where Nelson Mandela was imprisoned for 18 years of his 27-year sentence.

While the helicopter was nerve-racking, an excursion to the vineyards of the Western Cape was a no-brainer. We spent a day in the Franschhoek Valley. Grande Provence with its rolling hills, perfectly manicured vineyards, and spectacular food was the standout during our tasting adventure. On a later trip to Cape Town with Jet Black clients, I did a proper wine tour and visited four different vineyards, tasting entirely too much wine. It was all worth it to discover my favorite South African grapes: chenin blanc, viognier, and zinfandel.

Lingering tensions from apartheid can still be felt throughout the country. In recent years, there has been a spate of xenophobic violence directed at Black Africans from other regions, many of whom came to the nation seeking better economic opportunities. As a Black African, I enjoyed myself thoroughly in Johannesburg. But Cape Town was a different story. I was treated poorly by both white and Black South Africans. In a restaurant, a white South African woman bumped me out of the way and began talking to the hostess while she and I were mid-conversation. At another restaurant, a Black South African spoke to me rudely, but he used a kinder tongue with white patrons.

Despite my experience in Cape Town, I truly fell in love with Johannesburg because of the people that it brought into my life. For six weeks, I used Johannesburg as a jumping-off point for my exploration of countries in southern Africa. As is often the case when I travel, I am grateful to collide with so many beautiful souls along the way.

Omphi, a Cape Town expert, took me to Kalky's, a coastal restaurant known for its chips and freshly caught fish.

zambia

FOLLOWING SOUTH AFRICA, I visited Mozambique and Zimbabwe before making the easy drive across the border to Zambia. We crossed over the Victoria Falls bridge, which sits high above the Zambezi, a majestic river that forms the border with Zimbabwe. Entry into Zambia was quick, and the immigration officers were not at all distracted by the baboons moving about as if they worked there.

AFRICA

I stayed in Livingstone, an idyllic town nestled on the banks of the Zambezi. The boutique hotel, Sussi and Chuma, matched the town's charm with 12 luxury tree houses set on the shores of the river. Each evening we partook in sundowners, or sunset drinks, enjoying South African wine and hippo spotting along the water.

The Zambezi is one of Africa's longest rivers, flowing through five other countries. It is also the source of Mosi-oa-Tunya, more commonly known as Victoria Falls. On a sunset cruise, I saw several pairs of eyes belonging to massive hippos (they average more than 3,000 pounds [1,350 kg]) hiding below the surface.

I've made it clear that I am not adventurous. I have no plans to bungee jump from a bridge that crosses the gorge of Victoria Falls or zip line across it (two popular activities). But I did work up the nerve to visit Devil's Pool, nature's ultimate infinity pool on top of Mosi-oa-Tunya.

Devil's Pool is typically reachable mid-August through mid-January when the Zambezi's water levels are low. We hiked 20 minutes across huge boulders to reach the pool. As we approached, mist rose up to the top of the cliffs under a stunning Technicolor rainbow.

Devil's Pool is literally on the ledge of the vertical drop of Victoria Falls. I was a bit shocked as water rushed over the edge, forming one of the largest sheets of falling water in the world. Though the water in the pool was relatively still, I had to give myself a little pep talk. I prefer crystal clear waters where you can see what lurks beneath the surface. That wasn't what I got. As I hesitantly slid my body into the chilly waters, I started feeling little sensations on my legs. Our guide, David, told me they were fish. I tried to ignore both the sensation and the thought of fish eating me alive as I inched toward the edge.

You can sit on a small ledge and lean over to see the falls. David, cool as a cucumber, laid on the edge with his arms folded and legs out. I followed suit, sitting and posing for pictures. I even leaned my body slightly over the edge. This experience is definitely on the top 10 list of coolest things I have done. Later, when I saw the Devil's Pool from the Zimbabwe side, I had greater appreciation for my daring feat—the proximity to the edge of the rushing falls was even more apparent.

Though I could not imagine topping Devil's Pool, the next activity came close. On a traditional safari, I saw a zebra crossing—get it? *Haha.* That's for my British readers. I also saw impalas, baby giraffes, and African buffalo. Then I went on a walking safari to see a family of endangered white rhinos. Upon arrival, we were met by a gun-carrying ranger who is part of the group that protects and tracks the near-extinct species. With 24-hour surveillance meant to keep poachers away, you are able to get within 15 feet (4.6 m) of the rhinos while they rest. You can take the perfect selfie without being in any danger or risk interfering with the rhino's natural way of life. While the adult rhinos were sleeping, a cute baby was as curious about us as we were about him, walking close to and observing us.

Devil's Pool is a natural rock pool that sits on the edge of Victoria Falls. Hanging here is definitely one of the coolest things I've ever done.

namibia

I TRAVEL ALONE OFTEN. I have been to 89 countries, across six continents, solo. I enjoy soloing as much as I do traveling with friends. And then, there are the times I've traveled with near strangers. During my six weeks back and forth from Johannesburg as I explored southern Africa, I met many creatives from around the world. One of them was Wes, an emerging film director from El Paso, Texas. We met at a house party in

Joburg and instantly connected. I had intended to travel to Namibia alone, but I decided to invite Wes along, though I'd only known him a matter of weeks. Surprisingly, he was game, as was his friend Roman, who joined us so last minute that he purchased his flight while en route to the airport.

We landed in Windhoek, the capital city, and were met by our driver (and soon-to-be friend), Martin, who worked for Namibia Wildlife Resorts, a company that kindly sponsored our hotel stays and tours in Namibia. Martin laid out the company's itinerary for us, but it wasn't exactly what I had in mind. After a quick call to his management, we were given the OK to roam free and have the epic adventure that I wanted. The change led to a five-day road trip across about a quarter of the massive country. We spent about five hours in the car each day, but with me as DJ, several stops at Nando's (a South African fast-food chicken restaurant), and deep conversations, we had no complaints.

Just north of Windhoek, we spent our first night at a large resort. As we leisurely roamed the property, I looked up and my mouth fell open. For the first time in my life, I had an unobstructed view of the Milky Way. The clear Namibian skies bore the spectacular body of the universe's work, with thousands of stars shining above. It was more breathtaking than any photo had ever made it seem.

The next morning, we made a five-hour journey to Sossus Dune Lodge in Namib-Naukluft National Park, which surrounds part of the

AFRICA

Big Daddy, a sand dune in Sossusvlei, stands at 1,066 feet (325 m). Although I did not make it to the top, it was still a treat to slide down the soft sands.

Deadvlei, a white clay pan that transported me to another planet, was my favorite place in Namibia.

Namib Desert. Considered the oldest in the world, the Namib Desert is home to some of the world's tallest sand dunes. Monstrous mounds of golden sands stretched up to perfectly blue skies. In the bosom of these dunes lies Sossusvlei, a salt and clay pan, which was unlike any other landscape I have seen in the entirety of the world.

We dredged through the crimson sands, the colors changing as the sun moved across the horizon, to reach Deadvlei. The white clay pan transported me to another planet. The flat white land was accented by skeletons of 700-year-old trees that had succumbed to dehydration. Their desiccated bodies stand as natural art sculptures in the desert landscape. But what shook me most was the incredible serenity: no wind, no echoes, just the still silence of the desert.

With no movement or a single cloud in the impossibly blue skies, the idyllic landscape—dunes of red sands, flat yet beautifully textured ground, and an artscape of trees—looked like a surrealist painting rather than a tourist site. And we were four lone visitors.

After the sun set and evening fell, we marveled as dark skies took over. We decided to go back out into the middle of the desert, where we experienced some of the best stargazing in the world. In complete darkness, with no light pollution, we painted with lights. Using our cellphone flashlights and a long exposure, we made words in the black. I wrote "Be free." It was how I felt in the moment in this magical place, and how I felt about the direction in which my life was going.

The following morning, we peeled ourselves out of bed at 4 a.m. to head back to Sossusvlei to catch the sunrise. The crisp air in the early morning desert left me shivering as the sun peeked over the horizon. As the sun and the temps rose, we set out to climb Big Daddy, the biggest dune in the area at 2,625 feet (800 m). Though we didn't make it to the top, I felt like a kid as I slid toward the bottom, rushing down the softest sands I've ever felt.

One of Africa's most recognizable tribes is the Himba of northwestern Namibia, distinguished by the red clay—*otjize*—that they use in their hair and on their skin. In *Black Panther,* one of the elders on the king's court is a clear reflection of the Himba people. The red ocher is traditionally used to establish a difference between men and women, as well as to protect against Namibia's scorching sun and to keep the skin moist and clean. The Himba, who herd sheep and cattle, live in some harsh environments. While their images are familiar around the world, they make up just 2 percent of Namibia's population.

I asked Martin if we could visit a Himba village. Not knowing where they may be—they are a seminomadic tribe—he made no promises.

In Etosha National Park, we went on an early morning safari and got up close and personal with a few giraffes.

As luck would have it, we spotted a small village where several Himba women were selling woven and brass bracelets on the side of the road.

As we shopped, I was struck by the beauty of the women—their dark skin tinted red, the intricacy of their outfits, and their hair, which was styled with mud. Using Martin as an interpreter, I asked the women if they would dress me in their traditional attire. Confused at first, they talked among themselves before agreeing to indulge me.

I followed three of the women into one of their small mud houses, crouching to enter. Inside, I could stand up fully with a little room to spare, thanks to the domed ceiling. As I undressed, they grabbed pieces of clothing from around the house, each of them jumping in to add to my outfit. It started with a skirt, which was held up by a belt made of animal hide. Atop that, they fastened a second, decorative belt made of metal and beads around both my waist and neck. A few more necklaces were added—then we ran into a problem.

As the ladies stepped back and examined their work, they seemed to be having a small argument. One ran her hand over my head. I realized they had no clue what to do with my hair or, rather, lack thereof. Women's hair is very symbolic in Himba culture, and here I was with barely any. The styles Himba women wear reflect their tribe, the woman's role in the community, her marital status, her age, and her wealth. It can take hours—and a number of relatives—to create the elaborate and symbolic hairstyles these women wear. Along with the red clay, the hairstyles can incorporate everything from braids to goat hair to leather and metal accessories. Women wear a crown, called an *erembe,* made of cow or goat leather once they reach puberty or have been married for a certain period of time. One of the women grabbed a thin piece of cloth and tied it around my head before adorning me with a beautiful headpiece made of metal and leather. The outfit was completed by a pair of shoes, of sorts— very thin pieces of leather that did little to protect my feet from the earth beneath.

The ladies were giddy with excitement, and I was ready to be presented to the village. I emerged from the house and everyone was stunned, the Himba as well as Wes, Roman, and Martin. Though my bright orange lipstick and breasts that had not seen any sun as of late made me stand out, at a quick glance, I blended right in.

Before heading back to Windhoek, we made our way to Etosha National Park for a safari where we spotted lions, giraffes, zebras, and elephants, among other animals. Though it was not my favorite safari, we saw two giraffes fighting, a first for me. As the battling giraffes used their necks as swords, we were stunned into silence.

My travels are driven by my curiosity and a desire to see and understand how people live all over the world. It is important for me to make deep cultural dives when I travel. I try to immerse myself and experience as many authentic moments as I can. This was truly one of my favorite memories from my entire journey around the world. In this experience, I truly connected with the Himba women. Moments like these affirm what I know to be true: We are more similar than we are different.

Rarely do countries blow my mind, but Namibia did just that. The thing about travel is that you never know how it might change you. Namibia's beautiful landscapes, the stargazing, the kindness of the people, and the unbreakable bonds of friendship that were formed changed me for the better. In Namibia, I felt free, beautiful, and loved.

One of the highlights of my trip to Namibia was spending time in a small Himba village and learning about their culture.

Sudan

MY TRIP TO SUDAN happened on a bit of a whim. In early December, while I was still based in Johannesburg, I posted a video on Instagram in partnership with OkayAfrica. The video offered tips for traveling to various countries in Africa over the holidays and made mention of Sudan's capital, Khartoum. My friend Elkair left a comment that he was going home to Sudan for the holidays. I promptly invited myself along. Obtaining a visa

AFRICA

I took a moment to rest on a pyr-amid in Meroë, the former capital of the Nubian Kingdom of Kush, which boasts more pyramids than in all of Egypt.

while in the midst of travel is always a fun adventure. This one involved a couple of friends making sure my Ugandan passport made it to Pretoria, South Africa, and back, while I was using my U.S. passport to explore Namibia. Favors were called in at the Sudanese Embassy to ensure the five-day rush was met.

I landed in Khartoum dressed for the Muslim country of Sudan in loose-fitting black linen pants and a long-sleeve denim shirt that covered my bum. I topped off my look with a black scarf over my head. Though it wasn't necessary, I always err on the side of conser-vative when in Muslim countries.

Immigration and baggage claim were a breeze, but finding Elkair was a challenge. The airport was full of men—I do not recall seeing a single woman—most of whom were dressed uniformly in white tunics. My eyes darted left to right, up and down as I looked for my friend.

Around me, I heard no one speaking English, and when I looked outside, all I could see was an extension of the sea of white. I felt my heart begin to race and my palms moisten. I headed into a cell phone shop in hopes of using a phone. Men who lined up behind me were served first.

Impatient, I headed to a currency-exchange counter. Fortunately, the man behind the counter spoke English. I sheepishly asked to use his phone to call my friend, pushing the words past the lump in my throat, begging the tears not to fall. He obliged and even encouraged me to take the phone outside to ensure I found my friend. I managed

to reach Elkair. When I finally made eye contact with him, I breathed a sigh of relief.

That was one of the few times I remember being incredibly nervous during my travels, but I am also careful to tell this story. No one had actually done anything to make me feel afraid. People often ask me about countries that they have been trained to think are dangerous and impossible for tourists to visit. Sudan is on that list for many. If I say landing in the airport in Khartoum was scary, I would be doing the country a disservice.

My reaction was not a response to the country or its people. My reaction was the result of years of being socialized to feel nervous when I am completely surrounded by men. Fear is based on our perceptions, mostly. That is an important distinction to make when we tell our travel stories, because people will form opinions based on what we share. I am always mindful of the stories I tell for that very reason.

Outside the airport, Khartoum is a bustling capital with an official population of more than five million. Given the fertility of the land in otherwise arid conditions, ancient African civilizations developed along the banks of the Nile River in what is now Sudan. The two Niles—White and Blue—converge in its capital.

Omdurman is the most populated area in Sudan and has a buzzing souk. Though Elkair assured me I did not need to cover my head, I quickly realized that I was the only uncovered woman in the souk. Without a head covering or hair, many people in the market thought I was a man. Confusion really set in because of my bright red lipstick. I was a spectacle, again. As I tried on a gold headpiece, curious women began crowding around me. One woman exclaimed, *"Hay di bint*—Oh my god, it's a girl."

My Sudanese friends showed me the country's true culture. I fell in love with *fūl,* a traditional dish made of fava beans, chickpeas, tomatoes, chili, and cumin that's eaten with bread. I got an amazing haircut from a Turkish barber who added a delightful mini-facial to the standard service. I tasted lemon mint 7UP, a divine play on the popular lemon and mint drinks of the region. I got traditional henna on my left hand, which was so lovely that I regretted not also getting it on the right.

Sudan, a name derived from Arabic meaning the "land of the Blacks," has an extensive history that is lesser known than that of its neighbor to the north, Egypt. The history of the Kingdom of Kush, a Nubian kingdom whose territories covered parts of present-day northern

In front of Khartoum's gold souk, a woman knits hats that are popular with Sudanese men.

Sudan and southern Egypt, has many similarities to Egyptian history. In fact, the former Kush capital, Meroë, has more pyramids than all of Egypt. Sudan, with more than 200 pyramids, actually has the most pyramids of any country in the world.

The pyramids of Meroë are the crown jewel of tourism in Sudan, yet they receive very few visitors. Without the popularity of Egypt, Meroë does not have much tourism infrastructure. Getting to Meroë requires advance planning and permits. I was grateful to my new friend Khalid for arranging the adventure.

A long and dusty journey 120 miles (190 km) northeast of Khartoum takes you back in time to the former Nubian kingdom. We first arrived in Naqa, an ancient ruined city that boasts temples dating back to the fourth century B.C. Unlike ruins and ancient monuments I visited in places like Egypt and Greece, I was flabbergasted to find no ticket booth and no security, just ancient ruins for us to explore on our own.

One site had a very small gate—about two feet (0.6 m) high—to walk through. The groundskeeper, which may be an exaggerated title, was an older man who we only noticed midway through our exploration. Out of respect, we gave him a tip.

The ruins were beautiful. It struck me that, unlike in Egypt, the figures carved into these ancient ruins all had their noses—beautiful, wide, unmistakably African noses.

Sudan has more—and older—pyramids than any other country. In Meroë, you can visit them without any crowds.

After visiting Naqa, we took an off-road adventure 10 miles (16 km) north to reach the pyramids. We arrived late in the evening and planned to wake up the next day to watch the sunrise. After a futile attempt to get our group of 14 up in time, we all mounted our camels at 6 a.m. and rode just over a mile (1.6 km) to the pyramids. The sun beat us there.

It didn't matter. As we approached, I was floored by the sheer number of pyramids in front of me. To think I had never known these pyramids even existed before my trip. Unlike the crowds that gather in Giza, we had this place to ourselves. We roamed the historic grounds, and the

Sudanese American rapper Bas even shot the cover of his album *Milky Way* that December morning.

The kindness and softness of the human spirit move me most when I travel. Again and again I've witnessed those who do not have much still give to those who have less. This was also true in Sudan. Elkair's cousin Mohammed, who drove us around during my stay, has one of the kindest spirits I have ever encountered. Though he spoke minimal English, we found ways to communicate and connect deeply. One day, while sitting in traffic, a child was begging on the street and Mohammed gave him a bit of money, then asked the child to recite his alphabet. I was touched by the simple but generous exchange between the two. Afterward, Mohammed and I talked about how no matter where you are in the world, even poor children just want to be children.

The people of Sudan emit a warm energy that engulfed me. I'm often astounded that others think of the country as unsafe. I never found that perception to be a valid one. This is a place of millennia-old histories and beauty, one in which I found kindness in strangers and beauty in the landscapes. Travel has taught me to expect the unexpected. And to throw expectations entirely out the window. Forget everything you thought you knew and even what you have read or heard. Go see for yourself instead.

On a road trip from Khartoum to Meroë, we stopped for a roadside snack of fresh falafel.

eswatini

WHEN I VISITED ESWATINI, it was known as the Kingdom of Swaziland. Just a few months after my trip, the country's leader, King Mswati III, decided to use its precolonial name in an attempt to break with the lingering colonial past. My friend Rene and I drove to Eswatini from Lesotho, a quick jaunt on our way back to Johannesburg. It was an easily navigable trip for any driver and allowed us to explore the

AFRICA

countryside of two nations. At the invitation of the tourism board (one of only eight I received throughout all 195 countries), we visited Mlilwane Wildlife Sanctuary for a sunset game drive. This safari was unlike any other I had been on. We had to drive our own rented tiny sedan into the park past crocodiles and wildebeests, all the while hoping they didn't attack. Fortunately, these brilliant creatures ran away as we got closer, equally afraid of us.

At the lodge, we swapped our sedan for an open-air 4x4. This time we weren't at the wheel; thankfully, we were driven by our experienced guide, Stew. On the game drive we were served a bottle of crisp South African chenin blanc, the contents of which found their way onto my lap as we drove along the bumpy road. It was worth it to see impalas, little baby warthogs, mischievous monkeys, and a confusion of wildebeests with their babies.

The red dirt road was surrounded by lush plains with mountains in the distance. We came across large lakes with still waters and dense forests. Stew let us get out of the car when we spotted a dazzle of zebras—including babies with their mothers and couples clearly in love—standing in the open plains. After 10 safaris, I can confidently declare zebras and giraffes my favorite animals because of their beauty and noticeable personalities. To shoot a close-up of these naturally fashionable creatures was a dream come true.

The next day, we visited Mantenga Cultural Village, where we watched traditional dancers and learned about the cultural history of the Swazi people.

The traditional huts seen throughout the village are made of branches. The structures can last up to 10 years. Though they are more permanent now, the Swazi people used to move their homes more frequently. These branch structures allowed them to travel easily; it takes 10 to 15 men to move a hut.

Across Africa you will find a variety of traditional dances. I love seeing various dances around the world, among the African diaspora, because the linkages are always clear. Each dance focuses on a different part of the body: In Uganda, *kiganda* focuses on the hips; in Ethiopia and Eritrea, the focus is on the shoulders; in Eswatini, the focus is on the legs. Before Eswatini, I had only seen a traditional dance focused on legs in the form of jitting, a popular dance in Detroit in the late 1990s and early 2000s. The African spirit persists across centuries and geographies.

Watching the dancers was mesmerizing. The women were wrapped in a cotton fabric decorated in a red-white-and-black pattern that moved as easily as they did. Shells adorned their ankles and added a rhythmic noise to the enchanting beating of the drums. As men drummed, women danced in a group of eight. Their movements started slow and measured, moving forward and backward. As the drumming intensified, so did the dancing. Suddenly all of the women looked up, as if telling their leg "Go there," and each lifted a single leg from the ground to nearly their forehead. Their bare feet kicked up dust as they danced. The men, clad in animal skin and with fur accessories clasped around their limbs, danced with as much poise, determination, and grace as their female counterparts. As I sat and watched, I knew I was nowhere near as flexible. This was a unique traditional skill.

Eswatini is a rarely visited place, but in just two days, I found it offered so much in terms of nature and culture—without the crowds of some of the more popular countries in southern Africa.

In traditional Swazi dancing, the emphasis is on the legs. Mantenga Cultural Village is a great place to learn about Swazi culture.

antigua and barbuda

I PREFER A WINDOW SEAT when I fly. Anytime a plane descends, I am glued to the window like a child flying for the first time. The excitement of visiting a new place or seeing the old from the window of a plane always thrills me. As the aircraft descends through clouds, I often imagine being able to reach out and touch them just to see if they are as fluffy as they appear to the eye. I fled the cold of Detroit on a Sunday in January to

NORTH
AMERICA

visit the twin islands of Antigua and Barbuda. As we approached our destination, the deep blue Caribbean Sea below began to lighten and the shallow turquoise waters of the Antiguan coast came into view, lush green mountains just beyond them. Houses dotted the countryside. I spotted a marina in a bay near a golf course and people on watercrafts cutting through the warm waters. This, I thought, was the perfect way to enter my 100th country.

Antigua has been one of the Caribbean's top sailing destinations for centuries and hosts the most prestigious sailing week in the Caribbean. From my balcony at the Antigua Yacht Club and Marina, I watched the sunset, masts of million-dollar sailboats piercing the pink skies. After going down an internet rabbit hole of super yachts, I decided I need a friend with a yacht. I, myself, would prefer to be the friend with the private jet so I can skip those 5 a.m. flights.

Anyone who has been to Antigua will tell you to visit Shirley Heights, which offers the best views on the island, overlooking English and Falmouth Harbors. On Sundays, it hosts a party with mouthwatering barbeque, blaring music from local bands, and crowds of tourists and locals alike. It is an Antiguan staple not to be missed. But you should come back another, less crowded day to soak in the views and get the perfect photo. I happened to spot Bono gazing at the spectacular views on our second visit.

Bono sighting aside, it took until the day I was slated to leave Antigua to fall in love with the country. A perk of the travel influencer life is that we get invited to visit hotels in some of the world's most beautiful locations. I am selective about which hotels I visit and ensure brand alignment—and I make no promises of endorsement sight unseen. In Antigua, the marketing team at Cocobay Resort invited me and my friends to have breakfast before heading to the airport. Although I was impressed with the beaches flying into the island, prior to this breakfast I had not seen many sandy shores that blew me away.

That all changed when we walked into the Cocobay Resort. At last, I was blown away. Out the restaurant windows, the waters closest to the shore were an enchanting aquamarine. After breakfast and as my champagne flute neared empty, I started looking into rescheduling my flight to St. Kitts for the following day.

We were offered a tour of the resort's property and spent time on that picturesque shore, truly one of the most beautiful beaches I have ever seen. I swam in the infinity pool, lounged in a comfy hammock, and frolicked in the warm and welcoming waters. Then we were shown one of the suites—an all-white room with a private plunge pool and a bathtub on the deck. I knew I had to stay even though my flight was nonrefundable. I needed to take a bath in the morning, overlooking these waters and the mountains that hugged them.

I threw out that day's plane ticket, bought a new flight, bid my friends adieu, and enjoyed another 24 hours in paradise. In country 100, I fully realized the luxury and freedom I had created for myself. I didn't take the privilege of living this life and traveling the way I do for granted.

When I saw the breathtaking blue waters of Coco Beach in Antigua, I changed my return flight to enjoy them a little longer.

nigeria

THE THREE MONTHS BETWEEN Antigua and Nigeria were a whirlwind. I visited more Caribbean countries before flying home to Detroit. Then I checked off my remaining countries in Southeast Asia before meeting Elton in Bali to celebrate his birthday. In Bali, just over a year after I decided to take this journey, I filmed a video officially announcing my goal to visit every country in the world. I had waited to announce

my plans, aiming to get a few more countries under my belt before going public. I was shocked by how many outlets picked it up: *Forbes, Condé Nast Traveler,* and CNN, among others. It led to a huge bump on my Instagram to the tune of more than 40,000 new followers in just three months.

With less than 90 countries to go, I was on a high from all the press. But it quickly wore off. Following Bali, I made a quick three-day stop at home before a Jet Black trip to Senegal. I had planned to visit more countries in West Africa from there, but I had hit a wall. In a span of seven days, I took seven flights across 19,387 miles (31,200 km). I was completely exhausted. In Senegal, I decided to cut my trip short to spend two weeks in Detroit to rest. Nigeria could wait.

After my much needed break, I returned to West Africa to cross Nigeria off my list. The Federal Republic of Nigeria, home to more than 211 million people, is Africa's most populated country and the world's seventh most populated. Anywhere in the world you meet an African person, they are likely Nigerian.

Besides a decades-old joke about a prince who wants to give you money, Nigeria has given us Fela Kuti, the political activist, musician, and architect of Afrobeat, whose song "Zombie" can be heard on my record player regularly; the legendary writer Chinua Achebe; Ngozi Okonjo-Iweala, the first woman to helm the World Trade Organization; one of my favorite authors, Chimamanda Ngozi Adichie; and globally popular musicians, including Wizkid and Burna Boy. Nigeria gave us Nollywood, the world's second largest film industry after Bollywood, as

AFRICA

One thing I do in nearly every country is visit local markets. In Lagos, Lekki Market is my favorite. Don't forget to negotiate!

well as Hollywood stars Chiwetel Ejiofor and Cynthia Erivo. In the United States, the Nigerian American community garners significant success across industries and is the most educated ethnic group in America, even beating out white Americans. With all that Nigerians have given the world—including some of my favorite people in my life—it is no wonder they are some of the proudest people I have ever met.

If Africa were a country—reminder, it is not—Lagos would be its heartbeat. The vibrant West African metropolis of 21 million may intimidate some travelers and bring others to life. For me, it is the latter. Lagos is packed with yellow buses, *keke marwas* (motorized rickshaws), and *okadas* (motorcycle taxis) buzzing about. It is also home to a burgeoning tech and creative scene. The massive city is divided into the mainland and several islands, including Victoria Island and Ikoyi.

My first trip to Lagos was a mix of traffic jams, drinks, dinners with new friends and old, and a visit to the Kalakuta Museum, where I learned a small history of the empire that Fela built. I also hosted a small event to meet Lagosians who had been following my journey online. I often planned meet and greets in places where I had a large number of followers. These events were organized to help put faces to the countless commenters, continue to build my community, and share my experiences on a more personal level.

I also took a trip to Tarkwa Bay, a small island just off Lagos, where we made our own picnic as the waters of the Atlantic lapped the shores. At an epic J. Cole concert, a week after the release of his *KOD* album, I danced with the audience. I browsed Nigerian art in Nike Centre, completely charmed by its namesake owner. I negotiated for a new bag in Lekki Market and ate delicious bites at Nok. Lagos was a whirlwind, and it had me in its grasp.

Lagos is also where I learned a valuable lesson in kindness, positive energy, and the danger of assumptions. After grabbing a juice with my de facto tour guide, Toju, I realized a mile from the café that I didn't have my phone. We rushed back and searched frantically while trying to call my phone. The phone rang and rang. Finally, someone picked up but didn't speak. Using Find My iPhone, we hopped in the car and followed the GPS signal in what felt like a criminal chase. We found ourselves in the middle of a neighborhood with no one in sight. Feeling defeated, we went back to the café to look at security video footage. You could see me leave the store with my phone, and then unknowingly drop it in the parking lot as I climbed into the car.

The nightmare escalated. Whoever had my phone had turned it off, eliminating any possibility of tracking it. An hour and a half later, I insisted

that we look up the phone again. My luck, it had been turned back on. We called and this time someone answered. Thirty minutes later we met the man with my phone. It was clear he had not showered or eaten in days. He told us he had seen the phone on the ground and picked it up on his way to church. Relieved, we asked him if he was hungry and took him inside a small restaurant to buy him two meals, one to eat immediately and one to take with him. I gave him all of the naira I had and thanked him for returning my phone. Toju gave him his phone number, telling the man to call him every day until he found a job. The man never did call, but I believe karma is protecting this gentle soul.

I firmly believe in positive energy. The universe brought my phone back to me. Same with a stolen wallet in Los Angeles, a lost wallet in Detroit, lost credit cards in Johannesburg, and my passports and credit cards in the Philippines. Even in places with high crime rates, places people told me to avoid, I have always recovered everything I've ever lost or had stolen.

I was told I had to return to Lagos for "Dezemba," and so I did. From mid to late December through early January, people of the Nigerian diaspora return home. Beach clubs and nightclubs pop up and everyone is fueled by *suya* (a spicy meat skewer) and champagne.

No one parties harder than Nigerians (though Ugandans are a very, very close second) and Dezemba was a reminder of that. Lagos owes me nothing!

Lagos is a sprawling city perched on the shores of the Atlantic. The extensive coastline has many beautiful beaches.

guyana

I LANDED IN GUYANA on a rainy afternoon and hit the ground running. With only 48 hours in the country, I connected with Stacey, a travel agent, who created an itinerary that would allow me to learn the history of the country, see the major tourist attractions, and eat some delicious food. On short trips like this, I often rely on travel agents or local friends to show me the best of what each country has to offer.

SOUTH
AMERICA

As I drove from the airport to the capital city, Georgetown, the country felt familiar. Guyana is the only country in South America where English is the official language, though the majority of the population speaks Guyanese Creole. Culturally and demographically, it reminded me of Trinidad and Tobago. The banana trees and single-story homes with corrugated roofs were reminiscent of Caribbean islands. But more than anything, it felt African. It isn't always the way a country looks, but more often the way it feels.

The architecture in Georgetown is incredibly unique. On a walking tour of the city, I took in the colonial buildings, large wooden structures brightly painted and accentuated by white wooden shutters and balconies. We also visited St. George's Cathedral, which dates back to the late 1800s and is among the largest wooden structures in the world. Although the exterior showed its age, the interior, done in mostly dark wood, was well maintained.

The first meal I had in Guyana was actually Chinese food at New Thriving Restaurant, which Stacey assured me is the best in the Caribbean. The seafood soup, fried rice, grilled chicken with black bean sauce, grilled seafood, and Singapore noodles did not disappoint.

Why Chinese food in Guyana? Following the abolition of slavery in the mid to late 1800s, the British brought more than 14,000 Chinese people to Guyana to fill the labor gap on sugar plantations. Chinese people now represent less than one percent of the population, but the cultural impact is still present. The first president of Guyana, following independence, was of Chinese ancestry.

On the outskirts of Georgetown, I visited a hidden gem. I was dropped in front of a house, then walked down a narrow walkway to a backyard where I was greeted by a colorful mural that proclaimed, "Welcome to Backyard Café," a restaurant run by Chef Delven Adams. The eclectic restaurant is literally in a backyard filled with plants in rainbow-colored pots, with red and lime green benches, and energy that screams, "Welcome home." Without a menu, Backyard Café takes orders a day or two in advance. The food, much of which is made on a traditional stove, is ready when you arrive. We had a *pamplemousse* (grapefruit) salad arranged in the colors of the Guyanese flag, with red onion, cucumber, and tomato. This was paired with salt fish, coconut bake, pepper pot, and the customer favorite, steamed fish. We washed down the meal with fresh butter fruit (avocado) and passion fruit smoothie. The food was delectable, and the conversation was equally amazing.

To top off my whirlwind two days in the country, I boarded a 12-passenger plane and sat next to the pilot for a one-hour flight to Guyana's natural treasure, Kaieteur Falls. Flying at just above 10,000 feet (3,050 m), from the bosom of fluffy white clouds I gazed at rooftops scattered across the countryside. As we approached the landing strip, the mammoth falls came into view, surrounded by the expansive Amazonian rainforest, the Potaro River cutting through the lush vegetation. Kaieteur Falls is the world's largest single-drop waterfall by volume; it is four times higher than Niagara Falls and two times higher than Africa's Victoria Falls. I found it absolutely breathtaking, even after having seen all of the world's major waterfalls, including South America's other gem, Iguazú. This was also my first time flying over the Amazon rainforest, and my god, nature will never cease to amaze me.

On my quest to reach 195 countries quickly, I often didn't get as much time in every place as I would have liked. Though 48 hours in Guyana is nowhere near enough to explore the country, no matter how short or long my stay, so much of what I love about travel is being able to sit down with complete strangers and have open conversations. That is what gives me such a deep and beautiful understanding of the world. I come to know a place through the eyes of its people.

In the valley just beyond Kaieteur Falls, the world's largest single-drop waterfall by volume, the mist from the falls is ever present.

SNAPSHOT FROM NEPAL: In Kathmandu, Nepal, prayer flags fly high above Boudhanath Stupa, one of the largest spherical stupas in the world.

suriname

TRAVEL ALLOWS YOU TO BE A lifelong learner, if you let it. It is a crash course in history and anthropology. As we move through countries, we see how people live, learn about political and economic histories, and discover our similarities and differences. Despite its significant impact on colonization, you don't often hear about the Dutch Empire. But Suriname, a Dutch colony for more than 300 years, only gained

SOUTH AMERICA

independence in 1975. Located in the north of South America, Suriname is one of the three "Guianas": British Guiana, now Guyana; Dutch Guiana, now Suriname; and French Guiana, which remains a French territory. If you meet a Black person speaking Dutch, they are likely from Suriname.

Suriname was a beautiful and surprising adventure. But that adventure started with a middle-of-the-night arrival into the capital, Paramaribo. (It should be noted, the middle-of-the-night flights I took throughout my mission to hit 195 countries were the worst parts of this journey. And I took a lot of them.) After making it to Paramaribo, exhausted, I only got a few hours of sleep before having to wake up for an early morning drive into the interior of the country. The wake-up call was worth it. The drive highlighted Suriname's beautiful landscape: an incredibly green country covered in lush forest—a portion of which is the Amazon—which takes up nearly 95 percent of the land.

In Pokigron, a small town at the end of a paved road along the Suriname River, my friends and I boarded a traditional wooden boat fashioned from a tree trunk—thankfully equipped with a motor. We made our way three hours south to Danpaati River Lodge in the depths of the Amazon. As we sailed down the massive river, we were completely surrounded by rainforest that remained mostly still and untouched, aside from a few signs of life, such as women doing laundry on the shores.

In the rainforest, we took an excursion to a nearby Saamaka village. The ancestors of the Saamaka people were brought from Africa and enslaved to work on the plantations of the Dutch colony. Those who managed to escape settled in the rainforest. I was a bit shocked when we arrived in the village. It looked exactly like an African village, from the structure of the homes—roofs made from banana leaves or corrugated metal—to the people who looked like me. In fact, a few locals assumed I was Saamaka. The people we spoke with had a strong affinity for Africa and were very happy to see me there.

With few European interactions after their escape to the rainforest, the Saamaka connection to Africa remains deep. From women bending at the waist and brushing the ground with homemade brooms to yellow jerricans strewn about to freshly washed clothes hung on a line to dry in the afternoon sun, and even the way they cooked using charcoal, much of what I saw in the Saamaka village made me feel like I was in my mother's village in Uganda rather than in South America.

Back at the river lodge, the staff gave a traditional performance. The clapping, dancing, and singing cemented their direct connection to Africa. It is amazing how often I feel at home in foreign places.

While in Suriname, I took a sailing trip up the Amazon River and spent a few nights in the rainforest.

st. vincent and the grenadines

ONE OF THE BEST PARTS OF visiting all 195 countries in the world is seeing places off the popular tourist path. One of the least visited countries in the Caribbean is St. Vincent and the Grenadines, made up of 32 islands and cays. I visited two: the main island of St. Vincent, where the capital of Kingstown is located, and the private island of Mustique. I had big plans for my visit, namely getting my open-water diving certificate.

NORTH AMERICA

But the universe had something else in mind—a common occurrence on my adventures around the globe. Just before my arrival, I contracted an ear infection that was so unbearable I contemplated amputation.

With limited options, I had to forgo my scuba diving certification. Instead, I enjoyed a leisurely four-day stay in the island nation. On the island of Saint Vincent, I stayed at a small Airbnb for two nights. The house had two guest rooms and clear views of the Caribbean Sea. The second room was occupied by a Trinidadian woman named Ruby, who was a kindred traveling Taurus spirit. Married and retired, Ruby had just turned 81 and was in St. Vincent on a one-month solo adventure to celebrate her birthday. We spent evenings on the veranda watching the sunset and exchanging travel tales. She promised to make me rum punch when I visited Trinidad (unfortunately, we never got the chance).

Ruby and I explored the lush mountainous island with our driver, Kezal, who gave us a brief history of the country and ensured that we had the best meals of fresh fish, coconut rice, and fried plantains. The restaurants 4 Shells and Chill Spot were the best! And Belmont Lookout offered stunning views of the Mesopotamia Valley. We saw breadfruit being roasted on the side of the street. The starchy Caribbean delicacy was delicious; it's roasted whole, then cut open and served piping hot.

More than the food, I fell in love with the people on the island. Everyone was very welcoming, warm, and free-spirited. I met a group of guys dyeing their hair blond and, watching their fun for a brief moment, debated dyeing mine, too. At Indian Bay beach, Ruby saw "marijuana in the flesh" for the first time. It only took 81 years!

A 10-minute, unpressurized flight from St. Vincent is the island of Mustique. Noise-canceling headphones and earplugs helped manage the ear pain on the flight, but once I landed on the beautiful island, I had to visit the doctor for pain medication and another round of antibiotics. I was lucky that I wasn't often sick throughout this journey to 195, but this ear infection was a killer. If you are reading this and your five-year-old has an ear infection and you think they are being dramatic, trust me, they aren't!

Frequented by British royalty for decades (it was a holiday favorite of Princess Margaret's), Mustique maintains its position high on the list for jet-setters, even if its runway is too small for private jets. During my time on Mustique, I enjoyed a true vacation. Though my Instagram has convinced people that my life is one permanent vacation, I can assure you it is not. During the last half of my journey I dealt with back-to-back flights, layovers, frequently changing time zones, and lost luggage. People think I put my laptop on the beach and say "#todaysoffice," but that is not reality. Finding ways to maximize time on the ground in each country, engaging with the local culture, and working was, at times, exhausting.

On the tiny island of Mustique, a favorite of the British royal family, sunbathing at the Cotton House is the best way to spend lazy days.

Mustique was a much needed respite in the lap of luxury. I was hosted by the only hotel on the island, Cotton House. The phenomenal boutique hideaway has only 17 rooms and personalized service. This is a place where everyone knows your name, your favorite drink, and what you want for breakfast. Every Tuesday, people from around the island convene in the hotel's lounge for drinks and you never know who you might see. I saw one of the main cast members of Game of Thrones. Don't worry, I played it cool.

If you are looking for local food on the island, you must check out Lisa's. The bare-bones restaurant goes big on flavor. Be careful with the pepper sauce—I'm pretty sure it burned off part of my tongue.

Morning runs, afternoons on the beach, and evening drinks on the veranda led to a love affair with Mustique. In fact, I plan to spend my 40th birthday there with friends and family.

latvia

SO MUCH OF THIS JOURNEY around the world was knowing when and how to pivot. My trip to Latvia was planned during a nine-country tour, of which six were firsts. I didn't tackle countries continent by continent, which is the smart and efficient way to make this journey. But when I could get through a number of countries in one region at the same time, I took advantage. On this trip to Europe, that meant lots of one-way

EUROPE

flights, a couple car rentals, and one last-minute itinerary change thanks to a visa misunderstanding. Unable to get to Belarus as planned, I ended up adding two days to my time in Latvia.

Summer is my favorite time to visit Europe, and that proved true in the Baltics, too. The midsummer sun and cool sea breeze made for the perfect weather to explore Latvia. As we made our sunrise descent into the 800-year-old capital perched on the Gulf of Riga, the city came into view, as did the sprawling green countryside that surrounded it. From my window seat, the scene below was idyllic.

First on my to-do list was exploring Old Riga, the entirety of which is a UNESCO World Heritage site. At the top of St. Peter's Church, a Gothic building that dates back to 1209, I marveled at the panoramic views of the entire city.

But even in this stunning capital, I couldn't escape the realities of the world—something I've found to be true no matter where I am. In Riga, I came upon a gay pride event. Behind the barriers of the parade were supporters, as well as the expected haters, many of whom were older Latvian women shaking a thumbs-down at the revelers. My favorite sign among the supporters read, "Hate harms you and people around you." I couldn't agree more: Homophobia, transphobia, Islamophobia, racism, misogyny, and any other form of hatred only works to eclipse the beauty of our uniqueness in every corner of the globe.

I explored Riga with a local woman named Paula. We started with lunch at a cute rooftop restaurant, Herbārijs, where the floor was covered with an intricate black-and-white tile that complemented the glass walls, green plants, and the minimalist black-and-white decor. After lunch we stopped at Kaņepes Kultūras Centrs, a quirky spot with a small bar and a weekly events schedule that included "feminism for dummies," a "nonbinary workshop," and live music. Latvia, I was learning, was a surprisingly progressive place.

I love visiting cities to see what's at the heartbeat of a country, but the outskirts often offer more ways to relax. After a couple of days in Riga, we went into Latvia's picturesque countryside, full of rolling green hills and villages that are as charming as they are beautiful. Of all the places in the world, Latvia is the rare one that made me want to buy a house in the country. Just 60 miles (100 km) outside of Riga sits Rumene Manor, a 19th-century neo-Gothic home that once belonged to Baltic-German nobility. The property has a 17-acre (7 ha) landscaped park and its own lake. I felt a wonderful sense of peace and calm here. It was exactly what I needed during this sprint through nine European countries.

Straddling the Daugava River, Riga, the 800-year-old capital of Latvia, boasts a pedestrian-only historic center.

kyrgyzstan

AFTER MY NINE-COUNTRY TOUR of Europe, I made my way, for the first time, to Central Asia. Elton and I boarded a plane in Stockholm for an 18-hour journey to the charming Kyrgyz village of Bokonbaevo. It took us two flights and several hours in a car to reach the quiet village on the south shore of Lake Issyk Kul in eastern Kyrgyzstan. Upon arrival in Bokonbaevo, our guide, Nazira, welcomed us into her home, where we

ate a simple breakfast of bread, jam, and meat in the company of her mother and niece. Then we headed into town to find a mobile shop so I could buy a SIM card; internet connection on my phone was key throughout my time traveling the world. I was still running Jet Black and had to coordinate trips with my team. I also needed to post on social media from each destination to feed the content machine. So in countries where my phone plan didn't work, I bought a local SIM card.

I often forget that in many places, I stand out like a sore thumb. As Nazira and I walked to the mobile shop, I noticed traffic literally stop and people staring at me. I thought to myself, Oh yeah, I'm Black. I was a rarity in this region. Most people in the country, and especially in the countryside, had probably never seen a Black person in real life. It's a surreal experience to be someone's first. I felt both very aware of the eyes on me and also that the people staring were more fascinated than malicious.

Our first stop was a sustainable yurt camp with solar panels. The yurts were outfitted with brightly colored fabrics and loads of pillows and blankets. It had been 21 hours since we'd left Stockholm, so Elton and I took the opportunity to take a two-hour nap. A woman prepared a pallet of pillows and blankets with nothing but love. It was the best nap of my life; it felt like being in the womb. After we woke, those solar panels came in handy for hot showers, a welcome relief given the late afternoon chill.

ASIA

On a mountaintop overlooking Lake Issyk Kul in eastern Kyrgyzstan, I was able to live out my childhood dream of sleeping in a yurt.

Well rested, we headed into the mountains overlooking Lake Issyk Kul. On our way, we saw a huge herd of sheep and chased after them as the ambivalent animals bleated "meh" in unison.

We continued our journey to a quiet valley in the midst of gorgeous mountains just in front of the lake. In this picturesque location we were going to raise our yurt for camping overnight. This is the kind of travel that childhood dreams are made of—sometimes my breath is taken away by the fortune of my own journey.

Yurts are a key part of the nomadic Kyrgyz culture. Easily transportable, they function as family homes as well as places of worship. They are also a symbol of craftsmanship and artistry in the community. For our humble abode, we were raising a 30-year-old yurt—and it was tough work. In Kyrgyzstan, they have yurt-making competitions; one of the men who helped with ours is on a team that can set up a yurt in just 12 minutes. The average time is two hours.

When raising the yurt, you have to pray before putting on the top. One Kyrgyz jokester was kind enough to pray that I find a prince. I think he had too much fermented horse milk. The drink, known as *kumis,* is a delicacy in this region. It is an acquired taste—one I recommend you don't smell first. To round out our Kyrgyz dinner that night, the kumis was paired with yak meat—and that I did not mind.

The next morning, I emerged from the yurt and took in the fresh mountain air. I often forget how bad the air is that I breathe every day until I go deep in nature. Feeling truly clean air hit my lungs reminded me how much work we have to do to preserve our planet.

We rode horses to get a better view of Lake Issyk Kul, the world's second largest saline lake after the Caspian Sea. Weaving our way up the mountain along narrow paths, we were afforded stunning views of deep blue waters and the valley that hosted us. It was so quiet and peaceful in those mountains that I was truly one with nature. I listened to the birds chirp as the crisp wind caressed my cheeks.

Though you can see almost anything and everything on the internet, nothing compares to the real experience.

After soaking in the views and taking a second to give gratitude for the moment, we started our descent. To my surprise, we headed off on a new path, one that looked scary, steep, and just wrong! What had been a beautiful moment in nature quickly turned into a descent to hell. We were sliding and falling down the side of a mountain, literally. Our horses and our guide had never attempted to descend the mountain on this side. It was steep, full of loose gravel, and awful. We dismounted and tried to get down as carefully as possible. What was supposed to be an hour-long horseback ride instead led to the

destruction of my Toms shoes, extreme frustration, and the desire to get home immediately. I wanted to be somewhere with running water, electricity, and a bed that wasn't on the floor. Even the horses seemed to be questioning what the fuck we were doing.

Shaken but not broken, I took in my surroundings again once my feet were back on the grassy knolls of the mountain. The verdant green hills and natural beauty reminded me why I was falling in love with Kyrgyzstan. I wouldn't let one slide down the side of a mountain take away from what was otherwise my first foray into a region that stole my heart.

After our experience on the mountains, we returned to the capital, Bishkek. We did not have much time to explore the capital beyond a delicious dinner, as most of our time was spent trying to secure our Afghan visas. When we arrived at the Afghan Embassy, a very kind gentleman greeted us and offered us tea. Over our warm cups, I explained we were looking to obtain tourist visas for Afghanistan. We were kindly told the person who processes visas was out on holiday and would not be back for another 10 days. Another visa fail. We thanked him for our tea and left. I had no time to waste sitting around waiting on a visa. I had other countries to cross off my list. On to Kazakhstan we went.

Kyrgyzstan has roughly the same number of sheep as people. The animal is a cornerstone of rural livelihoods.

kazakhstan

UNLESS YOU'RE DRIVING YOUR OWN CAR, the only way to cross into Kazakhstan from neighboring Kyrgyzstan is by foot. So at the Korday border, Elton and I bid our Kyrgyz taxi driver adieu, walked through immigration, and were met by several taxis eagerly waiting for passengers on the other side. As two dark-skinned Black travelers, we were a spectacle everywhere we went in Central Asia.

It came as no surprise that the drivers moved toward us like moths to a flame.

Of the 10 or so men who surrounded us, none really spoke English. One driver put his phone up to Elton's ear so he could negotiate with his English-speaking friend while simultaneously posing for a picture with him. After a lot of back and forth, we were on our way to Almaty for roughly 20 percent off the initial fare for the four-hour ride.

Kazakhstan is probably the biggest country that you've never thought to visit. The former Soviet republic stretches from the Caspian Sea in the west to the Altay Mountains in the east, where it borders China and Russia. After the dissolution of the Soviet Union, the United States was the first country to recognize Kazakhstan's independence, in December 1991. At 1,052,100 square miles (2,725,000 km²), it is the world's largest landlocked country and the ninth largest country overall. The sparsely populated, Muslim-majority country has the largest and strongest performing economy in Central Asia, a fact that you become acutely aware of as soon as you step foot in Almaty.

When we arrived, we were floored by the visible wealth. We passed the Esentai Tower—the tallest in the city at a staggering 531 feet (162 m)—which houses a Ritz-Carlton; a Bentley dealership; and luxury stores like Saks Fifth Avenue and Prada. It was such a stark contrast to its next-door neighbor, Kyrgyzstan, that we quickly Googled where the money was coming from. The country's wealth comes from extensive and abundant natural resources, including petroleum, natural gas, uranium, coal, gold, and, well, the list goes on.

Most of our short visit to Kazakhstan was spent trying to obtain visas for Afghanistan and Uzbekistan. Thwarted in our plans to get an Afghan visa in Kyrgyzstan, we readjusted them to ensure our entry into the seldom visited country. It's remarkable that we could spend three days in a country and most of it hopping from one embassy to another dealing with bureaucratic red tape, but that was the reality of this journey. As a result, we didn't get a chance to see much of what Almaty had to offer, which includes a tsarist-era Russian Orthodox church and the Central State Museum of Kazakhstan. But to make the most of our trip, we left our hotel early to stop at Big Almaty Lake before our flight to Uzbekistan.

Located in the gorgeous, snowcapped Trans-Ili Alatau mountains a mere nine miles (14 km) south of the city, the alpine reserve is a stunning masterpiece of nature. The winding road up the mountains was lined with dense forest and offered views of the expansive valley below. When we arrived at Big Almaty Lake, I was stunned into silence. The sky was clear and blue, and the lake was a brilliant aquamarine. In the still of morning, with no one else around, I heard only the chirps of birds fill the air.

I am comfortable in the fact that I do not have to see and do everything on my first visit to a country. At the same time, on my journey to 195 countries, I was determined to make each visit count, to do something beyond just stepping foot within a country's borders. Yes, I could find myself on a bit of a time crunch in many of the countries I made it to, but there was always someone new to meet, something new to see. Big Almaty Lake made Kazakhstan completely worth the visit, and I'd go back just to stand in awe of her glory, as well as to see what else the country has to offer.

Located in the snowcapped Trans-Ili Alatau mountains, the natural alpine Big Almaty Lake is a stunning masterpiece of nature.

uzbekistan

I'M AN ENTHUSIASTIC EXTROVERT. It's a personality trait that has made travel—and connecting with the people I meet—easy and enjoyable. I can talk to a person as easily as I can talk to a wall, and I never let a language barrier get in the way of connecting with people. Case in point: Despite the fact that very few people spoke English, I fell in love with Uzbekistan. One of the five "Stans" of Central

ASIA

Asia, Uzbekistan is a double landlocked country with no access to waterways. That position strongly impacts its economy and makes for an extreme reliance on neighbors to access trade routes.

We flew into Tashkent, the capital, and hit the ground running. Our driver, Rusam, was an incredibly kind man, who—though he did not speak English—volunteered to be our guide. Getting past the language barrier meant lots of laughs and muddling through hand gestures. When absolutely necessary, Rusam would call someone to translate. He made one of those calls to be sure I understood the history of the Barak Khan Madrassa. It all worked out perfectly.

The patterns and textiles throughout Uzbekistan are sublime, from the traditional clothing to the domes of the mosques. But the markets had me head over heels. At the first shop in Tashkent, I was giddy as I came face-to-face with the beautiful Uzbek ikat design. The new-to-me design blends together bright colors in a unique pattern of shapes. The material is mostly used in jackets, though I had some fabric turned into pillows. Uzbekistan also has beautiful ceramics that feature the ikat design.

Seeing my joy at this small shop, Rusam took us to a much larger market where I may or may not have spent more than an hour trying on jackets in different sizes and lengths. I settled on two that have since become staples in my wardrobe. It really is a joy for me to find unique clothing, accessories, and home goods all over the world.

Uzbekistan's brightly colored buildings, ikat textiles, and incredibly welcoming people made it my favorite country in Central Asia.

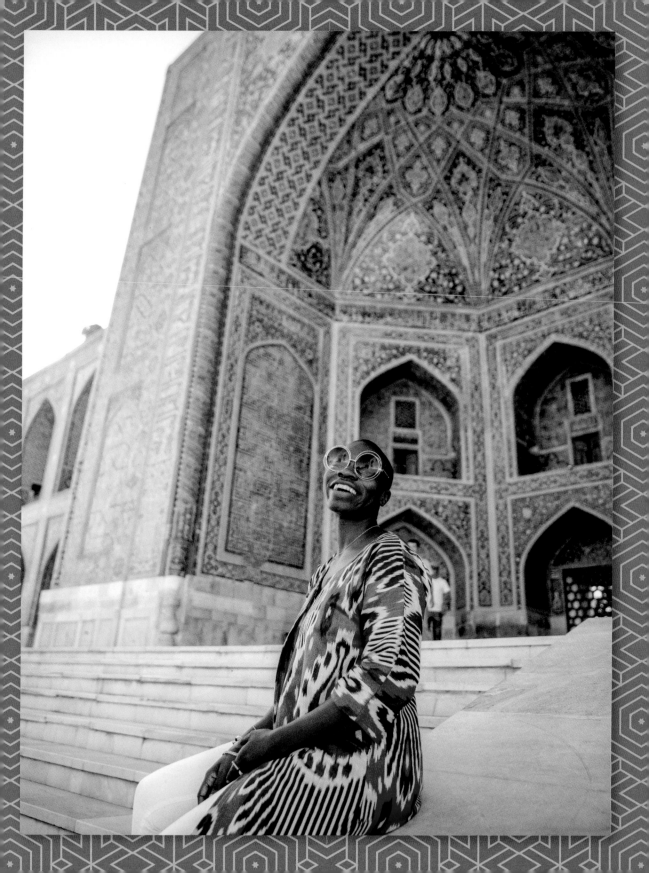

Dating back to the 17th century, Ak Mosque, also known as the White Mosque, is a must-visit in Tashkent.

Markets like this inspired me to start my brand, The Catch, an e-commerce site through which I sell products made by artisans around the globe.

While I was consumed with shopping, my and Elton's presence was causing quite a stir. People came from various stalls to gawk at us. One woman with a mouthful of gold teeth grabbed my arm and forced me to take a picture. I could do nothing but laugh and smile for the camera. Rusam quickly morphed from guide to bodyguard, swatting away people asking for pictures to grant us a little reprieve. It wasn't my first time becoming the object of local lenses, but it was certainly one of the funnier ones.

Before leaving the market, Rusam insisted we go to a bakery to see how Uzbek bread is made, as it is a daily part of their diet and there are many rites and rituals tied to it. The traditional bread, baked in flat circular loaves, is golden, flaky, and delicious.

In the bakery, no one spoke English, but the women managed to guide us through the breadmaking process, step by step. Even with the language barrier, an older woman began peppering me with questions and offering me some life advice. Using her hands, she mimed her thoughts. What was the vitally important message she had to deliver to a perfect stranger? Once she learned that I was 34 and single, she frantically gestured, "You need to start having kids! You're going to become old and ugly soon." She then kindly offered to introduce me to her son.

I couldn't stop laughing. She was emblematic of every auntie around the world, encouraging young women to get married and have children. And playing matchmaker with her son, no less! She was basically the Uzbek version of my aunt Ruth.

In her own misguided way, she was speaking from the heart. Even though I was a foreigner, she believed, "You're the same as everybody else and you need to be married and you need to have your kids. This is the basis for a good life." I believe her intention was valuing human connection. Though we may go about it differently, who can argue with that?

From Tashkent, we hopped on a train—in a luxury sleeping cabin that cost a whopping $9—to Samarkand. The city is stunning. I make it a point to visit mosques all over the world. While the Sheikh Zayed Grand Mosque in Abu Dhabi is my favorite, Uzbekistan's mosques as a whole take the prize for the most collective beauty across an entire country. The country is 88 percent Muslim, and while most people don't seem super religious and it didn't seem very conservative in the places I visited, you can see influences of the Islamic heritage throughout Uzbekistan. The bright colors of the tiles felt quite magical. The Shah-i-Zinda Ensemble is a complex of mausoleums and ritual buildings, some of which date back to the 11th century. The buildings are made of spectacular tile work in royal blue, turquoise, and emerald green. Though there is clear Persian influence, the architecture is incredibly, uniquely its own. The blue domes blended seamlessly into the sky above.

The complex of Registan stands at the heart of ancient Samarkand. Registan has three massive madrassas, which are colleges for Islamic instruction. Though we enjoyed the beauty of the complex, we were mobbed by masses of people who kept wanting to take our pictures. The unwanted attention put a damper on the experience. People did not approach us in a malicious way, but after several days of taking selfies with eager locals, we were over it. We truly missed Rusam and his bodyguard skills.

Though I found myself the uncomfortable object of too many cameras, the people of Uzbekistan were still incredibly welcoming and kind. In fact, Uzbekistan is definitely my favorite country in Central Asia, for its people, its patterns and textiles, and its sublime architecture.

afghanistan

ONE OF THE REASONS I wrote this book is to challenge people's assumptions about countries that are not the darlings of the travel industry and to showcase the beauty and joy that exists in every corner of the world, the forgotten places, the destinations others declare "scary." Yet, sometimes the reality of the world makes that mission hard to do. As I write this, the U.S. has pulled out of a 20-year

occupation in Afghanistan and the country has fallen back under Taliban control. As a result, the country may lose years of social progress and the economy is on the verge of collapse. I will not get political here, but I will say my heart is breaking for a country that gave me so much.

Afghanistan is one of a handful of countries that people immediately ask about when they hear I have been to every country in the world, and I welcome it. It offers me an opportunity to change people's perceptions. When thinking of Afghanistan, most Westerners conjure up visuals of war, terrorism, and strife. They see scenes straight out of *Homeland*. I'm here to offer a different perspective and a humanizing one. Because even after all the turmoil Afghanistan has faced (so much of which was brought on by outsiders), I found so much beauty, so much kindness, and so much strength in the country.

Getting to Afghanistan without military or government credentials was an adventure in and of itself. This was the first country I visited that was on the "do not travel" list under the U.S. travel advisories.

After failing to get a visa in Kyrgyzstan, we went to the Afghan Embassy in Almaty, Kazakhstan, where we were immediately taken to a small building close to the front gate. The man inside seemed to be the gatekeeper to the actual embassy. I briefly explained that we wanted tourist visas for Afghanistan and he immediately said no. Surprised, I explained my mission to visit every country in the world. He said no again, but at least allowed us to enter the embassy. Progress.

Several people inside the embassy got into a debate about our request. After 45 minutes of discussion and me Googling myself to

ASIA

Afghanistan is a country people often ask about, and what I can say is it is a beautiful country full of life and warm people.

The very rug that this carpet seller is sitting on now sits under my desk in Detroit as I write these words.

MUST-BUY: AN AFGHAN RUG

Just across from the Blue Mosque were several shops selling the rugs and tapestries that Afghanistan is known for. With endless vibrant colors in front of me, I took my time, exploring each of the shops. The rugs, made using a Persian style of knots, are made of vegetable-dyed, hand-spun Afghan wool. The proprietors of the stores were not pushy; rather, they were gentlemen. One offered us a cold drink to combat the heat we'd been suffering under all day. After some time and negotiation, I settled on a large rug, made in the iconic deep red, with designs of orange, white, and black yarn. It is lined with a turquoise blue fabric, with decorative strings on the end, and sits in my home to this day.

prove my mission and the size of my platform, we were told to get a letter of permission from the U.S. Embassy to go into Afghanistan. Though it hadn't been done before, they said it was the only way they would grant us our visas.

At the U.S. Embassy, I explained the situation to a consular. She was not friendly, but she confirmed they could indeed write the letter, which I would need to pay for. It was a Friday afternoon and the cashier was closed until Monday. We were leaving the next day. Despite offers to pay in cash, she denied us. Thanks, America.

Annoyed and disappointed, but still not deterred, we headed back to the Afghan Embassy. My plan was to beg, plead, and grovel. Then, a lightbulb went off. What if I write the letter?! And so, I penned a letter absolving the government of the Islamic Republic of Afghanistan for the responsibility of my safety. Our three and a half hours of effort was rewarded with a single-entry tourist visa.

We entered into the north of Afghanistan from the south of Uzbekistan, near the border city of Termez. About a half mile (1 km) before the actual border crossing, we boarded a free bus to the immigration building. Just like everywhere else in Uzbekistan, even the border guards wanted to take selfies with us, fascinated by two Black tourists.

After being stamped out of Uzbekistan, we walked about a half mile (1 km) across the Friendship Bridge, built by the Soviets when they invaded Afghanistan in the 1980s. On the other side of the Amu Darya River, we were met by kind and curious border officers. The entire office came out to see us, not only because we are Black but also because they rarely get tourists. The welcome was warm and made me even more excited to explore the country. After a few pictures and videos, we were stamped into the country and on our way.

We met our guide, Noor, who we had arranged to travel with through his company, Let's Be Friends Afghanistan, which we found via a Google search. We hopped in the back of a small sedan and made our way to a tiny hotel in Mazar-i-Sharif to change into clothes that Noor bought to ensure we were appropriately dressed. As a woman, I had to cover my head and my entire body, except for my hands. The outfit he picked out for me was a long burgundy tunic, with black and white stripes down the center, accompanied by striped black and burgundy pants. I was grateful for its light weight in the oppressive summer heat. Elton wore the traditional *perahan tunban,* a long white tunic with baggy white pants.

We ate breakfast while Noor dealt with a car problem. After nearly 30 minutes of waiting, I suggested I just pay for another car. Noor declined; he preferred to use a car and driver that he knew, leaving no

The Shrine of Hazrat Ali in Mazar-i-Sharif is one of the most stunning and unique mosques I have ever seen.

room for anything to go wrong. Having previously worked as a security adviser, he had safety protocols that he followed.

This brings me to the point I always make about some of the less familiar, "dangerous" places I've been: No country is completely safe, and no country is completely unsafe. When I'm in what are considered less safe regions of the world, I always hire a knowledgeable guide to feel more comfortable. They will know more about the security situation than any Google search or travel advisory website will.

The dusty roads of Mazar-i-Sharif were lined with shops in two- to three-story buildings and storefronts fashioned from shipping containers. Men roamed the streets in taxis, on bicycles, on foot, and in the back of rickshaws decorated in bright, bold colors and fabrics, similar to those I had seen in Haiti, Kenya, and Senegal. Noticeably absent were women. In fact, we would not see any until we visited the mosques.

Beyond the city, mountains towered in the distance. The arid landscape whizzed by as we made our way to Balkh, an ancient and historic city that houses Haji Piyada Mosque, the oldest in Afghanistan.

The guard at the mosque, once a Massoud guerrilla fighter (a military group that opposed Soviet occupation of Afghanistan in the 1970s and 80s), was a well-groomed man, likely in his 60s, dressed in a traditional green tunic with a gray vest on top. In one hand he held green grapes to snack on and in the other prayer beads. After a few moments with him, it was clear he was high—I could smell whiffs of hash in the air and noticed his slow, chilled pace. Although hash is illegal in the country, the law is rarely enforced because of cultural acceptance. The guard estimated he had consumed more than 165 pounds (75 kg) of hash in 30 years—yes, I asked. Later in the trip we were shown a "hash house" where people go to smoke, typically on Fridays.

At lunch I got another taste of Afghan culture—and I'm not just talking about the typical meal of chicken kebab, rice pilaf, veggie soup, freshly baked bread, and a small salad. At the restaurant, a Bollywood movie was playing on the TV and they blurred the backs, shoulders, and chests of the actresses on screen.

The highlight of our trip was the Shrine of Hazrat Ali, also known as the Blue Mosque. The majestic building shimmered in all shades of blue, yellow, and green under the afternoon sun. Persian-style white, black, and cream-colored tiles accentuated the facade. As we spent time on the grounds, I finally saw women. Many were wearing hijabs. Others wore the full body–covering navy blue burka that has become synonymous with the rise of the Taliban and radical Islam in Afghanistan.

It was clear that the Shrine of Hazrat Ali is a place where the community gathers. We saw children playing, women congregating, and men laughing together. We were the only foreigners, and our black skin made us stand out. It did not take long for a crowd to form around us. After one brave soul asked for a selfie, it became come one, come all. With smiles on their faces, some people simply stared while others took pictures. One man placed his baby in my arms.

I often wonder what happens to these photos of me. Do these strangers take them home to show their families and friends? Do they text the image? Post it to social media? I wonder what they say. I wonder if they ever revisit the photo like I do the images from my trips. Or do they just delete it when they need more space on their phone? For anyone reading this who has a random picture of me, I would love to see it and hear your version of events.

Afghanistan was the first of the so-called "dangerous" countries that I visited. Only 30 percent of the country was considered safe at the time I was there. Still, I never felt scared or unsafe. Instead, I felt joy watching people interact in their communities. I dined on delicious food just like in any other country, and I marveled at the beauty of a historic mosque. I am grateful that I had the opportunity to learn more about the political and cultural history, and yet I barely scratched the surface. Now, who knows what the future holds for Afghanistan.

bolivia

I CROSSED OFF 12 COUNTRIES in just five and a half weeks on my trip to Europe and Central Asia. With only a short break back in Detroit, I was on to my next leg, and continent: South America. Hyper-focused on the travel logistics of getting to the remaining 70-some countries, I planned to visit the last few countries I had left in South America in one fell swoop. Without thinking, I decided to visit Ecuador, Bolivia, Paraguay, and Chile

SOUTH
AMERICA

in July, which is winter in the Southern Hemisphere. Rookie mistake. I cursed myself as I added sweaters and socks to my suitcase.

I love winter wonderlands, skiing, snowshoeing, and an après ski as much as the next snow bunny, but "in-between" weather—those 40° to 60°F (4° to 15°C) temps that give you a brutal kick of cold to the chest in the shade but have you unzipping your wool coat in the sun—is my least favorite for exploring. It isn't quite freezing, but it definitely isn't warm. You are *never* perfectly comfortable.

I arrived at El Alto International Airport, the highest international airport in the world at 13,323 feet (4,060 m) above sea level. It felt something akin to a small SUV sitting on my chest once the airplane depressurized and I walked into the airport, which is nestled in the Bolivian Andes. But a few coca leaves and Tylenol later, I was almost as good as new, save the brisk 33°F (0.6°C) winds caressing my cheeks.

The best part of my four days in Bolivia was an expanse of land called Salar de Uyuni, the largest salt flats in the world. I prefer private trips that allow me to explore at my own pace. But traveling solo and with limited financial resources, I found myself on a group tour to the salt flats. I was picked up late and missed part of the tour due to some miscommunication. I had to share a back seat with two others. It was tight. And to top it off, I had unknowingly booked a Spanish-language tour.

When we entered the flats, my annoyance melted away. All I could see before me, beside me, and behind me was white, as if it were a savanna covered in freshly fallen snow. This spectacular natural beauty forced me into gratitude at a moment when I needed it most. Nature truly is divine in its ability to change our moods, to heal.

Two Korean girls on my tour had made plans to take the warped-perspective pictures that have made Salar de Uyuni popular on Instagram. I had no strategy or props with me, but with their help, I managed to take photos that made it appear as if I was climbing on top of and out of a Pringles can, fighting off dinosaurs, and crawling out of my Canon camera before riding off on a llama into the sunset.

The same girls insisted we go to the area of reflection. We drove to a spot on the flats where it looked like it had recently rained. There was just enough water to reflect the sky above. As the sun set, I turned my head and was struck by its magic. Tears filled my eyes. The orange. Pink. Blue. The reflection. It caused me to pause. To be still. To take it all in.

How insanely privileged I was to be standing there at that exact moment. I could have been born into different circumstances. I could be in a village with no running water or electricity. I could be finishing a day of work in a gray cubicle before heading home. But here I was, in the middle of Bolivia's salt flats, watching the most glorious sunset I had ever seen.

While at the Uyuni Salt Flats, I fought off dinosaurs on my journey to see a spectacular sunset.

solomon islands

I WAS MOVING RAPIDLY toward 195 countries, but the countries ahead seemed more daunting. They were farther away, harder to enter, and relatively unknown. Case in point: the Solomon Islands, located in the Melanesia region of the South Pacific. My curiosity about the Solomon Islands was piqued by images of its people—Black people with naturally blond hair. Melanesia is literally derived from a Greek word that

AUSTRALIA
AND OCEANIA

means "islands of Black [people]." As my public profile grew, so did the direct messages. One came from Ryan, who had seen me on CNN and wanted to know if I'd travel through the South Pacific with him. I typically would never travel with a stranger from the internet, but the South Pacific is a logistically difficult region, and Ryan had already done most of the legwork. I decided to go for it. This marked the only time during my entire journey that I traveled with a perfect stranger. We wound up visiting six countries together.

In the capital of Honiara, we met a driver, an attractive older Black man with deep dark skin and a head of white hair. Although his phenotype was distinct to the region, I immediately felt a kinship with him. It was the same with two local women, Debbie and Dorothy, who became our guides. We spent time chatting about our similarities, including our kinky hair and the struggles to find the perfect hair products. We talked about our skin tone and wondered when African explorers made it to the South Pacific. We also spoke about their deep desires to visit the African continent, to which they felt very connected. On the streets we met the son of a woman selling coconuts whose flawless brown skin was accentuated by blond hair, and a group of girls whose shyness was expressed by constant giggles from mouths turned red from icy treats. These people felt like reminders of home, of Africa.

It wasn't until I got home that I found out these descendants of Africa migrated to the isolated islands more than 400,000 years ago. Although their migration wasn't tied to the transatlantic slave trade, the Solomon Islands had a practice called blackbirding. At the behest of European colonizers, Black Indigenous people were taken from various islands to work in the sugarcane, cotton, and coffee plantations of Australia, Samoa, Fiji, and other locales. These operations continued through the first half of the 20th century.

Hearing of this history, I wondered why dark-skinned and Indigenous people were exploited the world over. What was it that drove Europeans to leave their homes and act as brutes in every corner of the globe? No matter the country or continent, there is a terrible history of the exploitation and abuse of darker-skinned people. I saw this again and again as I immersed myself in the history of each destination.

In the Solomon Islands, I flew my drone for the first time. I launched it from my balcony and within seconds, the drone flew straight into the leaves of a coconut tree. I panicked. Ryan tried to rescue it with a ladder and pool skimmer, to no avail. Finally, a hotel security guard scaled the tree to retrieve my drone. I showered him with so much gratitude you would've thought he'd rescued my actual child out of the tree.

For this shot, I swam to the deck, scraped my toe and knee on the very sharp coral, climbed up the steps, laid down, and posed.

On a cloudy afternoon, we headed to Visale beach in western Guadalcanal. From the beach, I noticed a large platform in the middle of the water and thought it would be perfect for a shot with my drone.

For some reason, I was paralyzed with fear of entering the water. I love to spend time in the water, whether snorkeling, paddling a kayak, or lying on a yacht, but I don't like to touch the bottom of any body of water; the deep sea is more my cup of tea. After a little coaching from my inner go-getter, I hopped in, swam to the deck, scraped my toe and knee on the very sharp coral, climbed up the steps, laid down, and posed. This is the life of an influencer—it's not all fun and games; it can be life and limb.

The bravery I needed to take the perfect picture wasn't the only reminder of my current status as an influencer and world traveler. On Guadalcanal, I was invited to take part in an interview about my journey with a local radio station. This kind of attention served as a welcome reminder that people are always watching (and listening to) my story, even in the most remote places. The journey had officially become bigger than me. I now had an amazing opportunity to inspire other people to jump on a plane and see the world. What an honor, a privilege, a motivation to make it to the finish line.

nauru

BY THE TIME I WAS IN COUNTRY 132, I was traveling smarter. I maximized my trips by visiting as many places in one region or on one continent as possible. That's how Ryan and I ended up going from Brisbane, Australia, to Nauru, the world's smallest island nation with a land area of only 8.1 square miles (21 km²), a little more than a speck in the vast South Pacific Ocean. Its nearest neighbor lies 190 miles (306 km) to the east

and only two airlines fly there—it's no wonder the island receives less than 1,000 visitors a year.

Nauru was not always so obscure. The tiny nation had large natural phosphate reserves that were exploited by Australia and the United Kingdom until independence in 1968. The newly formed government purchased the rights from both the Brits and Australians (yes, they had to purchase the rights to their own natural resources), which overnight made Nauruans some of the richest people in the world based on income per capita, second only to Saudi Arabia.

Unfortunately, the wealth did not last very long. The U.K. and Australian operations had led to severe environmental degradation and a steady decline in reserves that began in the early 1980s. By the year 2000, there was virtually no phosphate left. Nauru is now relatively poor with incredibly high unemployment rates. The country relies on Australia for imports of packaged foods. One significant source of income was housing refugees in the Australian detention center, until it was closed in 2019.

The entire country, sitting in the middle of the turquoise sparkling waters of the Pacific, was fully visible from the window of our plane. But more than its shockingly small size, our entry into Nauru served as a stark reminder of how travelers of different races are seen the world over.

Ryan, a white man, proceeded to the immigration window first. I followed closely behind, but I was immediately and aggressively blocked by a large Nauruan man. Annoyed, I told him Ryan and I were traveling together. Here's what happened next:

AUSTRALIA AND OCEANIA

Anibare Bay was formed by the underwater collapse of a volcano that sits underneath Nauru. What remains is an idyllic beach dotted with coral formations.

The dark spots in this image, which I had thought were coral before entering the water, are actually plastic bottles and other waste.

Officer: Are you sure?
Me: *rolls eyes* Uh, yeah.
Officer: How are you together?
Me: *rolls eyes*

He then took both of our passports and held them up next to each other.

Officer to Ryan: Are you together?
Ryan: Yes. I mean, we are traveling together. We aren't married. Our names don't match on the passports.
Me to Ryan: He's not checking our names. He's checking to see if my passport is real.
Ryan: *blank stare*
Officer: *moves arm*
Me: *annoyed AF yet not surprised*

This, my friends, is traveling as a Black woman, even in the most isolated of places.

Our host, Trish, met us at the airport to walk us to her home—yes, walk. The island is *that* small. She and her husband, Mathew, operated one of only a few Airbnbs in Nauru. Their home sat directly behind the airport, overlooking the landing strip, which doubles as one of the main roads. Mathew told incredible stories of his time as the foreign minister. One time, when Mathew entered Miami, the customs officials did not believe Nauru was a real country, despite his diplomatic passport.

Nauru has been through some things and it shows. There are clear signs of erosion on the coasts, which have eaten away at the beaches in the north. The palm-lined streets were fairly empty. Of the few structures that existed, many were abandoned. There were few restaurant options. Fresh, unpackaged food was hard to find. This was far from a tourist destination.

But we quickly came upon a beautifully decorated barbershop. Inside we met Fouad, a 26-year-old artist turned refugee turned barber from Iraq. He'd arrived five years prior, but his barbershop was only two months old. After years of thinking he would be able to leave the island, Fouad finally opened his barbershop, which represented a loss of hope. Thanks to immigration laws and bureaucracy, he was unable to leave the country. He readily admitted that he didn't enjoy living on Nauru. Can you imagine leaving your home in desperate search of a better life, only to be sent to a minuscule speck of land where you know no one and are not allowed to leave?

REDUCING SINGLE-USE PLASTIC

The only way to truly stop the plastic crisis is for producers to cease production. Until then, we can all do our part by making small shifts in our lives. I fail at some of these sometimes, but the goal is to be more conscious, reduce my use, and help spread awareness. Little things you can do to reduce plastic:

1. Always carry a reusable water bottle.
2. Travel with a reusable cup when flying.
3. Opt out of using plastic bags, even when it means carrying things in your arms.
4. Use only one trash can in your hotel room if they are lined with a plastic bag.
5. Travel with reusable cutlery.
6. Request no plastic straw in your drink.

I drove a scooter for the first time ever in Nauru. It only took 30 minutes to traverse the perimeter of the 8.1-square-mile (21 km²) country.

Exploring Nauru is best done on a scooter. It takes around 30 minutes to drive the entire perimeter. Though I've long had fantasies of owning a Vespa, I never mustered the courage to drive one myself, even after three years in Italy. I figured the limited traffic on the island made for a safe place to try. As the wind blew over my freshly shaven head (yup, we weren't wearing helmets), I daydreamed of driving a pale green Vespa through the streets of Rome, whizzing past the Colosseum on my way to Pizzeria Remo in Testaccio. I digress.

We visited Buada Lagoon, a small, marshy pond surrounded by lush, tropical flora. Then we headed off in search of Command Ridge, a World War II relic and a radio and telecommunications tower that is the highest point on the island, a mere 215 feet (65 m) above sea level. A hospitable Nauruan and his son offered to lead us up the winding path to the top. We passed the old phosphate mines before reaching a small clearing. The tower was a fascinating glimpse into the history on this otherwise sparse island, and we could see out to the beautiful waters of the Pacific.

While exploring, we came upon a harbor with turquoise waters begging us to jump in for relief from the scorching afternoon sun. Before diving in, I used my drone to see a little more of our surroundings. On my screen I saw dark areas that I assumed were coral. Excitedly, I grabbed some fins and a mask. Then Ryan came out of the water and said, "Uh, you're not going to like this." A little scared and uncomfortable, I slowly slid in, terrified of what could be below the surface. Once I dipped my head beneath the water, I saw tons of plastic bottles and other waste lining the floor of the harbor. I was horrified.

Here, on one of the most remote islands in the world, were tons of plastic at the bottom of this beautiful body of water. I made a vow then and there to change things, beginning with my own habits. Now I use my platform to inspire others to do the same, from connecting with the hundreds of thousands who follow me on Instagram to speaking to leaders and policymakers at the IUCN World Conservation Congress. I have seen how problematic single-use plastic is around the world, but seeing it in Nauru had a profound impact on me. I hope to encourage real change on both the micro and macro levels.

On our way back to our Airbnb, Ryan wanted to get a peek at the refugee detention center. The trip required going off the main road and onto loose gravel that snaked its way through the interior of the country. I was driving as slowly as possible when suddenly my tire slipped. The scooter fell on its side, dragging me with it for about two feet (0.6 m).

I was shaken. Nothing seemed to be broken, but my right arm and leg were on fire. Blood was coming from a few places on my body. I had used my right arm to protect my face, and the skin on my upper arm was gaping.

Fouad, a 26-year-old artist turned refugee turned barber from Iraq, gave me a much needed haircut. He'd been in Nauru for five years.

We flagged down a pickup truck, but there was no way to get the scooters onto the back. Ryan told me I had to get back on. It was the only solution. With my hands shaking, I climbed back on the scooter, which fortunately still worked, and slowly drove back toward civilization. On the way, we had to go down a small hill. Fear crippled me and I fell again, mistaking the gas for the break. I walked down the hill, leaving Ryan and some passersby to bring my scooter down. I wanted no part.

Trish, Mathew, and Ryan helped nurse me back to health. Trish made a concoction of noni fruit and coconut oil for my wound. I am sure her home remedy is how the gash completely closed in just 10 days and left only a small scar. I have not driven a scooter since—I've added it to the no-go list along with bungee jumping and skydiving. It's the passenger seat for me.

This was the only time that I physically injured myself while traveling. I've traveled to 195 countries now, and I have to thank the universe for keeping me alive and mostly in one piece.

marshall islands

THE NEXT STOP on my South Pacific tour was the Marshall Islands. The Marshall Islands are remote. Hawaii lies approximately 2,500 miles (4,000 km) to the west, and the Philippines 3,000 miles (4,800 km) to the east. This was not an easy place to get to, but its warm waters and palm tree–lined beaches beckoned. As someone who knows close to nothing about World War II, I was grossly unaware of the islands' importance and

AUSTRALIA AND OCEANIA

relationship with the United States. The Bikini Atoll, one of the island nation's 29 atolls, serves as a graveyard for many of the U.S. Navy ships used for extensive nuclear testing in WWII. In 1944, the U.S. drove Japan out of the Marshall Islands and began what was called Operation Crossroads on Bikini. The military and scientific experiment tested the impact of atomic bombs on Navy vessels. In one test, for example, an atomic bomb was dropped on about 80 obsolete WWII vessels. And in 1946, the Navy carried out the first underwater atomic explosion, which sank nine ships. The testing came to an end in 1958, but it took until 1985—and a lawsuit—for the U.S. to agree to cleanup efforts after it became clear radioactivity levels on Bikini were dangerously high. Levels are still high on Bikini—too high for people to live there—but the waters were opened in 1996 for scuba diving among the sunken warships, making the Marshall Islands a top diving destination. (A more fun fact: The bikini bathing suit was named after this atoll!)

The sparsely populated country is centered around the capital, Majuro, home to the islands' only international airport. Given Majuro's tiny size, you can see water from nearly everywhere you stand. Navigating the island is easy: There is one main road that is full of shared taxis—think UberPool with a fixed rate of 75 cents for any distance along that road.

Our cab driver incidentally had worked in Rogers, Arkansas, and attended university in the United States. This wasn't as uncommon as you'd think. Access to American universities is part of the Compact of Free Association, which allows Marshallese people to freely

relocate to and obtain work in the U.S. With a population of more than 4,000 Marshall Island immigrants, Arkansas has the largest Marshallese community outside of the small island nation.

Still not certified to scuba dive, I settled for hopping to Eneko Island, which is said to have one of the best beaches in the Marshall Islands.

We were amply warned about the lack of amenities on Eneko, so we stocked up on packaged American imports and a fruity beverage with 5 percent alcohol that was sold near the dock. Snacks in hand, we boarded a speedboat with a few locals. We could see the depth of the ocean giving way to shallow turquoise waters, exposing the coral reefs surrounding Eneko. The boat got as close to shore as possible, and we waded through ankle-high water the rest of the way. Eneko is full of vibrant palm trees and soft sand, but I really fell in love when I flew my drone and saw the true beauty of the very narrow island from above.

Never one to miss a photo op, I spotted a palm tree hanging over the rocky terrain and decided to make the climb, despite the pain from the scooter accident in Nauru. Ryan filmed me on all fours, making my way across the narrow tree that was crawling with yellow ants. They could've been poisonous for all I knew. Yet I managed to get an absolutely gorgeous shot of me lying on a palm tree in paradise. (See, I'll do almost anything for a good shot.)

Eneko Island, said to be one of the best beaches in the Marshall Islands, is even more beautiful from above.

palestine

AFTER MY LAST STOP in the South Pacific, I made my way to the Middle East. A week of work in New York City served as a long layover between the disparate locations. There are 193 member nations of the UN and two nonmember observer states, including the state of Palestine. Palestine comprises the West Bank and the Gaza Strip—a tiny piece of land that lies on the Mediterranean Sea and is bordered by Egypt

to the south and Israel to the east and north. With a total area of 141 square miles (365 km²), slightly smaller than my hometown of Detroit, and a population of nearly two million, Gaza is the third most densely populated area in the world. Since 2007, Israel has enforced a sea and air blockade of the Gaza Strip. As a result, the population is unable to freely leave or enter. The West Bank is a much larger territory—2,183 square miles (5,654 km²)—on the Dead Sea and shares borders with Israel and Jordan. Although the population of 2.7 million has more space, only a small portion of the West Bank is under Palestinian control.

I entered Palestine from Israel through the Qalandia checkpoint, crossing the large wall that surrounds Palestine. Israeli military authorities searched us, but it was a very smooth process. Once in Palestine, I was taken to the Ministry of Tourism, where I was told a bit of the history and geographic landscape of the West Bank.

Prior to my visit, I did not know much about the Israeli-Palestinian conflict beyond the 1990s trope "Peace in the Middle East." In my mind, Israeli "settlements" looked like temporary housing with scaffolding. In reality, the West Bank is divided into three areas: Palestinian authorities control Area A; Israel and Palestine jointly administer Area B; and Israel administers Area C. Of the three, Area C is the largest. To drive on roads in Area C, you need Israeli plates. This limitation makes traveling within the West Bank difficult for Palestinians. To top it off, many parts of the roads are enclosed by walls and fences. My guide, Rizek, a Jerusalem-born Palestinian, had Israeli plates, which made it possible for me to see a significant portion of the West Bank.

The narrow streets of Bethlehem's historic center, lined with homes made of white stones, are reflective of a city that spans millennia.

Rizek took me to Jericho, one of the oldest continuously inhabited cities in the world, first inhabited in 9,000 B.C. We visited Hisham's Palace and St. George's Monastery before making our way north to Nablus. While in Nablus, we had a chance to visit the incredibly busy market. The narrow streets were lined with stalls and people selling fresh produce, souvenirs, sweets, dried fruits, and grains. I bought some dried mangoes, as well as ceramics and brass wares that I simply could not resist.

The highlight of visiting Nablus, though, was eating *knafeh,* a traditional dessert found throughout the Middle East. Nablus is the hometown of the dessert, which has been exported widely. I'd had it before in Lebanon. The dessert is made with semolina soaked in simple syrup and layered with cheese. The cheese used here was a soft goat cheese made in the surrounding villages. It is generally agreed throughout the region that the Nabulsi version of knafeh is, in fact, the best.

At Al Aqssa Sweets, the oldest knafeh bakery in Nablus, the long line made it clear this was the place to try the local delicacy. Chopped on a two-foot-long (0.6 m) baking tray, our knafeh was served on a small white plate with a plastic spoon. We stood against a wall outside, like everyone else, to enjoy it while it was still warm. The gooey, sweet, borderline diabetes-inducing dessert was everything I needed it to be and more. I've subsequently tried knafeh in a number of other countries; the only place that compares is a small shop in Amman, Jordan, called Habibah. (You have to go to the original location downtown by the Arab Bank. I promise, you will not be disappointed.)

We rounded out our day with a trip to Ramallah, the administrative capital of the Palestinian National Authority (PNA). We visited the tomb of Yasser Arafat, chairman of the Palestine Liberation Organization and the first president of the PNA. The tomb, which is guarded, sits in a small complex with a museum where you can learn more about Palestinian history and Arafat's work.

Afterward, with our stomachs rumbling, we ended up, at my request, having Popeyes and treating Rizek to this American specialty for the first time. I rarely eat fast food when traveling or at home, and I was truly shocked to see a Popeyes in Ramallah. But after several weeks of travel and bouncing between continents, it was a welcome treat.

I overnighted in Bethlehem. Known as the birthplace of Jesus, the city is home to the Church of the

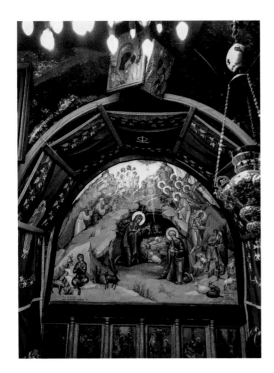

The Church of the Nativity in Bethlehem is considered to mark the actual location where Jesus was born.

Al Aqssa Sweets is the oldest *knafeh* bakery in Nablus. It's the perfect place to try the insanely sweet dessert.

Nativity, within which sits what tradition considers the actual birthplace of Jesus. Located in a grotto, the sacred site is marked by a 14-point star surrounded by marble. Although the famed church is Bethlehem's biggest draw, I enjoyed strolling through the narrow streets of the historic center and reflecting on the city that spans millennia. Homes made of white stone were scattered about in dense clusters, many with green doors, arched windows, and metal balconies. I felt like I was stepping back in time. Having read the Bible a time or two, I tried to imagine myself centuries ago, walking the same streets as the biblical figures once did.

My experience in Palestine was enjoyable yet shocking. Palestinians are welcoming, warm, and showed an immense level of resilience. The history here is incredible and rich. The knafeh alone is worth the trip.

On the other hand, I was completely dismayed by the walls running through the West Bank, the inability of Palestinians to move freely throughout their own country, and the so-called settlements, which looked more like permanent cities rather than the temporary housing I had imagined. One settlement has a population of nearly 80,000 people. At checkpoints managed by the Israeli military, the guards were very young and heavily armed. It was a reflection of what Palestinians face every day, and the deep, long-rooted history of its conflict with Israel.

Despite the difficulties, I found that the Palestinian people push forward, finding ways to continue living life in these conditions.

jordan

IF I WERE THE RANKING TYPE, Jordan would fall into my top five favorite countries. Situated in the Middle East—my second favorite region after Africa—Jordan is bordered by Palestine, Israel, Syria, Iraq, and Saudi Arabia. The tension, civil wars, and challenges surrounding this area may give other people pause, but in reality, Jordan is one of the safest and more liberal countries in the Middle East. It is also one of the

ASIA

most beautiful. I explored Jordan with Experience Jordan tours. Our first stop was Amman, the capital city, where I visited the archaeological site of the Citadel. Afterward, my guide, Emad, and I had *mansaf* for lunch. The Jordanian national dish is made of lamb cooked in a yogurt sauce and served atop rice. We followed up the delicious fare with *knafeh* from Habibah Sweets—the pastry was a close second to the version made in its origin town, Nablus, in Palestine.

Amman was, without a doubt, different from most other Arab cities I had visited. We saw people out and about at restaurants and bars in numbers that exceeded the typical crowds in other Middle Eastern countries. People openly enjoyed hookah, good music, and alcohol. I was even introduced to Jordanian wine in the tasting room of the Jordan River winery—the Cabernet Sauvignon Limited Edition was the standout.

When I checked into the W Amman hotel, which hosted my stay, I got a one-of-a-kind experience—one that cemented my status as a travel influencer. The staff put surprises around my room to celebrate my journey so far. They gifted me a beautiful globe and peppered the room with images of me from around the world. As I circled the room looking at the pictures, I was reminded just how far tales of my journey were reaching.

The Treasury, situated behind me, is the most iconic building in Petra. Be sure to check the weather before you visit. It gets very, very hot.

After two days of exploring Amman solo, my friend Nyanquoi arrived and the adventure really began. Our tour guide turned auntie, Maha, was one of the first female tour guides in the country. She and six other

women pioneered entry for Jordanian women into the service sector in 1994. Although it challenged gender norms, they were determined to push forward and create a path for more women. Now there are 67 female tour guides in Jordan.

Along with our driver, Ahmad, we departed for five days of exploring the Hashemite Kingdom. Our first destination was Petra, one of the Seven Wonders of the Modern World. On our way, we stopped on a cliff for a gorgeous, uninterrupted view of the golden brown desert dotted with cypress trees in the valley below. We also made a quick stop in Little Petra, a lesser known archaeological site where buildings are carved into the sandstone canyons at a smaller scale than Petra, as the name suggests. The site, thought to have housed traders on the Silk Road, is much less crowded. We enjoyed having more time and space to explore the ruins.

The ancient Nabataean masterpiece that is Petra was built in the fourth century B.C. and served as the capital of the Nabataean Kingdom, home to an estimated 20,000 inhabitants at its peak. The vast complex covers an area of 102 square miles (264 km²) and has so many sites it would require several days to see them all. We focused our efforts on the most iconic site, Al-Khazneh, or the Treasury, which is believed to have been the mausoleum of King Aretas IV.

To reach the Treasury, we walked one and a quarter miles (2 km) from the entrance through the Siq, a beautiful canyon. The surrounding cliffs provided some shade and a bit of relief from the brutal mid-September sun. I do not recommend traveling to Petra in summer. It was disgustingly hot and made the entire ordeal absolutely exhausting. Maha, ever so wise, brought along tiny white disks that, when put into water, turned into refreshingly cool little towels.

Each step through the Siq brings a little piece of the Treasury into view. When we finally arrived in front of the imposing 131-foot (40 m) intricate structure, we could only stand and marvel. Who cared about the heat? The Treasury is carved directly into the reddish sandstone using an architectural design that originated in nearby Alexandria. The structure has ornate columns and carvings of Egyptian and Greek goddesses. It is a true wonder.

A young man assured us he could get us to the best viewing point of the Treasury. Anxious for an epic photo, we agreed to follow him. The location scout was wearing flip-flops—how much of a journey could this be? Turns out, we were heading *up* the mountain. Our guide moved quickly and skillfully as Nyanquoi and I followed slowly behind, struggling to find our footing and using our hands to hoist our sweaty bodies to the next platform. But at the top, we discovered a one-of-a-kind view of the Treasury. Rather than the traditional angle, we were

The Amman Citadel sits atop one of the seven hills of Amman, giving uninterrupted views of the capital.

looking *down* on the gigantic structure. The new perspective made the climb entirely worth it. You rarely see this point of view in the widely circulated photos of Petra. I was grateful to have made the effort. But after snapping a photo, I dreaded getting back to the bottom.

From Petra we went to Aqaba, a city perched on the shores of the Red Sea, with views of both Israel and Egypt at its borders. We enjoyed the refuge of the cool waters, then headed to a small restaurant called Barracuda Seafood. We feasted on sautéed shrimp in a cream sauce, fried whole snapper smothered in a blend of fresh peppers, and fried shrimp with french fries. It was the best meal I had in the country.

After a quick haircut at Ahmad's barber—I always try to keep up, no matter where I am on the road—we went off to Wadi Rum. The beautiful and magical valley in southern Jordan is surrounded by granite and sandstone and home to the Bedouin Zalabieh tribe. Eco-adventure tourism throughout the area is a big economic driver for the Bedouin. We stayed at Sun City Camp in a "Martian Dome" nestled in the desert oasis—it felt like we had left planet Earth. This was my favorite stop on our trip through Jordan. Wadi Rum's soft red sands juxtaposed against the rugged tall mountains were emblematic of the area's otherworldly beauty.

The sheer enormity of Wadi Rum meant we could easily explore without many other tourists buzzing about. Maha told us about the endemic plants and rocks and their various uses. I loved hearing that sandstone was used as a lipstick. She taught us how to use it ourselves, rubbing the reddish rocks against one another, wetting her fingertip, and applying the dust to her lips. Even in the desert, they know how to be chic.

We shared a bottle of red wine as we watched the sun disappear and the pink-stained sky turned black. Back at camp, we were served a delicious dinner of chicken, carrots, potatoes, and lamb made in a massive pot buried in the sand. As a bit of a nightcap, we went back out into the desert, built a fire, made tea, and stargazed until we dozed off. Without light pollution, we could easily see millions of stars flickering overhead.

Before we left Jordan, we stopped at Maha's house to say goodbye. She gave me a dress from her closet as a symbol of our friendship. I couldn't travel with alcohol into Kuwait, my next stop, so I asked Maha to keep my limited-edition bottle of cabernet until I could return to pick it up.

It took me another year to get back to Jordan. I crossed into the country from Israel on my way back from Syria. Immigration stopped me because of my drone, which was illegal in Jordan. I called Ayman, the head of Experience Jordan, to help get me out of there with my drone. While he worked behind the scenes, I begged them to let me through—I was just heading to the airport after all. I showed the immigration officers an article about me that had been published in Arabic to plead my case. An officer laughed and called me CIA. Tensions lightened a bit and we bonded over my love of Jordanian food. Finally, with the help of Ayman's calls to various contacts, the immigration officers were convinced to let me leave with my drone in hand.

Though the experience wasn't fun, it highlights why I have so much love for Jordanian people. Though the officers were stern, they still treated me with dignity, respect, and kindness. This hasn't always been the case at other borders I've crossed around the world.

Before leaving Jordan, I went to Maha's home. She put together a beautiful dinner for me. We ate well, laughed hard, and had a teary goodbye. And yes, she had saved my bottle of wine after all that time.

When I go back to Jordan, I'm not going back as a tourist, I'm going to see friends and people I consider family. To Jordan I say, *Bahebak.*

The sandstone mountains and red dunes of Wadi Rum, a desert in southern Jordan, are truly otherworldly.

china

BEING BLACK AND VISIBLY AFRICAN abroad is an experience in and of itself. In many parts of the world I have found myself the focus of attention. For many, I am the first Black person they've seen outside of their TV screens. It's an odd feeling to become the target of a stranger's gaze or camera lens. Though I am most often open to meeting people and taking pictures, sometimes it can be overwhelming. I am reluctant

to say so, but some of my more distressing experiences with this have been with Chinese tourists, no matter where I have been in the world.

China, teeming with more than 1.4 billion bodies, constitutes nearly 18 percent of the world's entire population. With a diaspora of more than 50 million people, it is nearly impossible to visit any country without meeting a Chinese person. Although I don't believe the intent has ever been harmful or racist, my experiences dealing with Chinese tourists has been aggressive. In Laos, Chinese tourists chased me after I asked them not to take my picture. In Moscow, Chinese tourists confronted me, wanting to take my picture without my consent. It was so bad that I ended up revisiting St. Basil's Cathedral just after sunrise to have the peace to take in the church without commotion.

I am not proud to admit my trepidation going into my visit to China, but these experiences had led me to be wary of what I'd face in the country. I often speak about tuning out biases, but in this case my experiences led me to have some of my own. Given my misgivings, I only planned a short visit to China. In full transparency: The Great Wall was the only real attraction for me.

At the time, Americans could receive a 144-hour visa on arrival in Beijing as long as you stayed within the region. Planning was a breeze, and I was whisked from my hometown of Detroit to the sprawling 3,000-year-old urban capital on a nonstop flight.

With my past experience in mind, I was prepared for excessive staring and ogling upon arrival, but it didn't happen—at least not immediately. I made my way easily through immigration, met my

Dating back to 206 B.C., and at a length of 13,171 miles (21,197 km), the Great Wall of China is more impressive in person than I ever could've imagined.

driver, and headed into the city. I was beginning to feel a small sense of relief.

In Beijing I stayed in the Dongzhimen neighborhood, which was marked by small narrow streets called *hutongs*. These traditional streets date back to the 13th century and are typically marked by big, beautiful *paifang,* or archways. In a city of nearly 22 million, the streets can become a bit crowded, but this is part of the novelty of visiting Beijing. Plus, I was plenty comfortable after visiting cities like Manila and Dhaka, where the streets are even more packed.

I stayed in a home where no one spoke English. I could enjoy breakfast and take in the crisp autumn air in their beautiful courtyard. With bicycles everywhere, I was reminded of my year in Japan and hopped on a bike to explore. I took a calligraphy class, where I learned the history of the ancient art form and the nuances of holding the brush upright, the perfect amount of ink, and the grace with which one writes. My final exam was writing a phrase of my choosing on a traditional fan. I chose "Be positive." It's the mantra I try to follow throughout my life, and I needed the reminder after my wariness of China. I still have that fan on display in my home. I also took a kung fu class led by Baoxuan, who had trained in the art since he was a child. I had no clue that kung fu is more philosophy than physical strength. Relaxed muscles are more powerful than strongly engaged muscles—who knew! Although I won't be engaging in any fights soon, it was a welcome introduction to an ancient art form and a surprisingly enlightening way to spend a day.

I was mainly in China to visit the Great Wall, which was more impressive in person than I ever could've imagined. With a length of 13,171 miles (21,200 km)—the first sections of which were built between 220 and 206 B.C.—it is hard to comprehend how such an architectural feat was completed without today's technology. I asked my guide to take me to a quieter section of the wall with fewer crowds and we wound up in Jinshanling, about an hour and a half from Beijing. Being able to take in the breadth of the Great Wall with minimal crowds allowed us to move at a slower place, stopping often to just gaze on its beauty, which was truly endless. The ancient stone wall is flanked by lush greenery as it rolls over the mountains. This is a site that should be on everyone's bucket list.

I was pleasantly surprised to find that Beijing feels equal parts ancient and modern. With places like the Tianning Temple, which dates back to the 12th century, juxtaposed against the CITIC Tower, completed in 2018 at a staggering 1,731 feet (528 m), this Asian powerhouse's might is ever present. It's a green city that is also teeming with life: In a park, I watched retirees doing tai chi, playing poker, and crocheting—all

seemingly enjoying their old age. At the Temple of Heaven, where emperors of the Ming and Qing dynasties went for annual ceremonies to pray for a good harvest, I saw throngs of retirees photographing the gorgeous temple. One even stopped and *kindly* asked to take a picture with me. That request wasn't a bother.

I enjoyed Beijing more than I had expected, but I still had my frustrations. My visit coincided with Chinese National Golden Week, a holiday during which many domestic tourists visit the capital. The Forbidden City was impossible to see with all the crowds. As I waited for my friend, my fears came true: I was accosted by countless numbers of people wanting to take my picture. Most didn't bother to ask my permission. The back of my head and the front of my hand are probably on a couple hundred Chinese cell phones. Beijing's lack of diversity made me a novelty—and one that was attracting aggressive spectators.

I was also frustrated by the extreme cultural differences. The staring, taking pictures without permission, pushing, spitting, loudness, and lack of English proved to be more than I could handle. I always try to remain respectful and open-minded of other cultures, and I did. But it is also important for me to acknowledge when a culture or a place just doesn't suit me. China was one of a few of these places on my journey. To top it off, I got fined $72 for overstaying my visa by one day thanks to meeting a new *friend*. And I am pretty sure I signed a paper saying I can never enter China again. But that's a story for another time.

Tiananmen Square was packed with tourists from around the country during the National Day Golden Week holiday.

north korea

THE DEMOCRATIC PEOPLE'S REPUBLIC OF KOREA (DPRK), its formal name, is a relatively easy country to visit via several companies that organize tours and visas in partnership with the government. That is, unless you're American and your government forbids you from going. Lucky for me, I have a Ugandan passport. North Korea is one of the countries I am most often asked about because of its reputation and secrecy.

ASIA

But I was never afraid of traveling to North Korea; I only had a deep sense of curiosity. From the American media, I thought of North Korea as a place where the sun did not shine, the sky was never blue, and everyone wore gray. I understood it to be a country that is repressive of its citizens, maintains a communist way of life, and stands as one of the most isolated nations in the world. Also, I knew it is a place where you should follow the rules (which you should do in any country you visit).

The day before heading to the DPRK, our tour company held a briefing to go over the dos and don'ts of travel in North Korea. The rules were simple: No religious propaganda, including Bibles. No porn. No taking pictures of military officers or construction workers.

I boarded the Air Koryo flight, the national airline, with the other members of the tour group, as well as some Chinese tourists, North Koreans, and, to my surprise, a small group of Black people sitting in first class. The immigration process at the small, frills-free airport was straightforward. As we waited for our luggage, I spoke to the African gentlemen I had seen on the plane. Turns out, one was the new Nigerian ambassador to North Korea.

Our three guides ushered us onto a bus to the capital, Pyongyang. The drive through a rural area was calm. We didn't see many people on the streets, though we saw some working the land. Once in the city, you could tell that the country is not very exposed to the rest of the world. Nowhere do you see advertisements, brightly colored clothing or jeans, or Western brands in the supermarket.

Like in many countries with lingering communist governments, the capital city of North Korea, Pyongyang, felt like a time capsule.

Thousands of performers participate in the Mass Games, an elaborate display of athleticism and pageantry.

MUST-SEE: MASS GAMES

The Mass Games are a spectacle of synchronized gymnastics, dance, and acrobatics. We watched the performance at the Rungrado May Day Stadium, the biggest stadium in the world, with a capacity of 114,000. With up to 100,000 performers, the games are considered the largest human performance in the world. Each segment tells a different story and introduces beautiful costumes: The military portion has synchronized fight scenes; the high kicks of ribbon dancers dressed in red and pink put the Rockettes to shame; and men's gymnastics included stilts and trampolines. The people in the stands hold up colored cards to create a background image that changed more than 50 times. The Mass Games was easily the most phenomenal performance I have ever seen.

Pyongyang did, however, have numerous skyscrapers, large apartment buildings, and a multitude of government buildings and public squares, just like you see in other capital cities.

We saw all of the main tourist spots in Pyongyang on our very prescriptive government tour. We went to Kim Il Sung Square, named after the country's founding leader. It sits on the bank of the Taedong River, a beautiful waterway that snakes through the capital. I couldn't get over how empty the streets were. I didn't see many people, save for the smartly dressed traffic ladies who moved with such precision that they almost seemed robotic. There were also very few cars, just the occasional blue-and-white city bus.

We visited the Kumsusan Palace of the Sun, a massive mausoleum for two former leaders, Kim Il Sung and Kim Jung Il. You are not allowed to carry anything in your pockets or any bags. You enter through a metal detector followed by a machine that cleans your shoes. Another machine cleans you with powerfully blown air before you walk into the room where the leaders' bodies are on display in clear sarcophagi. (North Koreans know a thing or two about hygiene.) Other rooms display the honors and titles that the leaders received from around the world.

The mausoleum wasn't the only overt ode to North Korea's leadership. Throughout the country are numerous statues and displays, including a larger-than-life version of Kim Il Sung's signature. We even saw flower species bearing their names. Juche Tower, on the banks of the Taedong River, was named for the ideology of Kim Il Sung. From the top, it offered spectacular and expansive views of Pyongyang and its surprisingly brightly colored buildings. Apparently, in 2012 North Korea's leader, Kim Jong Un, announced that the buildings in the city were too gray and so they were painted.

To get a feel for what normal life in Pyongyang is like, we went to one of the main metro stations and were able to ride for a couple stops. The station and train felt retro—the green-and-red cars dated back to 1973. On the station walls were huge paintings of the leaders and copies of local newspapers on full display. When we emerged from the station, I noticed a lot of people riding bicycles, which seemed to be the most common mode of transportation. One evening we went to a bar—full of people—for a beer tasting. North Koreans love their beer so much that it is included in the monthly food ration. I don't often drink beer, but I thought North Korean beer tasted pretty good.

At Mount Myohyang, three hours north of Pyongyang, we visited the International Friendship Exhibition. Thousands of gifts from foreign leaders and organizations were on display, including a signed basketball from Michael Jordan. Having been to 141 countries by this point, I had fun seeing gifts from nearly every country in the world.

What I found most fascinating about North Korea was just how normal it often felt. Of course, I wasn't taken to any labor camps or prisons, so I cannot share the worst parts of North Korea. But I haven't done that in any of the countries I've visited.

Our trip was tightly controlled. We went only where they wanted us to go. But life still shone through. In the mountains, we saw people working the land and tending to their homes. They were clearly not rich, but they did not seem to be living in abject poverty either. In Pyongyang, I saw families playing in parks, schoolchildren on field trips, a couple looking lovingly into each other's eyes, people going to work by subway, a bride and groom taking wedding photos in front of major monuments, and co-workers drinking in bars after work. The people I met were shy, kind, and curious. One of my North Korean guides had lived in Angola to learn Portuguese. Maybe everyone wasn't as closed off to the world as we thought.

In the end, people are just people, and you can respect a culture separate from its government. Sure, some of what I saw was different, but North Korea wasn't the most unusual country I visited; Turkmenistan (page 340) gets that award.

The Taedong River, flanked by buildings on its shores, flows through Pyongyang. As the sun rises in the early morning, the fog lifts.

madagascar

MADAGASCAR, THE WORLD'S fourth largest island, was part of my multicountry trip to the African sovereign nations in the Indian Ocean. The islands in the region, including Comoros and Mauritius, are not well connected, so to accomplish this ambitious goal, I had to break Madagascar into two visits: two days in-country ahead of the only flight to Comoros that week, and another six days in Madagascar on my

way back. Because of the country's massive size and my limited time, I had to decide between visiting the beaches in the north or the interior of the country. Having spent a lot of time exploring beaches around the world already, I opted for the latter. My entire itinerary was planned by Jonah, the Malagasy owner of a tour company called Ramartour, and his team. Whenever I don't have a friend in a country, I try to book private tours through locally owned and operated agencies that are providing work opportunities to the local population and leaving the bulk of the profits in-country. Alongside the job opportunities, I find these tours provide the best insider knowledge to the countries I'm visiting.

The Malagasy people are unlike any other Africans I have seen. They are a mix of the Bantu of East Africa who migrated to the island centuries ago and Southeast Asian migrants from islands such as Borneo and Timor-Leste. The result is a people who are a beautiful blend of African and Asian physical features—with really long names, both in spelling and syllables. I first encountered this in the capital city, Antananarivo—a bit of a tongue twister itself—which is shortened to Tana. Malagasy names are typically long because they essentially form full sentences. For example, Andrianampoinimerinatompokoindrindra is the name of a 17th-century prince. His name translates to "the prince who was given birth to by Imerina and who is my real lord." The former president of the country, Hery Rajaonarimampianina, holds the world record for the longest name of a head of state.

Cultural history aside, I wanted to see Madagascar's famed lemurs. We made our way to Andasibe-Mantadia National Park, a rainforest

AFRICA

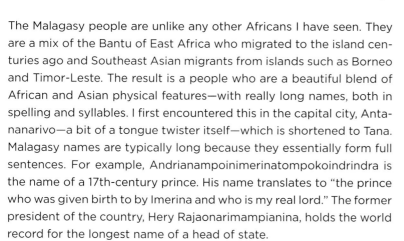

Antananarivo, usually shortened to Tana by locals, is the tongue-twisting, bustling capital city of the world's fourth largest island nation.

home to 11 types of lemurs. On our trek we spotted many *Indri indri,* one of the largest living lemurs, which have white fur and long limbs, and heard their renowned singing. To get more up close and personal, we went to "lemur island," where the animals, used to tourists, readily jump from tree to person and back again. When a small brown creature with orange eyes first jumped on me, I jumped too. But soon, I got comfortable with their little tiny fingers rubbing my head.

After our animal encounters, it was time for the number one item on my Madagascar bucket list: the Avenue of the Baobabs. Though I had seen the famous African tree in other countries, I made it my mission to get to the west coast, where the trees were concentrated into a road of sorts. It took 12 hours in the car, each way, from Antananarivo to Morondava. The bumpy roads and cramped legs were worth it.

When we arrived in the late afternoon, there were fewer than a dozen tourists. I felt like I had the regal trees all to myself as I stopped and stared, giving gratitude for nature's magic. The massive trees were a stunning testament to time, standing beautiful in their shape and form against clear blue skies. As the sun began to set and the trees cast their shadows across the road, I began to cry. I cried for the beauty of their silhouettes against the orange-stained sky and for all that I learned from the generous people of Madagascar.

Although so much of Madagascar's beauty is in its landscapes and wildlife, the people made the trip. I was charmed by the welcome reception I received in all parts of the country. Jonah taught me to say *fahasalamana* (cheers) over an ice-cold local beer at a tiny bar in a small village. We met kind locals in a fishing village who even complained about burning their feet on the sand in the blazing sun. There was also Jacques, who made bags on the roadside between Antsirabe and Antananarivo and happily adjusted one I purchased as he walked me through the design and coloring process. There were Hajaina and Prudence, my guide and driver, who served as translators and made nearly 30 hours in a car together fun and educational.

After years of travel, taking pictures and looking at sites gets old, but I can sit for hours talking to local people and asking a million questions about their lives. I got that in spades in Madagascar.

I was overjoyed by the simplicity of life in Madagascar. During a drive through villages and small towns, I wrote the following in my diary:

We've lost something in the West. Driving through Antsirabe early in the morning, you see people working in the fields, pulling people on rickshaws driven by feet. You see sweat on brows, laughter between

friends and strangers, community, and love. Here, in rural Madagascar, you can find a woman of 50 years carrying a basket with nine bricks on top of her head.

What is wrong with this way of life? Why should we go around the world "developing" developing countries?!

Sometimes life is not easy, or convenient, or efficient, but is this life less important, less valuable? In the West, we believe our way of life should be everyone's way of life, from exporting a false sense of democracy and hiding our corruption behind a faulty system to living lives that are built on the purest ideas of capitalism. It is not normal to have hundreds of thousands of dollars of debt, but we call student loans "good debt." It is not normal to have 47 pairs of shoes when you only have one pair of feet.

In so many "developing countries," I find freedom in being disconnected from Western ideals of vanity. Ideals that have us all feeling insecure. A focus on what people are wearing or if their shoes match their outfits. A focus on the body types of strangers and the public judgment of what we do not deem beautiful or acceptable.

Here, and in so many other so-called developing countries, there is a greater focus on community, on family, on living. Yes, for some, it is certainly about survival, and life is hard—minimal access to clean water, adequate nutritious food, etc. But people are doing what they need to do, which is often back-breaking work with very little results. This life, though, this simple life, seems so much more pure.

Avenue of the Baobabs in western Madagascar is reflective of the country's unique landscapes.

comoros

I AM NOT AFRAID OF A CHALLENGE. Making it to all 195 countries of the world proves that. I've taken hundreds of flights, had countless layovers, and dealt with difficult visa processes and discrimination at border control. And then, I've also dealt with countries that felt impossible to get to. With just one flight a week from Madagascar, Comoros is not particularly easy to visit. It requires some serious advanced planning.

AFRICA

That helps explain why this beautiful jewel is relatively unknown and has very little tourism.

Located in the Indian Ocean, Comoros comprises four major islands that lie between Mozambique and Madagascar. This southernmost member of the Arab League surprised and intrigued me.

The Indian Ocean is one of the most beautiful bodies of water in the world. It is warm, but not too warm, and full of colorful coral, vibrant schools of fish, and dolphins that enjoy playing with visitors. People often think of Zanzibar, the Seychelles, and Maldives when daydreaming of gorgeous beaches on this stretch of water. I want you to add Comoros to the list.

From the skies above Moroni, the capital on the island of Grande Comore, the white sand beaches are clearly visible, as are the crystal clear waters lapping the shores. Already familiar with the beauty of this vast ocean, I was still surprised as I laid my eyes upon the bright blue waters glistening under the Comoran sun.

Comoros gives me Zanzibar meets Lamu vibes. The mash-up of Swahili and Arab influences shines through culturally via the language (Comorian), the food, and the people. Although France colonized the country, there are not many remnants of its influence. In other former French colonies, you often see architecture or baguettes left behind, but in Comoros, the Arab influence overwhelms, particularly in Moroni.

The medina—the historic center of Moroni—is laced with narrow alleys that are a mix of shadowy little tunnels and the light of open skies. If you get lost in the ancient labyrinth, local people happily help you find your way. Inside the medina, many houses maintain their

I was taken aback not only by the stunning beauty of Chomoni Beach but also by the fact that we were the only ones enjoying it.

A fisherman takes his traditional wooden boat out to sea at dawn on the shores of Grande Comore.

Swahili architecture, including original doors that are regally adorned with wooden carvings and intricate metalwork. These doors highlight the importance of the ancient sultans who once lived behind them. The streets are full of little shops and the simplicity of daily life. In the afternoons you can see men playing local games like *mraha* (*omweso* in Luganda). Just after the call to prayer, men in white floor-length tunics and colorful *kofia* (cylindrical caps) congregate in front of the Ancienne Mosquée de Vendredi, which was built in 1427.

As on most islands, fishing is a key industry in Comoros. I woke early a few mornings to watch the fishermen head out. As I lay on the beach, I was impressed by the strength of two older, petite gentlemen moving a yellow traditional boat carved from wood. I smiled at their beauty and waved as they carried the boat to its parking spot on the shore. They waved back.

Led by Yassim, a local and my official guide, we took a day trip to Chomoni Beach, about 20 miles (32 km) outside of the city. We pulled into a dingy parking lot full of gravel and little bits of trash blowing in the light summer breeze. Despite the unbecoming parking lot, the beach just beyond its edge instantly jumped onto my list of top 10 beaches in the world.

What struck me about Chomoni Beach was not just its alluring cobalt blue waters and the whitecap waves crashing on its pearl-colored shore, or the powdery soft sands that caressed our toes as we made our way into the gentle warmth of the Indian Ocean. Rather, I was stunned by the fact that we were the only ones there. In other countries, this beach would be home to an exclusive five-star hotel. Elsewhere in the world, instead of a local fisherman in a tattered shirt pulling fresh lobster from a cage, crustaceans would be handled by the assistant of a Michelin star chef and served at "market price" alongside a starch topped with imported truffles rather than the more accessible locally roasted breadfruit.

While we waited for our fresh—and affordable—lobster to be delivered from a nearby shack, we discussed Comoran tourism, or the lack thereof. I have an affinity for countries that have yet to exploit their tourism potential, places deemed unworthy by the global powers that be.

Comoros has better beaches than Mauritius yet receives less than half of its tourism. Haiti sits on the same island as the Dominican Republic yet only receives attention when in need of billions of dollars of international aid. How do we determine which countries are worthy of tourism? Do they require stamps of approval from travel experts working within an industry that is decidedly Eurocentric? Or do we just wait for tourists to go beyond the beaten path, ultimately improving, in some small way, the lives of communities ready to welcome them with open arms? For that matter, would it even be to a country's advantage to invest in tourism, or are their cultures and climate intact only because they receive so few visitors? Are the risks of becoming a global hot spot—overtourism, increased waste, a fundamental change to the local culture—worth the increase in capital?

These are questions I found myself asking on the isolated beach in Comoros. I don't know that I have the answers.

In a country like Comoros, where 42.4 percent of people live below the poverty line, they could certainly benefit from a few euros, yen, and dollars. But the government would need to create proper infrastructure to be sure to avoid the damages of overtourism.

I certainly enjoyed the uncrowded beaches of Comoros and the locals who treated me like family. On that day on Chomoni Beach, after tasting some of the best lobster I've ever had—without the inflated prices—I relished having the unspoiled shores all to myself.

In Moroni, the capital, I photographed these Comoran children in the narrow alleyway after we took a picture together.

saudi arabia

IN DECEMBER 2018, Saudi Arabia began, for the first time, to issue tourist visas in an effort to decrease reliance on oil. Though the visas were tied to the attendance of a sporting event, concert, or cultural festival, the move sparked an immediate spike in tourism; people had been waiting for decades to see what the kingdom had to offer. I jumped at the rare opportunity. As a result, I was part of the first group of

non-Muslim tourists to explore the Arabian behemoth, visiting with a visa tied to the Formula E Diriyah ePrix electric car race.

The Kingdom of Saudi Arabia is the largest country in the Middle East. It is also the most important country in the Islamic faith as the home of both Mecca and Medina, Islam's first and second holiest cities, respectively. Mecca, thought to be the birthplace of Prophet Muhammad, is strictly forbidden to non-Muslims. Medina includes the Prophet Muhammad's burial site. Non-Muslims are allowed in Medina, with restrictions.

ASIA

I left Detroit for Saudi Arabia with five weeks of travel ahead of me. Though I have perfected my packing system, I am not a backpacker who can live off just five outfits for weeks on end. What that means is that I had more than 60 pounds (27 kg) of clothing, shoes, and toiletries packed for Riyadh and my subsequent destinations. But in Saudi Arabia's capital city, I found myself empty-handed. My bag hadn't made the journey. In fact, I did not see that suitcase until I returned home.

This was one of at least 15 times that my luggage did not arrive with me. For a time, it happened so frequently that I started to think I was cursed. Though my suitcase contained so much of what I needed, I was too tired from traveling to care. I simply filed my lost baggage claim and made my way to the Four Seasons Riyadh.

After a late welcome dinner, Saja, an amazing Saudi Arabian female footballer and changemaker who I had connected with over Instagram, brought me a couple of abayas (robe-like long-sleeve floor-length dresses that women were legally required to wear in Saudi Arabia until the end of 2019) and scarves.

I visited Saudi Arabia in December 2018, when for the first time ever they allowed foreign tourists into the country. The capital, Riyadh, was my first stop.

I spent the first full day exploring Riyadh, outfitted in a black abaya and the previous day's travel outfit. I was grateful my mother had taught me to always pack a clean pair of underwear in my carry-on. Mommy saves the day again. Along with seeing many cultural sites, I was able to talk to Saudi women about how the country is changing. Though change is slow going, many of the women I met expressed excitement about laws being lifted that banned them from driving. Throughout the Middle East, the restrictions on women vary from incredibly strict—like in Saudi Arabia before the Crown Prince Mohammed bin Salman began easing laws—to liberal, like in Jordan, where women enjoy social freedoms. Since my visit to Saudi Arabia, more laws have been lifted, I hope giving women slow, but steady, progress toward more freedom.

One of the highlights of my trip was a visit to the Edge of the World, a series of cliffs running along the Tuwaiq escarpment that offer uninterrupted views across a barren valley. The Four Seasons set up a luxury tent on the cliffs, complete with a full lunch service of grilled lobster and lamb chops, masterfully cooked, in the middle of nowhere, by Chef Mahmoud. I will never understand how they made a molten chocolate brownie out in the desert.

To get even better views, we took turns flying in a microlight, a tiny aircraft that had me shaking in my boots. The aircraft was so small, it looked like a gust of wind would take it down. I overcame my fear (sometimes I can be adventurous in the truest sense of the word) and hopped on for a 10-minute flight over the Edge of the World. The sweeping desert and sandstone cliffs below helped to calm my nerves.

Of course, our reason for being in the country was the historic Formula E race, which was being held in the Middle East for the first time. Due to traffic, we got to the race just as it was ending. Luckily, we were just in time for another event. At the post-race concert featuring David Guetta, history was made again: It was the first time in Saudi Arabia that men and women could attend a concert in public together. I will never forget the high energy. Barriers were being broken. What a time to be alive.

An hour-and-a-half flight from Riyadh lies Jeddah. Perched on the Red Sea, it is Saudi Arabia's second biggest city, its commercial center, and its most liberal city. Jeddah is also the gateway to Mecca, 40 miles (64 km) to the east. On my flight, I could see pilgrims dressed for Umrah.

Not to be outdone by the Four Seasons, more than 20 members of the Ritz-Carlton staff were outside the hotel to give me an outstanding welcome, including a dozen roses. Let me

My stay in the Royal Suite at the Ritz-Carlton Jeddah, coupled with the kindness of the staff, left me feeling like a queen.

tell you, Saudi Arabia knows how to do luxury: I was put up in the Royal Suite, a 5,300-square-foot (492 m²) "room" that had a bedroom, two living rooms, a butler's room, full kitchen, office, dining room, balcony, and a bathroom and closet roughly the size of my one-bedroom condo. Knowing I'd lost my luggage, the Ritz had Lamey Couture send a selection of designer abayas. They even sent me home with a robe that had my name stitched in Arabic in gold thread.

If you had told me that day in a parking lot when I decided to leave my nine-to-five that my choice would lead to this—I would have left corporate America much sooner. From leaving everything behind to teach English in Japan to this; you couldn't tell me I wasn't a princess.

I explored real life in Jeddah with my friend Alex. We took in the city's history on an evening visit to Al-Balad, which dates back to the seventh century and maintains much of its original architecture and charm. The unique buildings were made of limestone. Given its position on the Red Sea, Jeddah turned into a merchant city, and those who could decorated their homes with intricate wooden balconies and shutters, which have become emblematic of the city. Some were painted green and blue, giving a brightness to the city center. We explored the old houses to see how people lived back in the day. In juxtaposition to the progress of today, the women's rooms were located above the men's so women could see the men, but the men could not see them.

As the sun went down, the city came alive with merchants and men playing dominoes on the street and meeting friends in cafés.

Just outside of Riyadh lies the Edge of the World, dramatic cliffs in the middle of the desert.

Somalia

I LEFT SAUDI ARABIA TO SPEND THREE WEEKS tackling my last five countries in East Africa. Somalia forms the eastern point of the Horn of Africa. With 2,071 miles (3,333 km) of coastline, it also has the longest coast on Africa's mainland. Of the country's 15.5 million people, 85 percent are ethnic Somali, making this nation Africa's most culturally homogeneous. I traveled to Somaliland, a self-declared sovereign state, still considered to be part of Somalia internationally and by the UN. Somaliland has its own government and a representative office (equivalent to an embassy) in Washington, D.C. They have their own currency, flag, visas, and passports. Although traveling to Mogadishu, the capital of Somalia, requires extensive planning and security, traveling to Somaliland is very safe and easy.

AFRICA

I went alone to Hargeisa, Somaliland's arid capital, but met up with several locals through social media, including Faisa and Khalid. This was an unexpected benefit of building my online community: Connections made virtually across all parts of the globe led to long-lasting friendships and in-country tour guides.

Hargeisa is a densely populated city. Moving through town often meant sitting in traffic and carefully crossing the road as *tuk tuks* (motorcycle taxis) buzzed past. My days in Somaliland were packed from morning to night, but the best memories came from the market. As we made our way through the labyrinth of stalls, we stopped at one run by a man named Ahmed who was selling a variety of fabrics. I settled on a striped black-yellow-and-red fabric, which I had known my whole life as a Ugandan pattern. I was shocked to see Somali traditional dancers wearing it the night before. I had argued with my new friends that the pattern was, in fact, Ugandan, reflective of the colors of our flag. They insisted it was culturally Somali. Throughout Africa, I find many cultural similarities, which is largely due to the past migration of people and thus cultures, largely pre-colonization.

Somalia has the world's largest population of camels, and on the side of the road, just outside of Hargeisa, we spotted a small caravan.

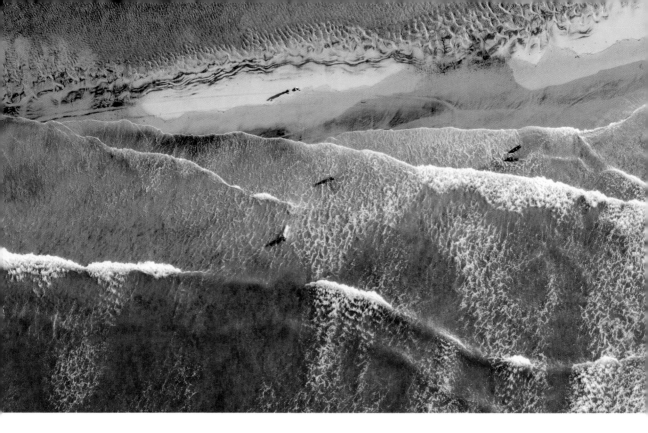

A bird's-eye view of Berbera, the former capital of British Somaliland, located on the Gulf of Aden

I purchased the fabric for the equivalent of $3 and found a tailor who would make me a *baati,* a very simple, traditional housedress. The tailor told me that it would take him just a minute to make the dress. In disbelief, I told him I would time him. It took him just under two minutes and cost just $1. Two and a half years later, I still pack that dress with me everywhere I go. That is craftsmanship at its finest.

At the souk I spotted some fake Balenciagas ("the ones that look like socks," according to Cardi B), housewares, clothing, and more fabric. At one point, we passed a stall and a man yelled out, "Hello, Uganda!" It stopped me in my tracks. I went back and asked him why he said that. He simply replied, "I just guessed." I was floored. I am often recognized as African, but rarely do people accurately guess my home country.

Always looking to make deeper connections, I asked a number of men we met throughout Somaliland what makes them happy. In the market, a man said women make him happy, specifically dark-skinned women. "I love people who are my color," he said. At a camel farm, Abel said, "The one thing that I love in the world is my religion." A beautiful answer that I felt people the world over could connect with, no matter the doctrine they subscribe to.

This sense of connection and community is one I related to deeply. I truly feel connected to people no matter where I am, but I feel a special kinship with African people the world over. As Ghanaian president Kwame Nkrumah said, "I am not African because I was born in Africa but because Africa was born in me."

Somalia is home to the world's largest camel population, so of course I was excited to visit a camel farm. The farm I visited was outside of Hargeisa, in Woqooyi Galbeed, an administrative region in western Somaliland. At the farm, I entered a pen full of young camels that were as curious about me as I was about them. They started chewing on my veil, attracted to the little pearl-like beads. I rarely drink dairy milk, but I had to try fresh camel's milk, a local delicacy. My stomach was turning a bit before I tried the very fresh, still warm milk. I slowly put my mouth to the bowl as all of the Somali herders watched and . . . it wasn't that bad. On the second sip, I realized that it was quite sweet. Though I wouldn't drink a whole glass, I'm glad I gave it a try.

We took a spur-of-the-moment day trip to Berbera, the former capital of Somaliland that sits on the coast of the Gulf of Aden, just across from Yemen. The ancient coastal city has been continuously inhabited since 400 B.C. and served as the capital of the British Somaliland protectorate.

During the two-hour drive, we stopped for lunch at a Yemeni restaurant named Al Yemen Al Saeed Restaurant. It was the best meal I had in Somalia. (No surprise, since Yemeni food is my favorite.) We were served slow-roasted meat prepared in a stew; freshly roasted chicken made on an open fire, served with potatoes and carrots; and fresh Yemeni bread that I have come to know and love. It is similar to naan but lighter and flakier.

At the beach, I was in my happy place. Water brings me so much joy, but here I only got my feet wet. In this conservative country, women must swim fully covered with a hijab. The bikinis and one-pieces that I pack weren't allowed.

Faisa and her friend Amina wore leggings and long-sleeved shirts and played in the salty water. Meanwhile, I stood on the shore and flew my drone to get a bird's-eye view of a tiny portion of Somalia's extensive and beautiful coastline. Just before the tide engulfed the sandbank I stood on, I was able to capture a selfie. The rising tide shocked us. Within five minutes, we were racing back to the car as water overtook the entire beach.

On our drive back to Hargeisa, we belted the lyrics to Adele's "Someone Like You" and I smiled to myself at all the friendships I had made during the journey, and at how within minutes strangers easily become friends.

eritrea

ERITREA IS OFTEN CALLED the North Korea of Africa due to its over-bearing isolationist regime. It is largely off-limits to tourists. It was only in 2018, the year I visited, that the governments of Ethiopia and Eritrea began to normalize relations following one of the continent's longest-running and bloodiest conflicts. Tensions subsiding, Eritrea was beginning to open up. But a visa for Eritrea is still notoriously hard to obtain.

Ugandans are the only nationality that do not need visas to enter the country. My Ugandan passport came in handy once again.

Stepping into Eritrea is like traveling back in time. Though it was colonized for less than 50 years, Italy's presence looms large more than 80 years after its departure. Asmara, the capital, is known as "Piccola Roma" (Little Rome). Having lived in Rome for nearly three years, being in Asmara felt a bit strange. It truly felt like the Eternal City. I had a cappuccino and cornetto standing at a bar, just as I would in Italy. From the window of my hotel, I could see a pastel yellow building, weathered by time, the metal gate on the storefront . . . it all felt like an exact replica of a street next to the Ostiense metro station in the heart of Rome. Eritrea felt familiar.

In Asmara, I saw a capital city that was full of life. We visited the Great Mosque of Eritrea, a beautiful building whose minaret stood proudly above the city. At Enda Mariam Cathedral, an Eritrean Ortho-dox Tewahedo Church, we watched female worshippers clad in white congregate out front and children chase birds. We passed an open-air market where fruits, vegetables, legumes, and spices stood ready for inspection by passersby. We toured the post office, which felt like what I imagine Rome was like in the 1940s, with its stained glass windows and marble counters, a distinctly Italian design. Inside, there was a painting of the mosque, the Orthodox church, and the Catholic cathe-dral, a beautiful testament to Eritreans of all faiths living in harmony. This harmony was juxtaposed by the Ministry of Education, which sits in a building in the shape of an inverted F, for Fascist. (It was designed

AFRICA

The charming streets of Massawa feel like a step back in time, with buildings that tell the tales of the once vibrant city.

this way by architect Bruno Sclafani and originally served as the head-quarters of the National Fascist Party.)

In Eritrea I was again reminded of the distance that news of my journey had reached. At a coffee shop, a man from across the street, Mussie, approached and told me he had seen me on Instagram. It still blows my mind that someone in a city like Asmara, with incredibly limited internet, would recognize me. Though I shouldn't have been so surprised. With fewer than 50 countries left, I had 70,000 invested Instagram followers anxiously awaiting the climax of my journey—only half of whom were based in the United States.

Roads, left by the Italians, twist and turn like serpents through Eritrea's dry and mountainous countryside. We drove to Keren, the nation's second largest city. At a livestock market we saw camels, cattle, sheep, donkeys, and goats being sold by men dressed in white tunics and turbans paired with blue and gray vests. The market was clearly the center of community in Keren.

At a small restaurant just outside of Keren, a woman gathers greens to chop, which will go into a stew, served atop injera.

We ate injera with shiro and tibs, washed down with Habesha beer, the first beer I have seen with a Black face on the label. The term *Habesha* was historically used to refer to northern Ethiopian Highlands Orthodox Christians. Over time it has become more inclusive. Within the diaspora, it is often used to refer to all people of Ethiopian and Eritrean heritage.

While walking around Keren, people often referred to me as "the African." At first, I smiled at the name. Then, as it continued, I thought, What do they think they are? At a club, I had a nearly violent run-in with a man who, very angrily, barked, "Your black ass." Only then did I realize many of the Eritreans were othering me as "African."

There has long been tension within the Habesha community in regard to skin tone–based discrimination. Though people from the Horn of Africa (including Ethiopia, Eritrea, Djibouti, and Somalia) have a different phenotype than East Africans, I had not realized that some do not consider themselves to be African. As someone who is visibly African, I have come to expect negative reactions while traveling, particularly in Europe and the United States. But to experience this discrimination on the African continent left me saddened for what

colonialism has done to these people. This topic deserves an entire symposium, but I couldn't let my experience go unsaid here.

Paved roads snake through the mountains in the dramatic landscape of the Eritrean countryside.

Our last road trip in Eritrea took us to the coastal town of Massawa, perched on the Red Sea. We relaxed on the beach under the unrelenting December sun. Massawa has an annual average temperature of 86°F (30°C), making it one of the hottest cities in the world.

After cooling off in the Red Sea, we headed to the Imperial Palace, whose initial iteration dates back to the 16th-century Ottoman period. The present-day building was completed in the late 1800s and was used as a winter palace by Emperor Haile Selassie, whose iconic lion statues still stand on the grounds. Though the palace is dilapidated now, the carefully laid blue tiles and precise archways showed the grandeur of what once was.

In some ways, Massawa reminded me of Havana, a beautifully aged city with lots of charm. Though many of the buildings are abandoned, there is an elegance to the town. If you see past the dust and consequence of time, you can find beauty in the archways framing windows and balconies that overlook narrow streets.

I was surprised by Eritrea. I did not expect to fall in love with it, to find so many places to see, or to feel like I needed to return to see more. But my return trip would have to wait. I was off to country 150, what some might consider one of the most dangerous places in the world.

south sudan

AS 2018 TURNED TO 2019, the new year marked the last year of my journey. With 45 countries left on my list, I had to shift my deadline from my birthday in May to my father's birthday in October to reach the finish line without being completely exhausted. And I still had some tough countries into which I needed to gain access. South Sudan, the world's newest country, was one of roughly 13 countries labeled "Level 4: Do Not

Travel" on the U.S. State Department travel warning list during my journey. While I was planning my trip, an acquaintance connected me with someone who formerly worked at the U.S. Embassy in Juba, South Sudan's capital. That person texted a warning: "During my time there many were killed and raped." I replied, "Same as what's happening in the U.S. and many other countries in the world. Such a difficult time we are living in." He exited the WhatsApp group shortly thereafter.

I do not follow U.S. guidance on travel. From my experiences abroad, my education in international development, and my stint at the United Nations, I have a very clear understanding of the political biases that manifest as travel warnings and visa hurdles. These warnings are often for people who "look American"—by that, I mean white people. When I was in South Sudan, no one on the street guessed that I am American. It was the same in Iran, Libya, the Central African Republic, and many other places on the list of countries deemed unsafe for Americans to visit. I feel I can travel safely in these countries because people assume I am, first and foremost, African.

Planning my trip to South Sudan was a herculean feat. I had to rely on the deeply built network I had made through years of traveling. Just try to follow this: My friend Kamiel's little sister Kyla, who did an internship in Geneva at the UN, connected me with a South Sudanese friend of hers who lived in Nairobi. That friend connected me with Nyankuir, who happened to be in Juba visiting her mother at the time

I spent several hours in a cattle camp outside of Juba, and I was impressed by this woman's ability to balance on her toes while milking the cows.

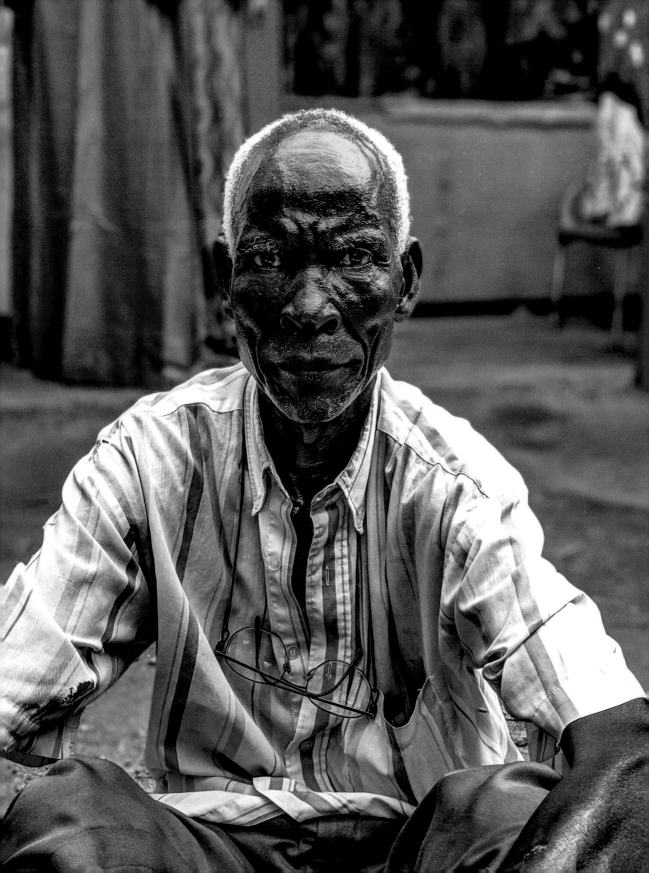

of my arrival. Talk about good timing, because Nyankuir made my trip to South Sudan unforgettable.

As we descended over Juba in early January, I saw only dry desert until we neared the Nile, her fertile lands covered in green trees. Juba came into full view as the wheels touched down. The airport was a mere three weeks old when I arrived, a reflection of the country's newness and the area's history of exacerbated political strife.

The security was extensive at River Camp, my home during my time in Juba. Two very large gates, which seemed more like walls, made it feel like I was entering a fortress. But once inside, I discovered an oasis.

The accommodations at River Camp were basic, but the location, perched on the shore of the Nile, was anything but. The property's D'Nile Bar is a popular watering hole for the extensive number of humanitarian workers, embassy employees, and foreign press living in Juba. I met many of them during my nights at the bar and learned a little bit about the persisting conflict through their eyes. Having worked in development, it deeply disturbs me how often people working to "help" people think so poorly of those they are helping. This is most often the case in places the industry calls "non-family duty stations," areas deemed too dangerous for workers to bring their dependents but that come with substantially higher pay. In South Sudan, I was disappointed to hear that many people there under the guise of helping considered the locals to be uncivilized and incapable of running their own country.

What I experienced in South Sudan was beauty and kindness—the actual opposite of what I was hearing from the people at D'Nile who hadn't left their privilege at home. It started with lunch under a large neem tree. With relief from the oppressive heat, we sat on plastic chairs and ate local dishes, including freshly stewed fish. Nyankuir, her friend Abul, and their cousin gave me a crash course in South Sudanese history. They told me the story of Dr. John Garang de Mabior, Nyankuir's father and the leader of the country's 21-year struggle for liberation. He was killed in a helicopter crash in 2005.

Always heartbeats of a city, markets are like large community centers where you can buy necessities and laugh with friends. Such was the case at the Konyo Konyo market, where I shopped for fabric and tasted honey so freshly harvested that bees buzzed around me as the sweet nectar dripped from my lips.

But what I love most about markets are all the characters you meet. I noticed an old man sitting on the ground and was struck by the beauty in his eyes. His dark skin glistened in the scorching afternoon sun. He didn't seek the shade like the rest of us. His face was accen-

In Konyo Konyo market, I was struck by the beauty in this gentleman's eyes. Perhaps more than struck; I was mesmerized.

tuated by snow white eyebrows and hair. The lines on his face expressed decades of life lived. I assumed he was a beggar, as did others who were giving him money as they walked by, but his clean clothes suggested otherwise. In fact, he was a retired father who was bored with all of his kids out of the house. He came to the market to entertain himself. The money he received was just a bonus. He allowed me to take his photo only after he put his glasses on for the picture. He even gave me a slight smile. I asked if I could take a photo without his glasses. I wanted to capture the full breadth of his face and those mesmerizing eyes. He kindly agreed. These two images are among my favorite portraits I've ever taken. Every time I look into his eyes, I am transported back to the market in Juba. They tell a story of a life and a place.

As the afternoon rolled on, we made our way to the shores of the Nile, enjoying a cool breeze as the heat began to subside. On our way, we stopped in a small village where we were invited to try *shetha-shetha,* a local brew made of sorghum and described to me as ginger wine. Though traditionally prepared by women but only consumed by men, I was happy to add shetha-shetha to the list of local brews I had indulged in around the world. Variations of homemade alcohol dot the globe, each using local ingredients and recipes passed from generation to generation. In Uganda, we call it *mwenge,* and it's made from bananas. We have moonshine, typically made from corn, in the United States. Kazakhstan has fermented horse milk. No matter the ingredients, all of these drinks share a high potency. Homemade alcohol can cure all illnesses from your body or make you blind. It's strong. I never manage more than a few sips.

The highlight of my adventure in South Sudan was visiting a cattle camp on the outskirts of Juba. Cattle are hugely important in South Sudanese culture. As one man said when I asked how many cattle he owned, "That's like asking me what's in my bank account!"

I saw more cattle than I could count, including calves sucking on their mother's teats—one was just two days old—and large males with incredibly long horns that I kept ducking and dodging. The camp had brown cows and white cows and gray cows, cows with spotted hides and solid hides. The people living in the camps know exactly how many cows they own and exactly which ones are theirs, even as the animals graze in shared spaces. Herders live close to the cattle, in temporary dwellings that are easily moved as the cows run out of grass. The herders live as a community, following traditions that are hundreds of years old. The cattle serve as their source of food and income and are even used for marriage proposals and bride-prices.

We spent almost three hours in the camp, meeting people and trying to avoid piles of dung. Curious children followed us around, and a woman balanced on her toes as she milked a cow with remarkable efficiency. The elder of the camp was a beautiful woman whose face looked like she had seen at least 100 years on this earth. A calf was aggressively drinking its mother's milk, which reminded me of friends telling me how painful breast-feeding can be. As we made our way out of the camp, I met a man named Daniel and asked what my bride-price would be. He said a maximum of 30 cattle. At five feet seven, I am considered short in South Sudan and thus not as valuable. A woman who is taller and from a prominent family could rake in as many as 200 cattle. I attempted to argue my way to a higher price to no avail.

After hours in the sun, milking and falling in love with and running from cattle, we left the camp with cow dung on our feet and sweat dried on our brows. I reflected on the day under a tree with a cold beer in hand. I was grateful for my time in Juba, this place that is so off the radar, so "other" to the rest of the world.

Seeing how I fit in, Nyankuir's friends gave me the Sudanese name Nyankiir, which means "daughter of the Nile," a fitting name for this Ugandan woman.

Life in Juba formed on the shores of the Nile. The massive river cuts straight through the city.

malawi

LIVING ABROAD HAS A WAY of making the world feel small. I met Henry from Malawi while living in Rome. He was in town visiting my friend Grace, and we kept in touch. It only made sense to reach out to him when I finally made it to his home country. Although Henry wasn't available, his assistant, Mark, accompanied me on my tour of Malawi's capital, Lilongwe. In true Jessica fashion, the first place I asked to see was the market, so Mark

AFRICA

brought me to the bustling Lizulu Market. But to get there, we had to cross a rickety wooden bridge, slightly tilted and held together by ropes. The bridge, covered in discarded plastic bags, costs 50 kwacha (roughly six cents) to cross and it's best *not* to hold on to the shaky railing as you make your way. As I nervously stepped onto the bridge, I prayed that I wouldn't end up in the brown murky waters below. But I'd do anything for a good market.

Safely on the other side, we found the massive market, a simple wooden structure with a corrugated roof. People were selling denim of all colors, secondhand clothing, chickens, vegetables, and all kinds of necessities. Mark insisted I try the freshly fried potatoes, and I was happy I did. In the shop, each person had a role: Someone peeled potatoes, another cut them, and someone else fried and sold the tasty treats. The potatoes are served right on the counter and you eat them standing up with a toothpick. They were divine, perfectly salted and crispy.

In the market, I saw more familiar sights beyond just the bustling stalls. A group of men played *bao*, a game of marbles that is found in many countries around the world. I had seen this same scene in Zimbabwe, Botswana, and Uganda. Though I was invited to play with them, I did not fare very well because the rules were different from the Ugandan version.

Mark and I drove to Chipasula, a town just outside of Lilongwe, for a haircut at his barbershop. Johnson, the owner and a Congolese refugee, had used African ingenuity to fashion an old car seat into a barber's chair for his clients. My haircut cost 69 cents! Johnson's story and ingenuity, just like the refugee turned barber I had met in Nauru, were reminders of what people will do to provide for themselves and their families. Refugees are not "always looking for handouts," just an opportunity at a better life.

Next, we went to a *shabin,* a spot where people drink *kachasu,* a very strong (no surprise) locally made alcohol that tastes similar to moonshine. Shots of the grain alcohol were being sold and poured into glasses fashioned from a bottle top and a small portion of a plastic bottle. Everyone watched me wince as the trail of fire made its way down my esophagus, no doubt sprouting an immediate hair or two below my shirt. I still purchased 200 milliliters (about seven ounces) of the beverage at 48 cents to add to my collection.

For the last leg of my trip, I made my way to Lake Malawi, the fifth largest freshwater lake in the world. At the shore, I boarded a boat to Nankoma Island, a private island and home of my host, the Blue Zebra Island Lodge. As the boat took me across the blue waters, I found it hard to believe we were on a lake and not an ocean—I could not see the other side. Though I went during the rainy season—not my best idea—to spend even one night on the gorgeous lake was worth it, if only for the sunsets. The lodge— designed with luxury accommodations built into a rustic, natural setting—successfully engages the local community, which allowed me to interact with a number of Malawians on the property.

I explore African cities the same way other travelers take on European hubs. In Malawi, I went to restaurants and bars, did some shopping, and got to experience how locals live. I'm looking forward to going back to see more sights and have a little more kachasu.

In Chipasula, I went to a *shabin,* a spot where people drink *kachasu,* which is a very strong locally made alcohol, similar to moonshine.

libya

AT THE TIME OF MY VISIT, Libya was facing instability and wasn't issuing tourist visas. But getting to Libya turned out to be much easier than I imagined. Through a tour company, Wadi Smalos, I was able to get a business visa and work around the bureaucracy. But there's always a *but*. I needed to get visas to Niger and Mali before I left for a short Canadian vacation ahead of the next leg of my journey. Niger and

Mali were easy enough, but when my logistics coordinator, Anna, called the Libyan Embassy in Washington, D.C., she was told the visa department wasn't open. I decided to go anyway.

At the Libyan Embassy, I quickly explained my dilemma and handed over my paperwork. I may or may not have lied and said I hadn't gotten Anna's message that the visa department was closed that day. The woman, who was suspicious but kind, asked me to sit down. I was prepared to wait hours. After less than five minutes, another woman walked out and handed me my open passport with the visa inside. Tears filled my eyes as I said, *"Shukran, shukran—*Thank you, thank you." She gave a soft smile and went back behind the heavy door. I could not believe I had been given one of the hardest visas in the world in less than five minutes. My trip around the world has led me to believe in miracles—and the kindness of humans.

To reach Libya, I had to go through Tunis, my favorite city in North Africa. On the one-hour flight on Libyan Wings, I was surprised to receive a modest meal—more than you get on a five-hour flight in the United States.

The airport in Tripoli is small and hasn't been updated in decades. I was traveling alone, and I do not speak Arabic, so I was grateful when I caught the eye of Abubakar, my guide. As we made our way

AFRICA

When we entered the main complex of Leptis Magna, I was stunned. I have seen my fair share of Roman ruins, but none as intact as these.

Despite the political turmoil, daily life in Libya's capital, Tripoli, continues in simple ways, such as these men enjoying an afternoon coffee in a café.

to the city center, my eyes were glued to the window, watching the coastal city pass by. I imagined what Libya must have looked like in its heyday. Tripoli is a jewel perched on the Mediterranean coast, an oasis in the desert that the Italians colonized in the early 20th century. The colonizers built a sewage system, the first modern hospital, and an airport. Today, the architecture is covered with dust and shows its age. Following the revolution in 2011, everything in the country came to a standstill. Construction sites still have cranes suspended in air, rusted from more than eight years of inactivity. Buildings have holes in the exterior where, in the midst of war, bullets and rockets penetrated.

As you walk throughout the city, you quickly see that life, on the other hand, is not standing still. Men sit in cafés, drinking coffee and smoking *shisha* (water pipe tobacco), kids play in parks as their mothers stand watching closely nearby, and people stand in line at banks, waiting to start their days. What I saw was a welcome reminder that no matter what is happening in a country politically, everyday life continues. For most in Libya, that life is filled with many unknowns. Resilience is a beautiful thing.

As part of my journey, I am constantly asked about safety. People regularly ask about places they've heard are "dangerous" or about how I feel traveling as a woman, particularly as a Black woman. I often surprise people when I tell them that I've very rarely felt unsafe in a place, and when I have, it's not in a country they'd have expected. Here's my rule of thumb: Before visiting any country—and I mean any country, not just those on the so-called "do not travel" list—I ask local people about the safety of their country. I don't look at the U.S. State Department warnings to make travel decisions. Many times, those warnings are made based on political decisions rather than the reality of the country. Furthermore, I am visibly African. I will rarely be a target of kidnapping or harassment for money. I jokingly call that "Black privilege." No matter where I travel, I remember that something bad can realistically happen anywhere, and I try to be as safe as I can be while still enjoying an authentic experience in my destination. So rather than allow a government's vision of a country to dictate my travel plans—or fear of making them—I rely on local people to tell me the realities of their countries. That was the case with Libya. I asked locals in advance of arriving if it was safe to travel there alone as a women. I was told it was and felt I had no reason to worry.

Founded by the Phoenicians in the seventh century B.C., Libya was part of the Roman Empire. Roughly 50 miles (80 km) from Tripoli is

The amphitheater of Leptis Magna was built in A.D. 56. From the top, you have uninterrupted views of the deep blue of the Mediterranean.

Villa Silin, the first stop on our tour of Libya's ancient Roman ruins. The villa sits directly on the coast, providing endless views of the Mediterranean Sea. Its design and location left me green with envy. Having been buried in sand for centuries, the villa was only discovered in 1974, and it is remarkably well preserved.

The wealth and opulence of its original owner are displayed in the pristine 2,000-year-old floors, painstakingly detailed with shapes, intricate designs, and images of animals. With lavish, marble-lined baths, it was clear that whoever lived here was living the good life. Imagine your dream home standing 2,000 years later. They just don't build homes like they used to!

Leptis Magna is one of the best preserved Roman ruins in the Mediterranean, having been buried for centuries in the sands of the Sahara. The UNESCO World Heritage site was founded in the 7th century B.C. when Libya was under Roman rule. It was abandoned around A.D. 647 and sat unnoticed until the early 20th century. Our first stop within the complex was the amphitheater, which dates back to A.D. 56. As we stood at the top of the massive structure, I looked out at the deep blue of the Mediterranean, trying to transport myself back in time. We made our way down the stairs and through the tunnels to the main stage. Looking up from the stage, I felt so small. I pondered how the gladiators must've felt to face their opponents as crowds cheered and jeered through their exhausting fights, often to the death. I shuddered to think of the brutality, the cruelty.

I have seen my fair share of Roman ruins, but none as intact as the main complex of Leptis Magna. The massive archway at the entry was made of marble, and some of its elaborate carvings were still in near-perfect condition. I continued to feel small as we made our way through the enormous complex.

The palaestra, where sporting events took place, was surrounded by towering columns made of Greek and Italian marble. We passed ancient marble baths, saunas, and forums. I closed my eyes and imagined I was walking around draped in a white gown, making my way to a bath where I would have warm milk poured over my skin, preserving its suppleness. Lucius Septimius Severus, the first African Roman emperor, was born here. This fantasy could very well be a memory from a former life.

In a less well-preserved area there were large boulders, tons of rubble, and fallen columns. Among the ruins, I noticed part of a wall that had clearly been restored. On the arches were carvings of Medusa, the design used in the Versace logo. Migos' hit song played in my head as if it were the summer of 2013: "Versace. Versace. Medusa head on me like I'm 'Luminati." Bobbing to music only I could hear, I climbed over the boulders and onto a marble column. I posed just beneath the Medusa carving as Abubakar obligingly took my picture.

As we continued through the ancient city, Abubakar noted that the presence of the Libyan tourists we were bumping into was a sign that things were returning to normal. Yes, the tourists were a positive sign, but Libya still has a ways to go. Though I never once felt unsafe during my visit, Libya is far from being a tourist hot spot. The government's instability keeps it from welcoming 180,000 foreign tourists to the country as it did in 2007.

As I enjoyed the sunset over hookah with Abubakar and Emad, my driver, in Tripoli, I gazed out at the Mediterranean, wondering what Libya was and what it could be.

The intricate detail of the architecture in Leptis Magna shows the design prowess of the Roman Empire.

mauritania

THE CAPITAL OF THE ISLAMIC REPUBLIC OF MAURITANIA, Nouakchott, is located on Africa's northern Atlantic coast, in the middle of the Sahel, the semiarid region between the Sahara desert to the north and savannas to the south. I took an overnight trip into the Sahara with my guide, Mohammed, who spoke barely any English. I am so grateful to speak French, which made my experience in many countries more robust,

AFRICA

especially throughout West and Central Africa. French allowed me to learn about the cultures I was visiting and to interact with so many more people. It certainly helped me communicate with Mohammed on our trip to the desert.

Our destination in the Sahara was Chinguetti, a *ksar,* or Berber fortified village and medieval trading center. Located deep in the Sahara, Chinguetti is surrounded by endless swaths of the great desert and sand dunes small and large. You'll spot the ancient city from a distance by the minaret of the mosque standing high above the town. The minaret is said to be one of the oldest and most continuously working in the world, dating back to the 13th century.

The vastness of the Sahara is hard to grasp at eye level, with sand dunes that tower over you. But I had my drone. Despite having played in the Sahara's sands on multiple occasions, my tiny flying device allowed me to see more than I had ever seen before. For the first time, with a bird's-eye view, I saw the rolling hills of golden sands that reached the horizon and bled seamlessly into the clear blue skies, a work of art, a masterpiece of nature. From the drone's vantage point, I could see the oases that allowed for desert dwellers to live among the sands and palm trees, in houses made of reddish dry stone and mud bricks.

In the center of ancient Chinguetti, I was guided through a labyrinth of golden structures made of rock and mud. From time to time, goats crossed our path and villagers who sat in doorways greeted us. We made our way to the library, commonly found near mosques, as studying is very important in Islam. The care-taker of the library, a local historian, pulled out a piece of wood with six nails on it, which he used to open the door. This was an ancient lock and key system, dating back to the 13th century. Once inside, we were shown ancient texts, including one with poems used to teach Arabic grammar.

Living in the middle of the desert requires certain clothing to protect oneself from the elements. As such, Mauritanians have a very unique style of dress that you can see both in the middle of the desert and in the city. The men wear a white or blue Moorish boubou, a long tunic with large billowing sleeves, often with embroidery on the front. A long-sleeve shirt is typically worn beneath it, and depending on weather conditions, it is paired with a turban to protect the wearer from sandstorms and the extreme heat of the sun. You will sometimes see desert dwellers using their tunic to cover their neck and lower half of their face.

Life in Mauritania is simple. There are not many tourist sights, but I fell in love with the country's energy. Outside of the desert, Port de Pêche in Nouakchott makes it clear that Mauritania is a cultural mixing pot made of various tribal groups. As one of the largest fishing ports in West Africa, it felt like a cross between a fish market and a factory.

My two guides, Medina and Hamza, led me through a maze of hundreds of traditional pirogues (handcrafted boats) decorated in bright colors, piles of fresh and not so fresh fish, and uniformed men moving fish to storage rooms onshore with assembly-line efficiency. Hundreds of birds flew overhead hoping to snag a meal. I had never seen this many fishermen or boats on a single coast. The best part was that it was all local fishermen—no commercial fishing vessels in sight. Women sat on the shores, some watching their men work and others selling small goods.

Something inexplicable pulls me back to Mauritania. I want to dig deeper.

Mauritanians have a very unique style of dress. The men wear a Moorish boubou, which is a long tunic with large billowing sleeves.

mali

I LONGED FOR MALI. I remember reading *Sundiata: An Epic of Old Mali*, by D. T. Niane, a saga detailing the origin of the Malian Empire through the storytelling of a griot. I recall tales of Mansa Musa, the 10th emperor of the Malian Empire, who is considered to be one of the richest men to have ever lived. Timbuktu, a city referenced often, was a global center of learning for Islamic scholars from the 13th to 17th centuries. I've been

inspired by the famed photographer Malick Sidibé's studio portraits detailing life in Bamako in the 1960s. I think of *bogolan* fabric and dream of negotiating in French for large pieces of the textile to use in my home.

I made it to Mali in February 2019 but immediately hit a roadblock that had me questioning this entire adventure. I had planned to see Djenne, known for its adobe architecture, but security issues caused by Islamist militant groups in the region prevented me from visiting. Depressed and frustrated, I spent two nights in tears in my hotel room in Bamako, drinking less than stellar imported white wine and scarfing down french fries. I had been traveling solo for two weeks and was exhausted; being alone in francophone countries was taking its toll. I speak French, but not enough to avoid mental fatigue. And I was in countries without tourism infrastructure, which didn't make things easy. I was tired of visiting new places, tired of feeling obliged to post on social media, tired of the journey.

Once I stopped feeling sorry for myself, I connected with a woman named Mouna, who kindly guided me through the market in Bamako. If I couldn't see Djenne, I could at least go shopping. My first stop was a shop that sold bogolan, a handmade cotton fabric that is dyed with fermented mud. The famous cloth has come to symbolize Malian arti-sanal culture. It is quite expensive in the U.S., so I bought as much as I could afford and carry! I bought six large pieces, two of which I turned into a coat, which I had made in Burkina Faso.

In the market, I took in the people and culture. There were women with baskets on their heads selling mangoes, as well as "waist beads"

AFRICA

I had the distinct pleasure of meeting and shooting with Kareem, the son of the great Malian photographer Malick Sidibé, in Malick's famed studio.

(apparently used for sex), penis enlargement cream, and other "sex-essories" that surprised me in the majority-Muslim country. They also had masks, snakeskins, charcoal, and gold jewelry, including my all-time fave, Fulani earrings in all sizes. The twisted pieces of metal were made famous by women of the nomadic Fulani tribe, one of the largest ethnic groups in the Sahel and West Africa. I joked with shopkeepers and drank tea as we negotiated prices.

Mali clearly is a country of artists and artisans. Possibly one of its most famous artists is Malick Sidibé, who died in 2016. His studio, founded in 1960, is still open, and I had the opportunity to visit thanks to an old friend whose mom connected me with a woman named Massaran, who accompanied me to the studio. My network never ceases to amaze me.

The studio felt like a time capsule with its checkered floor and Sidibé's various backdrops, the most famous of which is a striped curtain. Sidibé's son, Kareem, shoots in the studio, having taken on his father's craft. He captured my image using one of his dad's vintage Hasselblad film cameras and regaled us with stories of his father. We even got to see some of the elder Sidibé's negatives from his portrait work. As a photographer, I was humbled by this beautiful experience. I am standing on the shoulders of giants, and I am forever finding new ways to be inspired and connected to those who came before me.

In Bamako, another photographer, Seth, took me around town on his motorcycle. With the wind in our faces and the city flying by, I held him a little tighter, my nerves pushing me to do so—or maybe something else. One evening we explored an abandoned train station, whose glory days could be seen through the dust, then went to a local bar and sat in a dark corner sharing a beer and whispering sweet nothings. I went to his photo studio, and we listened to good music, dressed up, and made art.

On my last day, Seth and I went back to the market to capture some video and photos. We met a few of his friends, and he told them about my mission to visit every country in the world. At first, they were incredulous. *"C'est impossible!" "C'est pas vrai!"* they exclaimed. I was still feeling burned out. Maybe it was, as they said, impossible.

Their disbelief soon turned to awe as I told them Mali was country 154 of 195 and explained how my personal goal had evolved into helping to change the world's vision of Africans. When many people think of Africans—and Black people in general—they most often think of stereotypes: poverty, violence, and migrants. I wanted to show a Black person traveling as a tourist, to share the stories of the seldom

I was fortunate enough to visit the Bamako Art Gallery only one month after its opening. The gallery works with 25 local artists in a variety of mediums. Upon entering, I immediately walked into a sculpture garden of pieces made with nails, a perfect setup for the gallery's amazing works. Inside was a woodwork room; a small shop with pillows, throws, and more interior design inspiration that had me drooling; and, my favorite part, the rooftop, where a traditional mud structure with a thatched roof and a floor filled with sand was the perfect place to watch the sunset over Bamako.

seen countries and people that I visited, to show the world in a way we are not used to seeing it. As I spoke, pride (on my part) and admiration (on theirs) took over. They called more people over to hear my story.

Dabia Keita (seated on the right) reminded me that my journey to every country was not just for me, but for everyone.

One man, Dabia Keita, said to me, *"C'est pas pour toi, c'est pour nous.—It's not for you, it's for us."* They encouraged me to keep going because this is a journey for all of us, and that I had to make sure to finish. These simple words nearly brought me to tears. At that moment I realized this entire journey to make it to every country in the world had grown so much bigger than me.

The journey was challenging in many ways. Living out of a suitcase is hard. I often felt lost in time and space. I had truly wanted to quit in the weeks leading up to Mali. But those men reminded me that this journey is about showing that the world is for all of us, including people of color.

That moment got me to the finish line. With 41 countries and eight months of travel left, I needed their words of encouragement more than they will ever know. Along with a renewed sense of motivation, those friends gave me three gifts—a key chain and two bracelets—as a way to seal a pact. They told me I must return when I finish to celebrate—and I will. With a *"Bon courage,"* we parted. To Dabia, Oussman, and all the others, thank you for pushing me forward.

SNAPSHOT FROM TONGA:
During a whale-watching trip in Tonga, we stopped at an unin-habited island and enjoyed the powdery white sands and impossibly blue water.

burkina faso

BURKINA FASO WAS THE LAST country I visited
after nearly a month spent in North Africa and the Sahel. Even with the
encouragement from those men in Mali, I was still exhausted when I
arrived in Ouagadougou (or Ouaga), Burkina Faso's capital. The 100°F
(38°C) temperature made my fatigue that much more palpable. I decided
to take things slow and enjoy a few lazy days toggling between a

AFRICA

1.5-liter bottle of water and a 1-liter bottle of ice-cold Brakina, the local
beer, while reading Elizabeth Gilbert's *Big Magic*. I came across a passage
that felt divinely timed: "Whatever it is you are pursuing, whatever it is
you are seeking, whatever it is you are creating, be careful not to quit
too soon . . . Don't let go of your courage the moment things stop being
easy or rewarding." It is easy to dream a dream, but the pursuit can be
incredibly difficult, especially when you are on that path alone. This was
a reminder to keep going. What awaits is beyond your wildest dreams.

Once I was ready to tour, I met up with a young and vibrant woman
named Ifrikia, a journalist from the Republic of the Congo who guided
me around town on the back of her scooter.

We visited the expansive Village Artisanal de Ouagadougou, which
is the best place in the city to shop for handicrafts and souvenirs. I
spotted the usual group of men playing a board game that looked like
checkers and talking smack as onlookers laughed and jeered.

The market had jewelry, painted artwork, and ceremonial masks (two
of which I took home) from the Bobo tribe, who predominantly live in
the country's second biggest city, Bobo-Dioulasso. Burkina Faso also
produces the traditional Faso Dan Fani, a striped woven cotton fabric
that became a national symbol under Thomas Sankara. He famously
proclaimed, "To wear the Faso Dan Fani is an economic, cultural, and
political act of defiance to imperialism." I had items made from this fabric,
as well as the *bogolan* fabric I bought in Mali. (I recommend having
clothes made in African countries. You can typically find great textiles

and amazing tailors. I've also had clothes made in Senegal, Benin, Nigeria, Burundi, Uganda, Kenya, and Somalia.)

Eager to get outside of the city, I hired a driver to take me on the three-hour journey to Tiébélé, a unique village near the Ghanaian border. During the drive, I saw a family of elephants crossing the road in the distance. I watched, in awe, as the family navigated their way through the woods. I was shocked, but my driver said it was a normal occurrence.

Tiébélé is home to about 300 Kassena people, one of the oldest tribes to have settled in what is now Burkina Faso. The unique windowless traditional homes, known as *sukhala,* are made using a blend of mud and manure. There are two styles of home: rectangular (for unmarried men) and rounded (for married men and their families). Each home has beautiful artwork, traditionally made by women and created using natural colors—red from laterite, black from basalt, and white from kaolin.

In Tiébélé, the walls of the buildings are painted, usually by women, with elaborate traditional designs using natural materials.

In the village, we witnessed everyday life: women cooking, a few people selling souvenirs, and men sitting and laughing under the afternoon sun. I was enamored with a woman doing her daily tasks in vibrant mismatched prints that stood out against the beige-and-black buildings. As I gazed out over the village from a rooftop, the stillness was interrupted by the voices of children running around and playing games.

Back in Ouaga, I connected with Benjamin, who I'd met through Instagram. He invited me to his school to talk to the students. I have always wanted to be a teacher, but my lifestyle cannot be supported on a teacher's salary. Fortunately, my journey allows me the chance to speak to students all over the world. In Ouaga, I spoke to two classes, sharing my adventures and teaching them about the continents and countries. If they learned nothing else, they now know there are 195 countries in the world, but I like to think they learned a bit more.

Teaching those students was another reminder of why my trip to every country in the world was so important. I could suddenly see the impact my own story could have on others. I may have left Burkina Faso exhausted and ready for a break—or a real vacation—but I was reinvigorated to complete my journey.

Trinidad and Tobago

AFTER A HECTIC TWO DAYS in Detroit unpacking and repacking, I found myself right back on the road again. With 40-some countries to go, I didn't have much time to waste. My already busy travel schedule was intensifying. That countdown and Elton's birthday brought me to the twin island nation of Trinidad and Tobago, the southernmost country in the Caribbean and my last country in North America. I could finally

check off one continent as completed. Trinidad had long been on my bucket list, and I knew going during Carnival was an absolute must. Carnival is an annual celebration that involves dancing, costumes, and soca and steel pan music. It is celebrated during the three days leading up to Ash Wednesday.

I had put off Trinidad's Carnival for a long time because it is a costly excursion. I have friends who have spent $3,000-plus on flights, costumes, parties, and accommodations. Not a lover of soca music, I questioned if I would enjoy it as much as my regular Carnival-going friends do. But in 2019, Elton's birthday fell at just the right time for 11 of us to take part, play *mas* (masquerade), and eat as much as we could of the delicious street food.

A regular Carnival-going friend ensured that I was prepared with a playlist of soca music to get my waist moving. She also helped me find the perfect shoes to survive all of the time on my feet while still looking cute. (Pro tip: Make sure you prepare in advance, because Carnival is a lot of walking and drinking, and minimal sleeping.)

After a nail-biting race to New York's JFK airport in a winter storm, an hour of deicing the plane, and five hours wedged in a middle seat (despite what you see on my Instagram, travel isn't always glamorous), I landed in balmy 80°F (27°C) temps at Piarco International Airport, just outside of the capital Port of Spain.

At nearly 3 a.m., I found myself in the lobby of our hotel wearing cut-off shorts, a modified tank top, and a bandana. We were heading out for J'ouvert, derived from a term meaning "daybreak," a celebration that continues until sunrise. I am not a big partier and am usually in bed by 10 p.m., so this took a lot out of me, but I was excited to

NORTH AMERICA

Carnival Tuesday is the main event of all of Carnival, where people dress in costume and rep their countries with flags. Of course, I repped for Uganda.

experience the event. We arrived in a park with hundreds of other revelers and stood in line for a rum punch to loosen up the muscles. About 30 minutes in, large plastic buckets of small sandwich bags filled with colored powder were passed around and a mad dash began. Blue, yellow, green, pink, and purple powder filled the air as bodies pushed close together, gyrating to the blaring soca music.

I lost count of how many rum punches I drank as night turned to day. And as I danced to music I didn't quite understand, I just knew I needed to "pick up something, anything, [and] run, run wid it!" as Mr. Killa's soca line told me to do. At one point, I was the thing that was picked up. As I sat atop my friend Jeff's shoulders, we moved to the beat, covered in paint, rum coursing through our veins.

After about an hour, the party began to move. Without knowing what was happening, we followed the music, the crowd, and the rum punch. A truck serving as a bar on wheels led the way; the partygoers following with arms outstretched, hoping one of the bartenders would bless us with the fuel we needed to make it to the end of the night, or morning, as the case may be. As if that weren't enough, one can only hold their bladder for so long. That meant necessary, hilarious, and mortifying public urination. And the cherry on top: This is exactly when someone recognized me from Instagram. During without a doubt the oddest time to be noticed, someone asked me for a picture just as I was about to squat. I am used to being recognized now, but please, if you see me squatting in public, don't ask for a picture!

We also have to talk about Trinidad's street food. Any conversation about street food that doesn't include Trinidad is not credible. My favorite dish is "doubles," made of two pieces of flatbread, called *baras,* filled with chana (curried chickpeas) and topped with chutney—a nod to the influence of Indian Trinidadians. You should also try bake and shark, a traditional Trinidadian dish in which baked (or fried) flatbread is used to sandwich shark meat, lettuce, tomato, and mango chutney.

Though that night was wild and required some serious recovery, Carnival Tuesday is the main event. Everyone told us that we had to play mas with Tribe, one of the most famous Carnival bands. Carnival costumes are like highly elevated swimwear. Women are clad in what can be described as bejeweled bikinis with accessories for the head, arms, and legs that shine brightly when the sun hits them. The men are topless, with outfits that complement the women. The group that you are with, and your location in the band, determines how elaborate your costume is. We decided to jump with Tribe's newest offshoot band, Rogue, and needed to dress the part. Rogue provided bright red and orange outfits and accessories that I paired with the most comfortable red sneakers the internet

had to offer. With a pop of red lipstick, I was "ready for di road."

That morning we went to the designated location to meet Rogue and had our cups filled with rum punch. It is amazing how resilient our livers are. The music started blaring and the drinks were flowing as the band started to move. We danced in the streets with friends and strangers alike.

Carnival is a beautiful and inclusive celebration. Everyone is in good spirits, and people of all ages partake. You drink with strangers and make new friends when you lose the ones you came with. And it is body positive AF. I loved the costumes, throngs of beautiful Black people adorned in jewels and feathers, and everyone repping their countries with flags. Of course, I carried a Ugandan flag with me.

After several more hours of chasing down rum punch, glutes that were tired of twerking, and a waist that could wind no more, I decided to cut it short, head back to my hotel, and then go to the airport, two days early. I was pooped.

Experiencing Trinidad Carnival is something that all travelers should do at least once, but it is certainly not for the faint of heart. It requires a type of Energizer Bunny energy that doesn't come naturally to me. Those memories are golden, but I was more than happy to rest my feet on the plane ride home.

The best part of Carnival was enjoying it with friends and creating lifelong memories together.

myanmar

IN FEBRUARY 2021, a successful military coup upended democracy in Myanmar, but the political climate in the country has been murky for years. Myanmar is an incredibly culturally diverse country, with 135 ethnic groups, the largest of which is the Burman. Formerly called Burma during the British colonial period, the country took its name from this ethnic group. The 2017 genocide of the Rohingya led to a

A S I A

humanitarian crisis with more than a million Rohingya refugees fleeing, as well as a number of sanctions from the United States. I visited in 2019, when a democratically elected government was in place. Though parts of the country were unstable, I did not feel it. Everyday life continued despite the political climate.

I arrived in Yangon, the former capital and largest city, with my friends Nyanquoi and Faten. Yangon is a densely populated city marked by colorful apartment buildings, Buddhist temples and pagodas, and the architectural remains of British colonization.

With 90 percent of the population practicing Buddhism, monks are a constant presence in the city. As we drove around, we saw monks clad in saffron-colored robes walking under umbrellas, attempting to hide from the sweltering afternoon sun. Close to sunset, we headed to Shwedagon Pagoda, said to be the most sacred Buddhist temple in Myanmar. Identifiable by its gilded stupa, the pagoda sits on a hill high above the city. A Yangon zoning regulation caps the height of buildings so that the pagoda's prominence in the skyline remains. It's the best place in the city to watch the sunset.

Yangon's Chinatown buzzes with life after dark. The pedestrian-only streets are lined with restaurants that have both indoor and outdoor seating. Following in the footsteps of Anthony Bourdain—one of my travel inspirations—we ate delicious traditional Burmese food at Lashio Gyi: fried whole fish topped with cilantro; grilled prawns; and a spicy prawn dish, all served with white rice and a very spicy chili sauce. We washed it down with an ice-cold local beer. The food throughout the country is delicious, but please note that the default is spicy as hell.

Located on the eastern shore of Kandawgyi Lake in Yangon, the ornate Karaweik Hall is modeled after an ancient royal barge.

Riding in a hot air balloon over Bagan provides the perfect aerial view of the ancient city's temples and pagodas.

We took a short flight from Yangon to Bagan, an ancient city that dates back to the mid-ninth century. At the height of the Pagan Kingdom in the 10th and 11th centuries, more than 10,000 Buddhist temples, monasteries, and pagodas were built here, of which more than 2,200 remain. You can still see them reigning over the skyline.

Bagan is an idyllic city. It was blazing hot while we were there, so we explored early in the morning to avoid the heat as much as possible. It did not seem to help. We borrowed bikes from our hotel and, against our better judgment, set out to ride around Bagan for a few hours as the unrelenting sun beat down on us. Without a plan, we stopped at random temples, taking refuge from the sun when we found an occasional indoor space. To add insult to injury, you have to be barefoot when entering temples. I am pretty sure I burned off a layer of skin on the bottom of my feet, but the beauty of the temples was worth the pain.

Many of the temples clearly showed their age, with decaying stairs and crumbling statues. Others—like the Ananda Temple, with four fully intact Buddhas covered in gold leaf—stood the test of time. At one temple, we met a wonderful group of high school students who asked me to take pictures with them; I obliged. The people of Myanmar were all incredibly kind and had a peacefulness about them. I wasn't bothered by their attention because of this kindness.

The logistics of visiting every country in the world were incredibly challenging. I made it even more difficult by timing my visits to specific events. I planned my trip to Myanmar, for instance, around when I could take a hot air balloon ride in Bagan, which is only possible between November and April.

We woke up at 4 a.m. so that we would be in the air to watch the sunrise. I was fascinated by the more than 30 humongous pieces of fabric laid across a giant field, each of which had a team of 15 to 20 people preparing it for flight. Once our balloon was fully inflated, we climbed into the large basket, and as the hot air began pumping, we slowly lifted off the ground. As we rose above the trees, the tops of the temples came into sight, and the sun seemed to follow us, illuminating our way.

Nyanquoi and I continued on to Inle Lake, made famous by the traditional fisherman working in the still waters. We spotted a fisherman perched on the edge of his boat. In his hand he had a large woven basket with netting, and he controlled a long stick with his foot, which he used to move the boat. As we moved closer, he began doing what seemed to be an acrobatic routine. Our boat driver explained that most fishermen work in the morning and that this man was only here for us to take pictures. I was disappointed; I like to see and capture real life and real moments rather than staged photo ops. It felt like Sri Lanka all over again. I obligingly snapped a few photos before heading back. It wasn't what I expected, and it made me reflect on the impact tourism has had on cultural traditions. How startling that foreign currency can change a place's way of life. How sad that we opt in for the show rather than the true experience.

On our last morning, Nyanquoi managed to convince me to take an hour-and-a-half drive to the Kakku Pagodas, a remote ancient site dating back to the 12th century. The oft overlooked site is a gorgeous labyrinth of more than 2,400 stupas. They vary slightly in design but are similar enough that they create a beautiful uniformity. It is easily one of the most beautiful human-made sites in the world. Throughout the complex, we saw local tourists and a group of very young monks clad in burgundy cloth exploring the temples. The monks were trying to secretly take pictures of me. In return, I secretly took pictures of them as they walked away.

This simple act in this "secret" place was a beautiful reminder of our shared curiosity about one another and the world we share.

Burmese cuisine is a delicious blend of sweet, sour, salty, and spicy. Heavily focused on vegetables and seafood, every meal satisfied.

iran

THOUGH I HAVE A LOT OF rules of thumb for traveling, I live by one as much as possible: I do not travel to new countries with a fear of the unknown. I do not allow what I read in the news to taint my idea of a country or its people. I know what to ignore. I try not to let biases influence me. I choose instead to live by what is true, to be in the moment. Iran was the perfect example of that. I relied on my Ugandan passport

to avoid the hoops Americans need to jump through to make it to Iran. Ugandans can get a visa on arrival, rather than having to apply through an embassy.

My trip coincided with Nowruz, the Persian New Year, a holiday that has been celebrated for the past 4,000 years. What I didn't know was that this wasn't the best time to travel to Iran. Iranians all over the country were flooding the tourist destinations, overcrowding the mosques, forcing me to skip some sites altogether.

I started in Tehran, where I met my guide, Ali, eager to see firsthand all the glorious tile that is exported around the world. The Golestan Palace, dating back to the 1500s, delivered. Blue, yellow, and green tiles jumped off the walls. Inside many of the buildings were brightly colored stained glass windows—red, orange, blue, and green, each representing a season: summer, autumn, winter, and spring, respectively.

In the palace, a curious two-year-old boy kept walking up to me and shaking my hand. This made more sense as I made my way around the rest of the country. During my time in Iran, I did not see another Black person, and I encountered quite a bit of staring. But I found Iranians to be incredibly polite, and the vast majority of people who wanted to take my picture asked respectfully.

The best way to see Iran, a massive country of more than 600,000 square miles (1,600,000 km²), is by car. From Tehran, Ali and I hit the road to Isfahan. Now the third largest city in Iran, it once stood as the capital of Persia and retains much of the grandeur of centuries ago.

In the center of Isfahan is Naqsh-e Jahan Square, one of the biggest

ASIA

Shiraz's Nasir al-Mulk Mosque, also known as the Pink Mosque, dates back to around 1888 and is one of the city's most popular sites.

squares in the world at 964,000 square feet (89,600 m²). On the perimeter are mosques, the entrance to the Grand Bazaar, and numerous shops selling everything from tile to copper cups to Persian rugs. During Nowruz, the square was filled with kids running, mothers preparing picnics, and families enjoying the warm spring temperatures.

On the east side of the square sits Sheikh Lotfollah Mosque, a true masterpiece of Iranian architecture, built in the early 1600s by Shah Abbas I. It was conceived as a private mosque for the royal court, and particular attention was paid to the tile work and calligraphy. Upon entering the main area, my jaw hit the floor. Multicolored tile covered every inch of every wall. The tiled dome, covered in bright yellow, is so beautiful even a heathen would declare *"Mashallah!"*

On the south side of the square is Shah Mosque, built by Shah Abbas I for the general public. The massive mosque features seven-color mosaic tiles, a unique design not seen in many other places. Its sheer size left me stunned. Persian mosques are the most beautiful in the world—and I've been to mosques in 13 countries, so I can safely make that declaration!

Isfahan is the center of handicrafts in Iran, so I had to do some shopping. I left with a massive Persian rug, a few copper cups for my bar, and the phone number of a tile designer for future reference.

One evening, Ali was kind enough to invite me into his home for a proper Persian meal. We ate *tachin* (a rice cake with saffron and chicken),

The winter prayer hall of the Pink Mosque is bathed in colorful light from the many stained glass windows.

khoresh bademjan (an eggplant stew with lamb meat), and *baghali polo* (a dish made with rice and fava beans). Over dinner conversation, I was pleasantly surprised to learn that most people in Iran's middle class are liberal. Many Iranian women uncover their heads as soon as they cross a private threshold. As conversation continued, one of the dinner guests expressed fascination that I travel while on my period. To her and many other women I know, traveling while menstruating is almost unthinkable.

I love when the connections I make allow me to have truly authentic experiences like this night—to *truly* know a place, meet its people, and see the way they live day to day.

From Isfahan, we visited Yazd, an ancient city whose narrow alleyways snake between houses. New boutique hotels covered with adobe plaster (made of mud and straw) gave the old city a brown hue. From a rooftop I got a lay of the land and its picturesque architecture: The city is dotted with colorful mosques and shrines, the most impressive of which is the glorious Jameh Mosque. The

14th-century mosque has the highest minarets in the country and two massive domes covered in red, green, and blue Persian tiles. The grandeur of the mosque is depicted on the 200 Iranian rial banknote.

Our last stop in the country was Shiraz, Ali's hometown. We visited Nasir al-Mulk Mosque, also known as the Pink Mosque, the name derived from the myriad pink-colored tile work that dominates the exterior facade and courtyard. The winter prayer hall is outfitted with stained glass windows. On the morning we visited, the sun came through, soaking the entire room in green, red, yellow, and blue light.

The Shirazis were very open-minded, and the city seemed much more relaxed than other parts of the country. It should have come as no surprise that Shiraz is known as the city of wine, poets, literature, and flowers. It is also considered to be the cultural capital of Iran.

My encounters with the people in Shiraz, and throughout Iran in general, prove to me just how dangerous misconceptions can be. So many people write off this beautiful country because of headlines they read, or worse, stereotypes of Muslim countries in general. Just like almost every other country in the world, Iran's politics are complicated. But that doesn't mean the country has nothing to offer, or that it is any more or less dangerous than any other place in the world. A country's politics, I have found, very rarely reflect a country's people. Iranians are warm, open, and welcoming, and many are quite liberal. Further, I would put Iran in my top 10 most beautiful countries in the world.

The "towers of silence" in the city of Yazd are used as sky burial sites by Zoroastrians, members of one of the world's oldest continuously practiced religions.

yemen

MY EXPERIENCE IN YEMEN was terribly limited by conflict and government restrictions. Though the region I visited was incredibly peaceful and serene, it is not a reflection of the entire nation. Flying into Sana'a was not possible, and flights to Socotra, a magical Yemeni island in the Arabian Sea, were erratically scheduled. Fortunately, I found a fixer in the "Every Passport Stamp" Facebook community who could take me

ASIA

into Yemen from Oman. I only had a couple hours in Yemen, but enough to officially cross off country 161.

Salalah, Oman, is perched on the shores of the Arabian Sea, and my short stay there prior to crossing the border turned into a beautiful and unexpected vacation. My visit to Oman and Yemen fell between 18 days on the road across four countries and another 24 days and eight countries before I would be in my bed in Detroit. I took time to lounge at my hotel's pool, soak up the sun on the beach, and have a quick interview with the *Oman Daily Observer* before enjoying room service in bed. It was a much needed break from my always-on-the-go lifestyle and a welcome rest before entering a country in turmoil.

My fixer, Azzam, picked me up early in the morning, along with another gentleman who was also visiting every country in the world. Together, we made the three-hour journey through the dry mountainous region of southern Oman, slowing down from time to time to allow camels to pass.

Azzam had organized everything in advance, so crossing the border was quick and easy. Once in Yemen, I was glued to the window, taking in as much of the country as possible in the few hours we had. As we drove toward Hawf, a small village where we would have lunch, I saw abandoned buildings and remnants of lives past, including a hotel that was erected to welcome tourists but never opened. I noticed a lot of plastic waste, even with no people present. Camels were everywhere, and we often had to slow down as flocks of sheep crossed the road.

We hiked a short distance on the coast to see the gorgeous waters of the Gulf of Aden. As waves crashed against the rocky coast, I lamented that such a beautiful country was being destroyed by conflict. Nature's beauty has no refuge from man's destruction. Yemen has experienced extreme tragedy and turmoil and—as of this writing—is in the midst of one of the worst humanitarian crises in recent years. It saddens me that we never see beautiful images from countries in conflict, as if beauty cannot exist inside of conflict, as if all these places have to offer is warfare and despair. I wonder how these places would be thought of differently, how they would be assisted and protected, if more photos and stories of their beauty and humanity, rather than their tragedy, were shared.

Metro Detroit has the largest population of Arabs in the U.S., so I had come to know and love Middle Eastern cuisine, with Yemeni and Lebanese topping the list. Royal Kabob is a Yemeni restaurant in Hamtramck that my family frequents. The rice pilaf, *shish tawook* (chicken kebabs), and tabbouleh always keep us going back.

We hiked a short distance to get a closer view of the stunning turquoise waters of the Gulf of Aden, off Yemen's eastern coast.

As we moved closer and closer to our lunch spot in Hawf, my mouth was watering. We finally arrived at a small restaurant, though that word seems too big for this one-man operation. The proprietor grilled very fresh fish from the fisherman across the street and made traditional Yemeni bread in a round clay oven. He used a stick to get the bread to adhere to the oven's walls. I later would see an older woman on the roadside making bread in a similar way in Georgia.

The small establishment boasted two long plastic tables and a few plastic chairs, enough seating for the lunchtime rush. Our simple and delicious meal was completed by *masoub,* a dessert of honey drizzled over mashed bananas and butter served on top of hot bread. It was the perfect meal, and while my time in Yemen was short, it was worth crossing the border to get a taste of this beautiful nation.

central african republic

KÖDÖRÖSÊSE TÎ BÊAFRÎKA, as it's called in Sango, the lingua franca, is a country largely overlooked, politically unstable, and far too often pitied by visitors. As one of the world's poorest countries, the Central African Republic (CAR) may lead many people to assume that it leaves much to be desired. I found otherwise. In advance of my trip, I had spoken to several people who each had negative thoughts of the nation:

I was told of streets littered with United Nations peacekeepers and of a boring capital city with not much to offer. Right before my trip, I saw images another traveler posted that felt patronizing and irresponsible. I was incensed, and the rage fueled my visit to the nation. I was on a mission to find beauty, happiness, positive stories of people who live in the CAR. I did not have to look far. I simply needed to look through the right lens—a lens that values every country in the world and makes an effort where many travelers do not.

The CAR's capital, Bangui, is expensive and difficult to get to, but I had to go. In the 10 days preceding my trip, I visited Iran, Iraq, Oman, and Yemen. I was exhausted, but I had to go. With a last-minute booking, I managed to wedge the CAR between visits to Yemen and Turkmenistan. I lost luggage in the madness of flying from Oman to Qatar to Kenya to the CAR; I was switching continents and countries like I was simply changing channels. Still, I had to go.

On my flight into Bangui, I was stunned by the beauty of the landscape. The Ubangi River—whose name I didn't even know prior to this trip—majestically cut through dense forest, forming the border between the CAR and the Democratic Republic of the Congo.

When I landed, I was bombarded by people who wanted to help me with my bags. As the carousel—after several rotations—came to a halt without my bag in sight, my stomach dropped. Another airline lost another bag. With *"non merci"* on repeat as I waited in line, my intermediate French kicked in for me to file my lost luggage claim. There was not another flight coming in for two days—the day I was leaving. It was 100°F (38°C) outside and I didn't even have a short-sleeve shirt.

Not letting my lost bag deter my efforts, I hopped in the car sent by

Desire, a local journalist, was kind enough to spend two days showing me Bangui from the back of a motorcycle taxi.

the hotel and was driven through the main thoroughfare, which was lined with stalls of fruits and shoes, among other necessities. Bangui had that typical African buzz: motorcycles speeding by, mothers with babies on their backs, men drinking beers at plastic tables and hawking mobile credits and chewing gum in traffic. Though Africa's 54 countries have distinct differences, I cannot help but smile at the similarities. I often refrain from speaking about the continent of Africa in a larger sense, but something about her entirety brings me to life. Riding on a motorbike, squished between my driver and a local guide—a journalist named Desire—I felt as at home as I have in any of her 54 countries.

In Bangui, I found beauty in simplicity, in characters I met, and in stories I heard. There was the woman who was roasting plantains on an open flame. Her smooth dark skin stood out against the red-and-green printed dress that fell slightly off her shoulders, her hair neatly plaited. There was Prince, who dropped out of school due to the political conflict and now sold bread—some days making 40,000 CFA francs ($73.44). There was the man selling mobile credits who agreed to allow me to take his picture but refused to smile. (Trying to get African men to smile with teeth seems impossible.)

In Bangui, I found splendor in simplicity. This woman's effortless beauty drew me in as she performed her daily task of roasting plantains.

We visited a market in town so that I could buy a shirt and see what else was on offer. While perusing the stalls, Desire asked if I wanted a coffee. My instinct was to say no, as the temperature crept toward 105°F (41°C), but I decided to enjoy a local staple. I splurged and ordered milk and sugar that was well worth the extra 13 cents—the coffee put hair on my chest and left my hands shaking as the caffeine coursed through my veins.

I stuck out like a sore thumb in Bangui, which didn't bother me much because people were curious and I was able to have interesting conversations. I met a group of young men who worked in the market and who kindly offered me a chair in the shade in a futile attempt to bring down my body temperature while I drank the hot coffee. We talked about politics, the ongoing civil war, and reducing single-use plastic, something they had never thought of before. After I quickly explained, they understood the importance. While sitting with them, I bought a shirt, and when asked if I wanted a bag to put it in, I looked at one of them with a knowing glance and he said, *"Non, parce que c'est en plastique!"* They may forget our conversation years from now, but I hope in some small way I made them think before grabbing the next plastic bag.

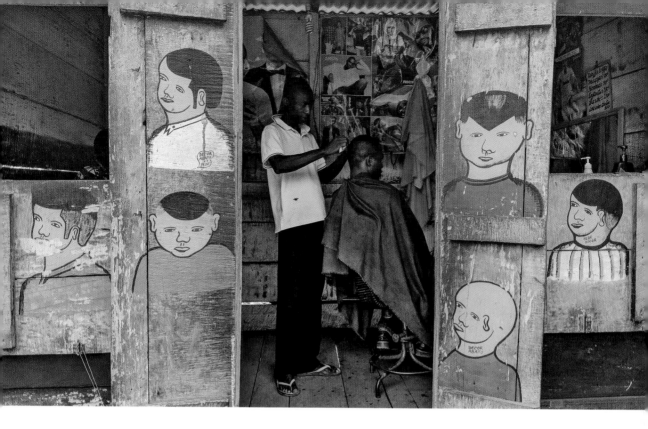

After finishing my coffee and our conversation, I spotted a man walking down the street pushing a huge cart full of charcoal. He was wearing flip-flops and his brow glistened, his pitch-black skin taut on his face. His name was Blaise. He told me that he had just pushed this cart 28 miles (45 km), a feat that most able-bodied men could not pull off. He had somehow managed to achieve his goal in four hours, a task that he does three to four times a week to support his wife and three children.

My visit to the Central African Republic made me consider in a way I never had the importance of Africans traveling around the continent and sharing stories with the world. When we tell our stories, most of us do not patronize each other, nor obsess over poverty and lack of material wealth. When I travel, I see people as they are. I do not define them by their circumstances or their wealth or lack thereof. I meet them where they are.

What I saw in Bangui, as I have seen all over the continent, was a beautiful city full of culture, love, joy, and people trying to survive despite the hand they've been dealt. What makes one way of life better, more full, richer than another? If you want to find suffering and poverty, it will be there. If you want to find joy and people living their regular lives in a dignified way, you can find that, too. It all depends on the lens through which you see.

Photographing barbershops all over the world reminds me that we are more similar than we are different.

Turkmenistan

TURKMENISTAN IS PERHAPS THE least known of the "Stans," the five former Soviet republics that compose the Central Asia region. Getting a visa to Turkmenistan is notoriously difficult, but after working with a tour company, Wild Frontiers, I managed to secure mine on the first try. Though it was my last of the Stans, I knew from speaking to other travelers that Turkmenistan was nothing like its neighbors.

ASIA

I arrived in Ashgabat, the capital, at 4:35 a.m. on a two-hour flight from Dubai. (Sometimes I wonder how my body even managed to survive this entire journey. The middle-of-the-night flights were brutal, but they were often the only option to get to rarely visited places.) The Ashgabat airport, built in 2017, is shaped like a bird and has lights that move in sync to make it seem as though the bird is flying. The all-white airport was shiny, new, and very empty, a sign of things to come.

Turkmenistan is easily one of the most fascinating countries. My experience in Ashgabat was quite bizarre. Closed off from the rest of the world—internet access is scarce—the dictatorship is fierce and the country receives fewer than 9,000 tourists a year.

My first impression of Ashgabat was similar to the airport: Everything seemed new, shiny, empty, and white. In fact, Ashgabat has a Guinness World Record for having the world's highest density of buildings made from white marble. It boasts 543 buildings outfitted with white marble from Turkey and Italy, collectively covering nearly 50 million square feet (4.6 million m²). If you own a car in Ashgabat, it must be white. When you leave town and reenter the city, it is expected that your car will be clean. Seriously.

When you are a dictator of the country with the world's sixth largest natural gas reserves, you do things like spend $90 million to build the world's largest enclosed Ferris wheel or what was once the world's tallest flagpole. Everything felt more for show than enjoyment as the streets remained largely empty and incredibly pristine. And Turkmenistan takes urban planning to a whole other level. The new area of the city is perfectly planned with the utmost attention to detail.

With 543 buildings, the capital of Ashgabat holds a Guinness World Record for having the world's highest density of buildings made from white marble.

Visiting the Door to Hell, which is in the middle of nowhere, meant camping and dinner cooked on an open fire.

With no advertisements on buildings and a lack of internet, Turkmenistan felt more like North Korea than North Korea did. I often felt as if I was being watched. In a country of nearly six million people, I rarely saw anyone on the wide, incredibly clean streets. When I did see life, it was women cleaning the streets or street sweeper trucks. I never saw people casually walking down streets or other guests in the hotel, and I only saw a few people eating in restaurants. I kept asking where the people were, but I never really got a straight answer.

On my last day, I pushed my guide, Tylla, the country's only female tour guide, to show me a bit more of normal life. We visited some areas on the outskirts of the city, where people live. I popped into a small grocery store to get a bottle of water, and it was nothing like the other parts of the city. There were other people in the store, and of course they wanted to take a picture with me. The area was not as modern, but it felt lived in. We went to a small mall where I saw the wealth of fabrics that married women had to choose from to cover their heads and their massive faux buns. I also learned that married women bite their scarves when in the presence of their mother-in-law because they should not speak louder than her out of respect.

We went to a food market where locals were shopping for fresh meat, spices, and other goods. I was quite the spectacle, and a number of people asked to take pictures with me. They rarely see tourists, and Black tourists are even rarer. A Black woman with no hair, I'm willing to bet, was a first for everyone in that market. I also met two female college students who, in line with their culture, wore red dresses and put their hair in two long braids.

Though there was still a lot of regiment in day-to-day life, it was refreshing to see *life* and *people* after such emptiness throughout the city.

The number one item on my Turkmenistan bucket list was the Darvaza gas crater, also known as the Door to Hell. The crater is about a three-hour drive from Ashgabat through the Karakum Desert. We arrived at the crater well before sunset and, honestly, I was unimpressed. The fire was burning, but it was quite anticlimactic and felt like a waste of a three-hour drive.

We set up camp about 200 feet (60 m) from the crater behind a small hill. Our driver, Vepa, who was watching a Gucci Mane video during our ride, packed the car full of everything that we would need in the middle of nowhere. He had tents, sleeping bags, fresh meat and vegetables, cookware, tables, and chairs. Though this overnight was very basic, we were well equipped. Vepa put up our tents and, with a bit of help from Tylla and me, made a nice little barbeque for dinner, including beef, chicken, and grilled vegetables cooked on a small fire made with wood that he gathered nearby. (Side note: To my future husband, I hope that you can make a fire in a desert in the middle of nowhere.)

Female college students in Turkmenistan wearing their uniform: a red dress and two braids in their hair

As the sun set, we made our way back to the Door to Hell, and I was stunned. The fiery pit is a sight to behold once the sun goes down. The orange glow was simply surreal in the barren desert. From the edge, you can feel the heat of the massive methane reserve that has kept the fire burning continuously for more than 40 years. The pit itself is otherworldly. The rocks and flames of varying sizes looked like the surface of another planet. We walked around and snapped pictures and gazed at this natural wonder before heading to bed.

Around 4 a.m. I had to use the bathroom, which I did under the brilliance of the night sky. Best bathroom ever! Afterward, I climbed to the top of the small hill to get one more glance at this mystical site. The glow of the orange pit coupled with a clear sky full of a million stars is a scene you cannot see anywhere else in the world. *Phenomenal* only begins to describe its beauty. I long for the day when technology allows me to snap a picture exactly as my eyes see. Bonus if I can capture the feeling as well.

georgia

TRAVELING AROUND THE WORLD can be incredibly complicated, and I was lucky to have a supportive community behind me. In particular, my incredibly selfless follower turned friend and logistics coordinator, Anna. A couple of words under an image on Instagram led her to assisting me with blog content and the logistics of my journey for the last 70 countries. After a year of working together, we met in

person for the first time in Azerbaijan, and she joined me on my adventures in Georgia.

Georgia is located in the Caucasus Mountains of western Asia. Just across the Black Sea from eastern Europe, it is a country where you can feel the influences of the entire region. We touched down in Tbilisi, the capital, on a gray and chilly April day. We were met by our driver, Mose, and our guide, Ia, whose striking red hair, abnormal in the region, led me to ask if she was local; indeed she is Georgian.

We didn't waste any time getting an introduction to this fifth-century city. We started in Metekhi, one of the earliest inhabited areas of Tbilisi. Today, the elevated neighborhood gives you a perfect view to the Old City below. Next we went to the Sulphur Baths, where the city began to come alive. Tbilisi, a word that means "warm place," sits atop sulfuric hot springs that make for great thermal baths. The Abanotubani area is where most of the bathhouses are found, and the Orbeliani Baths stood out with their colorful facade. The unmistakable Islamic architecture featured arches and stunning blue Persian tile work, evidence of a centuries-old invasion.

At the Orbeliani Baths, we rented a room with a sulfur hot tub that was around 113°F (45°C) for an hour for 50 lari, or $18.55. For another 20 lari each, or $7.42, we had five-minute body scrubs from a Georgian woman who rubbed me down better than any man ever has. It reminded me of the hammam experiences I've had in Morocco and Tunisia.

ASIA

Georgia, the birthplace of wine, has winemaking methods dating back 8,000 years. Traditionally, Georgian wine is made in a *qvevri,* a type of clay vessel.

The food in Georgia officially turned me into a foodie. Chasing the next best dish in Georgia was like a game. The country has a culinary prowess to which the rest of the world needs to catch up. Yet most lists of the world's best cuisines never include Georgia—or many countries outside of the Western world, for that matter. I am happy to give you the lowdown on places that your favorite travel site rarely talks about.

It started near the Orbeliani Baths at a quaint, understated restaurant called Culinarium Khasheria. The gorgeous blond wooden tables were accentuated by turquoise chairs and light fixtures. The meal kicked off with *guda,* a soft and spongy sheep's cheese, served alongside fresh greens and beautiful red tomatoes. Then we had a sublime *chikhirtma,* a soup made with chicken broth, mint, lime, and egg. As if things could not get any better, we had the succulent and complex *shkmeruli,* fried chicken smothered in cream, milk, ginger, garlic, and green *adjika,* a typical Georgian paste made with hot peppers.

Outside of Tbilisi in the Kakheti region, we stopped along the road at a small house where an older woman was baking bread. She was making it in a circular clay oven, sticking it on the sides to bake, similar to how I saw a gentleman making it in Yemen. I love sharing other cultures, especially with those who may never travel outside their home countries. I pulled up the video from Yemen and showed it to the woman, who was thrilled to see the commonality.

My favorite meal in Georgia was *shkmeruli,* fried chicken smothered in cream, milk, ginger, garlic, and spicy green *adjika.*

We visited Pheasant's Tears, an organic winery and restaurant started by an American artist and his partner. Rather than order from the menu, we allowed the owner and chef to dictate our meal. The food was stunningly fresh and light, with colors that popped. We had salad with tomatoes, onions, cucumbers, greens, and a delicious homemade dressing, then a beet puree served on crostini and topped with cilantro and other greens. Freshly grilled mushrooms, lightly seasoned to allow the earthy taste to shine through, rounded out our light lunch.

Back in Tbilisi we ate traditional *khachapuri,* freshly baked bread filled with melted cheese, and *khinkali,* meat-filled dumplings best eaten by first taking a bite of the corner and drinking the broth. Our final meal was at Shavi Lomi, a beautiful restaurant that makes you feel like you're in someone's home. We had beef shank cooked in saperavi wine and served

with creamy mashed potatoes and a side of fried chicken and grits. Every single day of our five-day visit, we ate well.

Then there was the wine. Georgia is the birthplace of the art of winemaking, which is a UNESCO intangible cultural heritage and dates back 8,000 years. Given this is wine's home, it is plentiful, delicious, and cheap.

In the Kakheti region, about 40 miles (64 km) outside Tbilisi, we visited the Giuaani Winery and were rewarded with beautiful grounds that were just as striking even with the rain showers that accompanied our trip. Here I saw firsthand the *qvevri,* a clay vessel within which traditional Georgian wine is made, as well as the underground spaces where they store the wine to age. After tasting too many wines, I wound up drinking wine from a *kanci,* a vessel made from a hollowed goat's horn. We also went to G. Vino Wine Bar, where the owner described the nuanced differences between commercially produced wines and natural wines. We drank sparkling wines and white wines, red wines and rosés. We drank wine made in qvevri and wines made using modern techniques. I learned new grapes, such as saperavi, mtsvane, and tsitska. And I brought home wines and drank them fast, reminiscing with each sip. While I loved exploring both the bustling cities and lush countryside of Georgia, it is the food and wine that will take me back again and again.

In the ancient town of Mtskheta, you can see the confluence of two rivers, the Aragvi and Mtkvari.

russia

AFTER 166 COUNTRIES, obtaining visas was becoming a new hobby, and each experience was different—ranging from the comical to the frustrating. On the application form for my Russian visa, they ask which countries you've visited in the past 10 years. I chuckled to myself as I attached my list as an addendum to my application. The woman working the window asked me what the extra

sheets of paper were. She was surprised and said they had never had someone apply who had been to so many countries. Luckily, my visa came through without a hitch.

The stern face that greeted me at immigration in the St. Petersburg airport rocked my nerves a bit. Having said goodbye to Anna in country 166, Belarus, I was on my own. I didn't know much about what to expect in Russia. The first question I was asked was, "What's your nationality?" Even as the officer held my American passport in her hand. (*Insert eye roll emoji.*) But soon enough I was allowed to enter the country.

For nearly a year I had been working with Four Seasons Hotels. Partnering with the luxury hotel chain meant that in exchange for a complimentary night or two, I produced content for my social media, sharing my experience with my audience. My time in St. Petersburg was made magical because of the Four Seasons Hotel Lion Palace, housed in a 19th-century royal palace in the Admiralteysky district. While in the City of Palaces, sleeping in one felt like the only logical option. The historic hotel exemplifies the opulent stylings of imperial Russia, and its impeccable staff makes you feel like royalty.

From my balcony, I was floored by the beauty of the gilded dome of St. Isaac's Cathedral, which is flanked by 12 bronze angel statues. It reflected the city's opulence, and St. Isaac's is easily one of the most beautiful cathedrals I have ever stepped foot in. The centuries-old building is filled with paintings and gold trimmings that rival churches of Rome. The paintings on the ceiling depict fantastical scenes from the Bible. The towering bronze doors are

Located in Moscow's historic Red Square, St. Basil's Cathedral is a brightly colored Orthodox church dating back to 1561.

covered with ornate sculptures. The Russians are some fancy folks!

Speaking of fancy, to enjoy Russia properly requires a bit of splurging—one needs to drink lots of champagne and eat lots of caviar. I did a tasting at the Four Seasons: The bubbly was ice-cold, and it came with two types of caviar, as well as salmon roe served with sour cream, chives, and other accoutrements. Caviar is definitely an acquired taste—it's briny and a bit fishy—but paired with the right cracker and champagne, it is a great appetizer. The tasting fit the indulgent nature of the Russia I experienced.

Caviar and champagne aside, Russian food was surprisingly delicious all around. At breakfast, I ate traditional pancakes made with cottage cheese and raisins. Lunch was borscht, a beet soup. And everything was served with sour cream, a Russian obsession.

But my favorite meal was in the home of one of my social media followers, Daria, who offered to host me. Whenever possible, I love to eat a local meal in someone's home. I feel there is no better way to experience the true culture of a place.

On my ride to her house, my taxi driver attempted to give me a tour of the city, in Russian. He extended his kindness by ensuring I made it into Daria's front door before driving off with a *"Do svidaniya!"* out the window.

Daria served a traditional meal of soup, bread, beets, and fried fish paired with vodka shots, also very common on Russian dinner tables. I added cherry juice to soften the bite. Daria served a dessert called *kartoshka*—dense chocolate in the shape and size of an American potato—a specialty in St. Petersburg.

Driving through the streets of St. Petersburg, you are regaled by the luxury and royalty of the city. The crown jewel is the Winter Palace, a part of the State Hermitage Museum. Commonly known as the Hermitage, the five interconnected buildings form the world's second largest art museum, which dates back to 1764, when Catherine the Great founded it with her own personal collection. When I went, lines were wrapped around the corner.

Luckily, I had a tour arranged by the Four Seasons. Inside, I got a feel for what real wealth was back in the days of European dominance. The architecture is detailed, the artwork magnificent, the carvings intricate, the chandeliers brilliant, and all of the gold! If you get a chance to visit, don't forget to look up. The gold ceilings, decorated with frescoes and intricate carvings, were the best part.

While visiting the museum was truly a dream come true, the crowds—which were shoulder to shoulder—proved to be too much. I ended up leaving sooner than planned. Because I have a three-year

The Four Seasons Lion Palace hotel in St. Petersburg offers uninterrupted views of neighboring St. Isaac's Cathedral.

visa, I plan to go back in the depth of winter, when I hope the freezing temperatures will mean smaller crowds.

On my way back to the St. Petersburg airport, I chatted with my driver about our personal travels. Though he spoke English, he mentioned his wife only speaks Russian. I asked if he gets tired of translating for her when they are abroad. He told me that he didn't have to. She manages to communicate with others despite language barriers and has taught him how to do the same. "Don't speak with your mind, speak with your heart," she told him.

That idea resonated with my feelings about the places I have been and the experiences I have shared with perfect strangers. I wish we all could get past our differences and realize it isn't about skin color, religion, or where you're born. When we get down to our core, we're all just people, all the same, all just a brain and a heart.

Moscow is a one-and-a-half-hour flight from St. Petersburg that you should not take. The two cities are connected by a three-and-a-half-hour train ride that allows you to skip all the fun of airport security and driving outside of the city center. I'm out here learning these lessons so you don't have to.

Russian cuisine did not disappoint: I enjoyed caviar, borscht, and blini, small pancakes typically served with sour cream and fruits.

Unfortunately, most of my sightseeing in Moscow took place in the back of a taxi because my time was spent running to different embassies to secure visas to Chad, Cameroon, and Venezuela. This is one of the downsides of visiting every country in the world on a time crunch: You spend a lot of your travel time planning your next destination.

Still, I was able to see plenty of Moscow's beauty. My hotel, the Four Seasons Moscow, sat just steps away from Red Square and the Kremlin. I became completely enamored with the bright colors of St. Basil's Cathedral, an Orthodox church in Red Square.

But it took me a while to enjoy St. Basil's. Whenever I walked around the historic city center, a number of tourists took my picture without permission, even when I was obviously disgruntled by the intrusion. It made sightseeing nearly impossible. I was left dodging camera lenses and finding ways to feel less uncomfortable, rather than focusing on the beauty of the city laid out before me. Thankfully, a very kind doorman from the hotel escorted me to St. Basil's early one morning so I could get a picture without becoming the object of fascination. It's amazing how much I have come to rely on the kindness of strangers.

One evening I spent an hour walking around Red Square, listening to music, and offering to take pictures of families and couples I spotted taking selfies. I bumped into three Black men from the U.S. One lived in Moscow and the other two were visiting. We became a spectacle in the busy square, but we were able to escape to a spot serving margaritas and Mexican food.

Before traveling to Russia, a number of my social media followers had told me that Russians don't like Africans or Black people. People inundated me with their negative experiences. But I went in with an open mind and positive attitude. Though there were moments when I became the center of attention—by tourists and locals alike—I was met with kindness from Russians at every turn. It was another reminder that one person's story is not the only experience to be had.

One of the most common questions I receive is, "Which countries are safe for Black people?" I understand where this comes from, but I hate the question nonetheless. Damn you, white supremacy, for the years of oppression and making people feel they won't be welcomed in different countries! Though I have certainly dealt with racism and anti-Blackness in my travels, it is nowhere near the majority of my experience. The positive far outweighs the negative. My hope is that the stories of my journey ease the minds of Black people who wish to venture to more parts of the world. Follow my motto: If something bad should happen, shake it off and keep going. The world is yours! It's all of ours.

The ceilings of St. Isaac's Cathedral are covered with paintings depicting scenes from the Bible.

guinea-bissau/guinea

THIS IS LESS A STORY ABOUT visiting two countries and more about the beauty of spontaneity and trusting strangers. I have been sharing my travel adventures on Instagram since 2012. As my community grew, more and more people connected me with others in various countries. When I posted my arrival in Guinea-Bissau on Instagram, a friend from Rome put me in touch with her brother, Cafary, in Bissau, the capital.

We met up my first evening for beers, and he helped acclimate me to the city.

The following day, I visited the local market, which was full of color. I saw green plantains and avocados, oranges, and red onions. There were heaps of green peppers, piles of brown potatoes and red tomatoes, orange carrots, and green scallions. A whiff of cilantro, my favorite herb, made me smile. The market was packed mostly with women buying and selling goods. I loved the hustle and bustle of it all. Everything brought me joy.

As I made my way to the port, the dynamics changed. While the market was filled with women at work, the port was filled with men working on the bright blue traditional fishing boats. On the boats were giant fishing nets and plastic tarps, jerricans full of gasoline, and men buzzing about as they readied the vessels for the next shift.

That evening, I met Cafary and his cousin Marvin for dinner. We started looking at Google Maps to see where they could take me next, with hopes of showing me more of Guinea-Bissau beyond the capital. I kept zooming out, seeing how close we were to Guinea. I had been lamenting the fact that I would have to return in June to cross Guinea off my list, due to logistics and a lack of time. Yet it was so close, and my visa for Guinea had arrived that afternoon. Serendipity seemed to be calling!

Anxious to cross off the neighboring country, I asked if we could go. At first, Cafary said no, claiming the border was too far. I kept pushing. It was just four hours from where we sat—I've driven much farther in a single day. Marvin joined my pleas, and after 15 minutes we decided we would go to Guinea. I thought we would leave in the

AFRICA

On the border of Guinea-Bissau and Guinea is a Fula village where motorcycles and feet are the primary modes of transportation.

morning, but they had other plans. *"Tout suite!"* Cafary said. Translation: "Right now!"

I was excited for our adventure, and around 10:30 p.m. we stopped at my hotel and their house to grab a few things. We finally hit the road at midnight.

Here I was in a car, in the middle of the night, in an unfamiliar country with two men I barely knew, on my way to visit another new country. Some of you may think that I am crazy or that I put myself in harm's way. I assure you I was fine. I am good at reading energy and always manage to find the right people. I am not afraid of other humans—and you shouldn't be either!

I stayed awake for as long as I could while we drove through the pitch-black rural areas of Guinea-Bissau, the headlights revealing nothing but road ahead and trees around us. I dozed off around 2 a.m., but the bumpy roads kept me from deep sleep.

Around 5 a.m., we entered a small Fula village on the border of Guinea. Though Google Maps showed a road into the neighboring country, we could not find it. We drove back and forth twice with no luck.

As the sun's rays began to peek above the horizon, signs of life began to appear. It was Ramadan, and the first person we saw was a Muslim woman. She refused to speak to Cafary, a man, while she was alone. We spotted a light in a house and a group of men on the porch. They pointed us in the right direction, but the road was closed. We decided to take a quick nap until the rest of the villagers awoke.

When we woke up, a man was approaching the car. I immediately covered my head, feeling more comfortable talking to men in this small and seemingly conservative Muslim village that way. He introduced himself as the one responsible for the border crossing. Foolishly, I thought he would just raise the gate and we would cross right into Guinea. No such luck! He wanted to charge us an insane amount to take the car across the border, and we refused to pay. Then, after two hours of explaining my goal to reach every country in the world, the customs officer hopped in the car and joined our spur-of-the-moment adventure.

A small gate was raised and we left Guinea-Bissau, then drove down a nondescript road

Upon entering Guinea, the immigration officer did not have the passport stamp, but he agreed instead to take a picture with me at the border.

through small villages, stopping to greet people. A few kids on their way to school hitched a ride on the back of our car. As we made our way farther into country 169, we saw women fetching water from a well, mango trees littered with dust from the evening breeze, and cashew trees with bright red fruit peeking out from green leaves. White bedsheets blew in the breeze beneath trees with bountiful red flowers. I noticed a man whose style was striking in this rural setting. He had on a straw hat that was frayed by time and a printed shirt whose original color was changed by the African soil. I took his picture just so I could remember his swag.

As we continued making our way deeper into Guinea, we came across the Kogon River, which could only be crossed by boat. Women were washing clothes on the riverbanks, and a small boat was preparing to cross, but not before those aboard emptied all the water from the bottom. It was unclear when a boat large enough to carry us and the car would come, so after a few pictures on the river bank, we had to turn back.

Though I was disappointed we couldn't see more of Guinea, I cherish that late-night drive with two strangers turned friends. I will forever laugh about the border guard who wanted to deny us entry but then came along for the ride! Our little adventure was short-lived, but it was one for the books.

The markets of Bissau, Guinea-Bissau's capital city, are filled with brightly colored, freshly picked fruits and vegetables.

cabo verde

CABO VERDE IS AN ARCHIPELAGO and the westernmost point of Africa. It comprises 10 volcanic islands just west of Senegal, its closest neighbor. During our four-day stay, Elton and I explored Santiago, home to the capital and largest city, Praia. Though other islands, such as Sal and Boa Vista, receive more visitors and reportedly have better beaches, Santiago was perfect for a taste of Cabo Verdean culture.

AFRICA

Cabo Verde was a Portuguese colony, and Portuguese architecture remains ever present throughout the island. Cidade Velha, in the south of Santiago, is the oldest settlement in the country, founded in 1462. Remnants of the colonizers are seen in its cobblestone streets and brightly colored colonial buildings.

Set on the shores of the Atlantic, Cidade Velha is the perfect place for a day trip. We enjoyed fresh fish at a small restaurant on the beach and watched children play in the chilly waters. As waves crashed on the rocky shore, the children ran away. When the waters retreated, the children threw rocks and yelled before the waves circled back in an act of revenge, leaving the young kids running back to shore again.

We hired a taxi to drive us about an hour and a half to Tarrafal in the north. We drove along winding roads that cut through mountains reminiscent of the mountainous landscapes of Jordan and Utah. At the beach, an energy in the air reminded me of Salvador de Bahia, Brazil, one of my favorite cities in the world. The beach was crowded, but not with foreign tourists and the hawkers who often sell to them. Instead, this beach was filled with locals playing volleyball, soccer, and Frisbee. One man was throwing a Frisbee so hard I wondered if his enviable obliques came from years of playing the game.

We lazed under the African sun, chatted with locals, listened to music, and admired the Cabo Verdean men, whose dark skin hugged their muscles. Santiago has *beautiful* people.

On our drive back from Tarrafal, the mountains lay in the path of the sun as it moved closer to the horizon. Clouds loomed in the distance. The entire scene felt mystical, and I asked our driver to pull over so I could take it all in and savor the moment. Out of the car, I asked out loud, "Is this heaven?"

On our last day, we explored Praia. In need of a haircut, I popped into a barbershop, then traversed the narrow streets, checking out different shops and enjoying a lunch of fresh fish. As I was constantly working on the road, I used the colorful streets as backdrops for a campaign I was shooting for a clothing brand. In the evening we went to a popular restaurant that served delicious local grouper wrapped in banana leaves and paired with steamed cassava. The restaurant also had live music, fitting for a country known for its music. All around Praia, you can have a drink or dinner and enjoy the tunes of local musicians in numerous places.

Throughout our stay in Santiago, we did not see very many tourists, which was refreshing because most of the world in 2019 felt like it was suffering from bouts of overtourism. Just before reaching Cabo Verde, I was in popular tourist destinations such as Cancun, Moscow, and Dubai. I saw firsthand how many of the world's top destinations cater to tourists at the sacrifice of their own culture. The overcrowded streets, the imported souvenirs, and the constant harassment from tour guides and shopkeepers are enough to keep me off the beaten path.

In Cabo Verde I could people-watch and have more authentic experiences. I loved watching locals enjoy their own beaches, a stark contrast from some locales with privatized beaches that cater to tourists over locals. I reveled in being where locals can afford to live and welcome the few tourists they receive. I enjoyed a space where locals took pride in their homes and were able to enjoy their land rather than stand to the side of visitors.

With 600 miles (966 km) of coastline across 10 islands, there is no shortage of Atlantic beaches in this small island nation.

gabon

GABON WAS MY FOURTH STOP on a multicountry tour through Central Africa. In a country with 84.5 percent of its landmass covered by rainforest, it was fitting that our first adventure took us deep into the trees. I was joined by my friend Sal, who had already visited every country in the world. A mutual friend connected us in 2018, when I announced my goal and he had completed his. He was great to lean on

AFRICA

for advice. His best recommendation was to get to the harder places earlier in the journey so I wasn't close to the finish line with tons of difficult-to-obtain visas. Having been in touch since I had more than 80 countries left, we decided to finally meet in Gabon, country 174.

Our guide, Nikita, told us it would be a two-hour drive to our destination in the rainforest. Two hours barely got us out of the city. When I inquired how much farther, I was told we would be there soon. Almost as soon as I asked the question, the paved road ended and a bumpy-ass ride ensued—so bumpy that at times our butts lifted off the seats. At the four-and-a-half-hour mark, we came upon a sign that read "Parc National des Monts de Cristal" and our hearts and butts were filled with joy . . . until we saw the bottom of the sign. We had another 26 miles (42 km) to go on an unpaved road.

The following morning, we were introduced to a park ranger named Eloge who would be our guide on a walk through the forest. Perhaps his bright green camouflage and professional hiking boots should have been a clue of what was to come. I was in my everyday wool sneakers and Sal wore Prada ones. (Yes, Sal wore Prada sneakers in a Gabonese forest.)

At the trailhead, we immediately started walking down a muddy slope. I looked at Nikita and laughed. "A walk?" What lay in front of us was a full-on jungle, the kind where your guide moves with a machete to cut down the brush. Just as that two-hour car ride turned into six, this "walk" turned into a hike, one that sometimes required us to use our hands to scramble up small rocky hills.

Despite being totally unprepared, we loved it. Our surroundings were stunning. We walked through knee-high green foliage and crossed rivers on large rocks. We saw waterfalls and bugs we had never seen before. It was all so ridiculous and amazing that all we could do was laugh.

Back in Libreville, we went out for a traditional meal. I opted for vegetables and rice and Sal ordered chicken. When our food was served, the waiter also brought us a local delicacy. He told us it what it was, but we couldn't translate. I am not an adventurous eater, so I opted out. Sal tried it while I took a video.

After posting the video on social media, it was brought to my attention that what Sal had eaten was a pangolin, a variety of species ranging from vulnerable to endangered. I was shocked and immediately removed the video from my page. Had we known, Sal never would've eaten it and I never would've filmed it. We would've politely declined.

In Gabon, 84.5 percent of the landmass is covered by rainforest. During my trip I explored the gorgeously lush Crystal Mountains National Park.

What ensued was a series of online attacks. I was accused of eating an endangered animal. Blog posts used incendiary headlines in an attempt to shame me. I do not check my direct messages very often, but when I did I was appalled by what I read. One troll wrote, "How can we find her and cook her?"

I was horrified to find out I had contributed to a lack of understanding around the pangolin's precarious status. But I was also dismayed to read so many abusive messages from those who have charged themselves with spreading awareness about its plight. This was a teachable moment, but several people chose to attack my character rather than kindly educate me on the issue.

It is impossible to know everything, which is why I love traveling and the community I have built on Instagram. We all get the chance to learn from one another every single day. But those lessons should be shared with kindness rather than shame. If you love animals, you should love humans too. It was a stark reminder of the vitriol on the internet and just one of the many reasons I have a love-hate relationship with Instagram. I'm out here trying to do my best. We all—yes, even public figures—deserve kindness in the face of unintentional mistakes.

sao tome and principe

TO REACH SAO TOME, located in the Atlantic Ocean off the coast of Gabon, I took a direct flight from Luanda, Angola. Transit between countries in Africa that had the same colonizers is easiest. Both Sao Tome and Angola are former Portuguese colonies, so my trip was a breeze. Not-so-ancient history still plays a crucial role in this part of the world, dictating access and borders, among other things. I do not tend to be picky about

AFRICA

food when I travel. I have picked bugs out of a meal and kept eating, eaten street food that my host recommended I not eat, and dined from kitchens that would not get an A rating from a food inspector. Yet, I have never had food poisoning. My stomach is coated with positive energy. I have, however, fallen victim to diarrhea. After dinner in my hotel in Luanda, I landed in Sao Tome with a stomach that was far from happy.

Having been glued to the toilet most of the night, I was nervous to head out for a daylong island tour with my guide, Fernando. I drank some water and begged my stomach to wait until I saw another bathroom. As we drove along the coast, my stomach felt like it was eating itself. I placated it with coconut water that we bought from a man on the side of the road. After a few hours on a beach, we went to a restaurant in a village for lunch and I finally felt OK enough to eat. Lucky me, my stomach had settled and the delicious food stayed in.

As we continued our drive, I was enthralled by the ocean views. The Atlantic-lapped shores had baobabs, soft golden sands, and palm trees. But for the most part, I saw no one enjoying the beaches. It shouldn't have surprised me. Despite being called Africa's "Heaven on Earth," Sao Tome is one of the least visited countries in the world.

I noticed several women washing clothes in a small river. With sheets, shirts, and underwear spread across rocks as far as the eye could see, the massive amount of clothes made the operation seem like a full-on laundromat. As I watched, they invited me to help. I politely declined. I have never been a fan of doing laundry—just ask my mom.

Fernando afforded me a deep dive into his country's culture. We had dinner at a simple but popular restaurant, where a woman grilled fresh octopus, flipping it with her hands. I drank the local beer, served in dark bottles with no label, as a soccer match played loudly on TV. We went to lunch the next day at a small restaurant owned by a beautiful woman named Gina. The space was decorated with swaths of brightly colored fabrics. As we devoured our lunch of grilled meat and bean stew, I laughed as my hosts ate their *fufu* (dough balls made from cassava) with a fork and knife. I had never seen an African do such a thing. *Garri, fufu, matoke* (green banana), and *igname pile* (pounded yams) are to be eaten with one's hands, specifically the right hand.

Here, life was different. It was simple, breezy, and full. It had similarities to other African countries yet was completely its own. Sao Tome blends island life with its unique heritage. I was all in.

In Sao Tome, women do not wear their hair short, so I stood out. One person yelled, "The man is wearing lipstick!" At an old church, Fernando overheard a young girl and boy discussing my gender. I approached and asked what they'd concluded. The girl decided that I shared a gender with her, but the boy thought I was his gender mate. It is fascinating the number of times that I am misgendered simply because of my hair. Though I do not have the largest breasts in the world, I would think, coupled with my cheekbones, the way I dress, and my typically bright lipstick, it would be obvious. But my experience has proved otherwise.

MUST-SEE: CENTER OF THE WORLD MONUMENT

Located at 0.18° N, 6.61° E, Sao Tome and Principe is the nation closest to the center of the world, where the Equator and prime meridian meet. We drove to the southernmost point of the main island and took a tiny boat across the crystal clear blue waters to Ilhéu das Rolas, a small island with fewer than 200 residents that straddles the Equator. We crossed through the sleepy village and took a short hike through the lush forest. Though it is not exactly at latitude 0° and longitude 0°, a monument marks the center of the world.

Sao Tome and Principe is the country that sits closest to 0° N 0° E, where the prime meridian and Equator meet. The location is marked by this giant map.

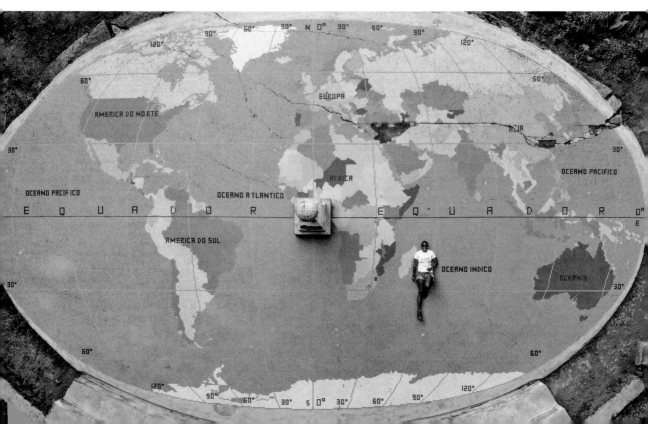

sierra leone

FROM ITS NAME, I always thought Sierra Leone, in West Africa, was a francophone country. In fact, the lingua franca is Krio, and it is anglophone. The country's name is thought to have come from a Portuguese explorer who called it "Serra Leoa," or Lion Mountains. An Italian explorer, however, introduced the modern name. This etymology got me thinking: Why do so many African countries retain names given to them by

AFRICA

European explorers? Cabo Verde, South Africa, and Nigeria, to name a few. Is it time for these countries to take back their heritage, or are the roots of colonialism just too deep?

Freetown, the capital, was established as a settlement for Africans, Americans, Caribbeans, and Brits freed from enslavement. I arrived at the city's Lungi International Airport on a cloudy day in June, not knowing that the airport was separated from the city by the Sierra Leone River. Once you get through immigration, you have to walk to a bus that takes you to a port. A 30-minute ferry brings you to Freetown. At first, I thought this was a very pleasant way to enter the country. But when I was running late for my departing flight and missed the boat, I thought it was actually inconvenient AF.

In Freetown, I was met by Madam Wokie, a Sierra Leonean clothing designer who reached out on Instagram when she saw that I was heading to her country. (I'll say it again: My community is amazing.) Her joy radiated from the inside out. I knew that I was in good hands. Finding out that we shared an exact birthday was icing on the cake. Her itinerary stunned me at every corner.

As we pulled into my hotel, I froze in disbelief. At the entrance was an enormous banner with my face on it! As if that weren't enough, Madam Wokie threw an event in my honor at her store. I had the chance to meet the mayor of Freetown and local people who had been following my journey. There was live music and drinks, and I was even able to wear one of Madam Wokie's designs. She takes hospitality to another level.

I learned a lot about Freetown's foundation through a civil war and about its battle with Ebola. We visited Fourah Bay College, the first Western-style university in West Africa, dating back to 1827. We went to Tacugama Chimpanzee Sanctuary, on the outskirts of Freetown, a refuge and rehabilitation center for chimps that are victims of the illegal wildlife trade, orphaned, or otherwise unable to fend for themselves. The whole city was a lesson in inhumanity and humanity, strife and resilience.

I also had a chance to pamper myself. I did this periodically throughout my journey to remind myself to slow down and relax, even if only for a few hours. It was necessary to keep from burning out or breaking down. In Freetown, I went to Nali Spa, which employs women from countries in the Middle East and Africa. It was one of the best massages I've ever had.

The highlight of my trip to Sierra Leone was the food! Why didn't anyone tell me how good the food is? Do other people not know? Probably not, if you think about how rarely Sierra Leone makes it on a top anything list. I did not have one bad meal in Salone, as the locals call it. Madam Wokie took me to Crown Bakery, which is so much more. This local favorite is popular with the lunch crowd. Although the decor was nothing to write home about, the food was delicious. I ate a meat stew served with jollof rice. Though it might start World War III, I will note that Salone's jollof is an excellent contender in the jollof wars.

Late one evening, we made our way to the beach to find a light bite. I allowed my host to order for me and received a goat soup. In the dark of night, my stomach growling, I dug right in. I took one large spoonful and was sure that I swallowed fire. My dining companions thought it was hilarious. When I shone the light from my cell phone into the bowl, the excessive pepper was evident. To preserve what taste buds I had left, I stuck to the large pieces of goat meat, which were a bit more forgiving. When you go to Sierra Leone, eat everything, but be sure to ask a few clarifying questions before digging in.

Though I visited Sierra Leone during the rainy season, which was not ideal, I got to enjoy Tokeh Beach, one of many on the country's more than 300 miles (480 km) of coastline.

Samoa

TRAVELING TO EVERY COUNTRY in the world requires a lot of flights. In 2019, I took 170 flights, flew 244,547 miles (393,560 km), and spent the equivalent of 25 days in the air. All that travel took me to 66 countries, 46 of which were new. Four of those 170 flights took me to the South Pacific nation of Samoa. A group of islands in the Polynesian region of the South Pacific, Samoa is incredibly far from Detroit. How far?

AUSTRALIA AND OCEANIA

Case in point: I left Michigan on July 11 at 8:29 a.m. and didn't arrive in Apia, the Samoan capital, until July 13. The dizzying 30-plus-hour journey and plane changes were worth the arrival in a lush paradise.

My time in Samoa was limited to three days, so I hit the water running. I quickly found myself on a boat heading out for some incredible snorkeling. Beneath the still waters, I spotted dory fish, made famous in *Finding Nemo*—yes, Dory is real! There were beautiful radiant coral and bright blue starfish, the likes of which I had only seen in Roatán, Honduras; Fiji; and Zanzibar. My only regret was forgetting my brand-new GoPro to capture the subaqueous adventures. Samoa boasts some of the prettiest and healthiest underwater ecosystems in the world.

Back at my hotel, I enjoyed a plate of *oka,* a traditional Samoan dish of local fish marinated in lemon juice and coconut cream and served with fried taro chips. As the afternoon turned to dusk, I laid in a hammock, listening to music as the wind swayed me softly from side to side. I watched the sunset and journaled, reflecting on my day and savoring the memories.

I woke up early for a full day of exploring Upolu, Samoa's main island. Upolu never lets you forget that you are on an island in the South Pacific. Along the coastal road, the wind blowing on my face through the lowered window, I took in the aquamarine waters glistening in every direction under the blue sky.

Upolu has a population of about 50,000 people, making it much larger than many of its South Pacific counterparts. But it still felt like a really big village. Most of the homes are single-story, colorful houses flanked by palm trees, with large covered porches that offer an escape from the sun.

We stopped for fresh coconuts on the side of the road. To my surprise, each came with a paper straw. The island has a ban on plastic bags and was moving to reduce all single-use plastic where possible. In this most remote of countries, they had enacted policies to preserve their reefs and larger environment from damage like I had seen in other parts of the world.

The number one thing on my Samoan bucket list was To Sua, a 100-foot-deep (30 m) swimming hole surrounded by lush tropical gardens. Water from the nearby Pacific Ocean fills the trench through a cave. At first glance, the wooden ladder leading into the abyss is intimidating. Strangers hyped me up to scurry down and jump in the cool waters. The ladder was steeper than I thought. In my flimsy black swimsuit, I could not help but think "You're welcome" to all the onlookers below. Finally at the wooden platform, I walked to the edge and jumped into the clear cool water. As I waded around, I looked up to the clear blue sky framed by the green trench. After a few minutes, I made my way back to the ladder and said a little prayer as I began the climb to the top.

The number one site on my Samoan bucket list was To Sua, a giant swimming hole that is a 100-foot-deep (30 m) trench surrounded by lush tropical gardens.

Tonga

I FLEW FROM SAMOA TO TONGA in an eight-seater plane that felt more like an UberXL than a commercial aircraft. The journey took us across the international date line and back again. I left Samoa on July 16, entered and exited American Samoa on the 15th, and arrived in Tonga on the 16th, all in less than three hours. Without a doubt, it was one of the most interesting flights of my trip—or at least the top five smallest planes.

AUSTRALIA AND OCEANIA

And it was well worth the time confusion because Tonga is my favorite South Pacific island.

I arrived in a very rainy Nuku'alofa, the capital city, and was concerned about the impending boat ride to the resort. Fortunately, as I ate amazingly delicious fish and coconut soup paired with a crisp New Zealand sauvignon blanc in Friend's Cafe, the gray clouds cleared. I had a picture-perfect boat ride to Fafa Island, a resort on an 18-acre (7 ha) private island that hosts up to 36 people. With barely any Wi-Fi, this was a chance to disconnect and relax.

I was welcomed to paradise with fresh coconuts, biodegradable straws, and a dense forest of palm trees in front of me. Each of the island's 13 *fales,* traditional thatched-roofed houses, offered privacy, beach access, and outdoor showers and toilets overlooking a lush garden. In the evenings, the close-knit staff played music and performed traditional dancing. Dancers rub oil on their bodies so that people can stick money to them as a sign of gratitude. Kava, a staple alcoholic drink made of a plant by the same name, was passed around. My one regret is that I only stayed two nights.

I typically wake up just before sunrise every morning. In Tonga, my body's natural alarm clock was rewarded with a sunrise over the incredibly still South Pacific. As the sun peeked above the horizon, it cast yellow upon the soft ripples, sunbeams dancing on the surface. It was the absolute perfect way to start each day in paradise.

My trip to Tonga was serendipitously timed for swimming with humpback whales. Our first day of whale chasing, island hopping, and coconut water drinking, we headed out into Pacific waters so crystal clear we could see coral as the boat sped over small waves. The deep blue waters soothed me, the large waves like rolling hills. After about 45 minutes, we spotted a humpback whale in the distance, its iconic tail surfacing briefly as it made its way back into the ocean's depths.

Swimming with whales is a lot of hurry up and wait. At the mercy of the regal creatures, we rushed to put on fins and dive into the water, only to lose sight of the giant mammals. That first day, we did not swim with whales, but we did make it to a deserted island surrounded by untouched coral reefs. We spent an hour on the island, snorkeling, eating lunch, playing with my drone, and jumping into the warm, bright blue waters from the top of the boat.

The following day was more successful. When we approached a gentle giant, it swam under the boat and I got nervous. I prayed it didn't breach and knock us over. Overcoming my nerves, I put on my fins, mask, and snorkel and climbed into the water. I made my way toward the massive creature, my nerves subsiding the closer I got. The humpback whale spun around, surfaced, and swam back down as the sunlight cut through the water's surface. The whale barely registered my presence, and a calm came over me. Realizing how small I am and how gentle these whales are was truly one of the most beautiful experiences I've had.

Back on land, I was invited to a beautiful event of a different nature. The Miss Galaxy Pageant Beauty of Oneness is a contest for *fakaleiti,* Tongan people assigned male at birth who have a "feminine gender expression." The show opened with the first ever winner of the pageant dancing to a remix of Beyoncé's "Single Ladies." Each round had beautiful, themed costumes. One was full of red lace and sequins; another featured dresses, capes, skirts, and tube tops fashioned from condoms. It was fun to watch tourists and locals alike enjoying the pageant. Hundreds of people cheered on the contestants. It was electrifying to see the performers strut across the stage full of confidence and receive so much love. Though fakaleiti face some challenges in Tonga, they are largely accepted. I wish this idea could permeate more cultures.

Completely surrounded by the South Pacific Ocean, Tonga's 170 islands offer much to explore beneath the surface, including beautiful coral reefs and humpback whales.

Tuvalu

THE ONLY WAY TO REACH FUN IS from Fiji or Kiribati. What is FUN you ask, besides a good time? FUN is the fitting airport code for the tiny international airport in the equally tiny country of Tuvalu. Composed of nine islands and a population under 12,000, it is one of smallest, most isolated, and least visited countries in the world. With only six flights landing in the country every week, it is expensive and difficult to reach.

Most people who visit are development workers or locals flying between the islands.

It was clear that I was the only tourist on the small plane from Fiji. A woman in front of me, Millie, was taken aback when she found out I was landing in FUN for fun. I sheepishly admitted that I had absolutely nothing planned. She offered to meet me in the late afternoon for an island tour.

On arrival, I got a real feel for how small this island was: The main road, which runs parallel to the runway, closes briefly whenever a plane lands. My accommodations were conveniently located, as it seemed most things were, next to the airport. With a little assurance from the woman at the front desk that I could not get lost, I set off on foot to explore.

Very few cars were on the road, just the occasional motorbike whizzing by. While I was there, the island was preparing for a conference and building living quarters for international guests. The brightly colored, seafoam green structures added a new and interesting dimension to the palm tree–dense landscape.

From the road and through a bevy of trees, I could see turquoise waters in the distance and decided to take a closer look. Once I got through the brush, an unspoiled beach with powdery white sand came into view. Just like that, I stumbled onto one of the most beautiful beaches I had ever seen.

Have you ever thought about what makes a beach beautiful? For

AUSTRALIA AND OCEANIA

Senee asked me if I wanted a coconut. Next thing I knew, he was climbing up a tree, a small machete in one hand, with impressive speed and skill.

me, it is white sands that move between your toes with ease, a backdrop of palm trees, and impossibly blue water. Special acknowledgment goes to beaches with mountainous backdrops (Copacabana in Rio De Janeiro, Camps Bay in Cape Town, and West Bay in Roatán).

On the beach, I began chatting with a man named Ben from the Netherlands. He was heading out on a small rowboat to a larger sailboat anchored offshore and asked if I wanted to join him. As he rowed us closer to the vessel, he talked to me about his NGO, Sea Stewardship, which worked in the Pacific Ocean to create awareness of global climate change. As we toured the ship, we discussed how small islands like this one are the most threatened by rising sea levels. The worst part is that they are hardly contributing to climate change. This is another reminder to consider how your behaviors can affect people tens of thousands of miles away. Climate change doesn't care about who did what. We will all be affected, even the innocent among us.

In the late afternoon, I met Millie for my official tour of the island. She drove me the entire length of its 11 miles (18 km). As we drove along the palm-lined streets, I noticed people lying in hammocks

In the early evening, Tuvalu's only runway turns into a community center, soccer field, volleyball court, and an extra-large mattress, where people sleep to catch a breeze during the stifling hot nights.

between trees, resting on benches, and doing as little as possible to avoid overheating in the summer sun. As the sun set, the blue sky turned pink and the clouds looked like cotton candy. The runway—safely without planes for the day—had been turned into a community center, soccer field, volleyball court, and extra-large mattress where many people slept to catch a breeze during the stifling hot nights.

The following day, Millie introduced me to her husband, Sam. He is a Tuvaluan politician who orchestrated the island's ownership of the .tv web domain. That decision yielded the money Tuvalu needed for paved roads on the main island. Millie and Sam kindly offered me their boat to explore some of the neighboring islands. Their friends Tekokoa and Senee joined me as driver and navigator, respectively. Tekokoa's son also came along for the ride.

We passed uninhabited islands brimming with palm trees. Even far from shore, the waters were clear enough to see the fish

swimming below. The first island we visited was the sparsely populated Funafala. It was an idyllic scene—our little boat was the only
thing on the golden sands, our four sets of footprints the only mark-
ers of human life. Senee asked me if I wanted a coconut. Is the answer
to that question ever no? Next thing I knew, he was climbing up a
tree with impressive speed and skill, a small machete in one hand.
He disappeared among the leaves, but soon coconuts began to rain
down, making his presence known. We enjoyed fresh coconut water
straight from their husks just as much as we enjoyed having this
pristine beach to ourselves.

We hopped over to another locale laden with palm trees and went
for a swim. Only one family lived on the island. Imagine that, only you
and your family living on a fairly isolated island. All the extrovert in
me could think was, Don't they get bored?

The charm of Tuvalu is in its unspoiled beaches and its community.
Everyone knows one another. Given its lack of tourism infrastructure,
I was lucky to have met Millie, whose kindness allowed me to explore
the country more than I thought possible.

Visitors in Tuvalu receive necklaces as gifts. The woman at the hotel
gave me one, and Millie, who came to see me off at the airport, gave
me two more. I keep them to remind me of the incredible kindness
of the strangers on this journey.

With a nationwide total population of just over 11,000, many of
Tuvalu's nine islands have very
small populations, the least of
which is 34 residents.

mongolia

I ARRIVED IN MONGOLIA after nearly one month exploring the South Pacific and South Korea. Mongolia is a vast country snuggled between Russia and China. With only three million people, it is the least densely populated country in the world. The most notable person of Mongolian descent, by far, is Genghis Khan, the founding father of the Mongol Empire, who lived more than 790 years ago. He is said to have

A S I A

roughly 16 million descendants living today. I knew that I wanted to go into Mongolia's countryside after seeing beautiful images of the massive Mongolian steppe. I was curious what rural life was like. Goyo Travel paired me with my guide, Buju, a nickname that means "curly." Buju is half Mongolian and half Angolan, the latter accounting for his curly hair and moniker.

As we made our way into the Mongolian steppe, I was surprised to see no paved roads, just vast open plains. Without roads or GPS, our driver knew exactly where to go. I asked Buju how, and he said he just knew. Simple as that.

Everywhere I looked, sheep were roaming, the population outnumbering people in the country. When sheep would block our path, we had to wait for them to run out of the way.

The plan was to stay with a nomadic family, but first we had to find them. When I asked how, Buju responded that the family had four girls. I was perplexed. How on earth would that help us *find* someone? How would we be able to spot four girls standing in the vast plains?

Later it all made sense. As Buju was explaining life in rural Mongolia, he told me that the round structures in this region—what I know as yurts—are called *ger* in Mongolian. It was then that I realized we were looking for four *gers* not *girls*.

Our host was Sanjmyatav, a name that my heavy English-speaking tongue clumsily pronounced. He and his family welcomed us with a warm meal of hot tea and milk and a fried bread that reminded me of *mandazi* in Uganda.

Sanjmyatav had more than 800 animals, including horses, sheep, and goats, so our lunch was very dairy heavy. In the interest of all things cultural, I drank my hot milk, ate the butter and cheese, and consumed more dairy in this single meal than I probably had in the previous year. We also had delicious fried meat, plain white rice, potatoes, and veggies.

Though there was no running water, they did have solar power, which was used very sparingly. Solar power has truly changed the lives of rural people around the world. From my mother's village in Uganda to this ger in the Mongolian countryside, I have seen solar energy allow more access and resources, from charging a simple cell phone to powering a small lamp.

Sanjmyatav and his family hosted us in the Mongolian Steppe, welcoming us with a warm meal of hot tea and milk in one of their four *gers*.

Sanjmyatav, who also works as a park ranger, took us out on his horses, which had the most enviable blond highlights I've ever seen. We made our way up the sloping hills and farther into the plains. We passed an ancient grave site that dated back to A.D. 6 and was said to be the burial grounds of noble people. We saw massive rains in the distance, but as luck would have it only blue skies followed us. After two hours—about one hour too long for comfort—we headed back to the gers.

We rounded out our day with a drive into the mountains, where we saw wild horses in the distance. Przewalski's horses are said to be the only true wild horses left in the world. I marveled at their beauty and the way they roamed freely over the wide expanse of land. As night fell, we noticed little bright eyes looking at us on our drive back to the gers. The headlights revealed gazelles prancing in the dark. It was like an unplanned mountain safari.

My time in the country was too short to see it all. I long to explore the Gobi desert, experience the Golden Eagle Festival, and see the towering 131-foot (40 m) statue of Genghis Khan in Ulaanbaatar. In Mongolia, the possibilities for adventure are endless.

bhutan

BHUTAN IS A NO-BRAINER FOR any traveler's bucket list. The government believes in "high-value, low-impact" travel, which leads to less crowded sites, a cleaner country, and a positive socioeconomic impact that doesn't dilute their culture. Nestled in the southern slopes of the eastern Himalaya, the Kingdom of Bhutan is one of the world's most unique and beautiful countries. Bhutan maintains a cultural purity that

ASIA

very few other countries have: It was never colonized, tourism only really began in 1974, and TV and internet weren't introduced until 1999. You don't feel the Western influence that is so prominent everywhere else in the world. This is a nation that measures its progress through the gross national happiness index rather than the standard gross domestic product.

On our descent into Paro International Airport, the Himalaya range came into view, its deep valleys and rolling green mountains scraping the dense and low-hanging clouds. The airport's short runway is wedged between 18,000-foot-tall (5,500 m) mountains. Fewer than two dozen pilots are able to land here; it is often considered one of the most dangerous airports in the world. I witnessed the skill of our pilot as we neared the ground and the plane was expertly maneuvered through the mountains, banking dramatically mere seconds before landing.

Idyllic. Picturesque. Stunning. Remarkable. Phenomenal. None of these words on their own can describe the beauty of Bhutan. The Himalaya are an ever present backdrop, and the Bhutanese architecture melds with the lush valley and its winding rivers. The air is remarkably pure.

The country has a calming energy that matches the kindness of its people. At the airport, I was met by my guide turned friend, Tshewang. He gave me a small wooden bowl and poured rice wine into it, a traditional offering when receiving guests. After a quick swig of the potent drink, Tshewang placed a white cloth called a *khadar* around

Adorned with colorful prayer flags, at a length of 520 feet (160 m), the Punakha Suspension Bridge can be a nerve-racking crossing. Don't look down!

my neck. This is offered as a welcome and for good wishes for guests' well-being. I happily received the welcome again at my hotel.

Nearly 75 percent of Bhutanese citizens are Buddhist, which is reflected in the way of life and much of the architecture. In each region you will find *dzongs,* or fortresses, characterized by massive doors made of wood and iron, high white walls, and red roofs. Prayer flags are seen throughout the country, major symbols of the Buddhist faith. From time to time, we saw monks walking around.

We went to a bar and I tried Bhutanese whiskey for the first time. The bottle, which read "Bhutan grain whiskey," made it seem scarier than it was. The whiskey was smooth and delicate, unlike other grain whiskeys like moonshine. I bought a bottle that still sits on my bar today.

The highlight of my trip was hiking to Paro Taktsang, better known as Tiger's Nest, a sacred Vajrayana Himalayan Buddhist site. Its monastery, finished in 1692, is built into the side of a mountain at an altitude of 10,240 feet (3,121 m). The two-mile (3.2 km) hike to the monastery begins at roughly 8,500 feet (2,600 m) above sea level and climbs more than 1,700 feet (500 m). I questioned what I had gotten myself into when I saw Tiger's Nest's staggering height from below.

The beginning of the hike was easy enough, with dirt paths and only a slight incline. We had an option to take a horse to the halfway point, but I opted to go on foot considering how tame the beginning was.

Tshewang, dressed in a *gho*—a knee-length robe-like outfit secured with a belt—was the perfect hiking partner. As I huffed and puffed, he walked in a much more relaxed manner, having done this hike more than 100 times. He offered encouragement, conversation, and laughter.

After about 30 minutes, we arrived at a fork in the road. He asked which path I wanted to take: the shorter but steeper path with better views, or the easier path. I chose the hard one. It was worth all the pain when I saw the expansive views of dense forest and the valley below. I kept stopping to take pictures (read: catch my breath) before finally reaching the halfway point, which had a cafeteria. Our final destination was still mind-bogglingly far away.

When I finally saw the entirety of Tiger's Nest, I was stunned by its beauty. The white building, accentuated with red details and a golden roof, sat in regal contrast to the brown mountain behind and the dense green forest below.

After descending then ascending one too many steps, we finally reached the monastery and had to leave our electronics behind. I was grateful for the forced unplugging. Without my devices, I paused to reflect not just on the beauty around me but on my journey to every country in the world, which was almost over.

I hiked to Paro Taktsang, or Tiger's Nest, a sacred Buddhist site on the side of a mountain containing a monastery built in 1692, at an altitude of 10,240 feet (3,121 m).

For most of my journey, I spent an inordinate amount of time strategizing and planning for the next country. I had been so hyper-focused on getting to the next place while simultaneously enjoying the country I was in that I hadn't reflected on how far I had gone. On this hike and during our quiet time in the monastery, it hit me. *Wow.* I'd made it to 190 countries—130 of which I had visited in just two and a half years. This journey toward the finish line had been at times a whirlwind. The experience had brought immense joy as well as serious frustration and tears. I had met so many people who graciously shared the best parts of their countries and cultures with me. On this mountaintop, each and every one of those moments and friendly faces came pouring in. I gave thanks to the universe for allowing me to create this life, to live it wildly, to live it fully.

The serenity was short-lived. On our way down the mountain, I was over it. I was exhausted; my body felt like I was dragging a ton of bricks. As a storm rolled in, Tshewang turned to me and said, "You just have to accept it. There is nothing we can do about it." We stood under some trees for 20 minutes in a futile attempt to wait out the heavy rain. I kept reminding myself to just accept it. We made our way down the muddy mountain, and Tshewang—ever so patient—put up with my complaints until I was inside the car. I had accepted a lot throughout this experience around the world. I was done "just accepting" for the time being.

I asked Tshewang to take me to a local place for lunch. I was the only foreigner inside the tiny establishment of just four tables. We started with an ice-cold local "super strong beer," as the Druk 11000 label claimed. Then we were served dumplings, white rice, dried pork, pork ribs, pumpkin soup, and a bowl of chilies. The pork looked like it had been pulled out of a hot chili bath. I was understandably nervous when it came with a glass of milk. Tshewang assured me it wasn't hot. What I learned: The taste buds of someone who probably had chilies in their baby bottle are different from mine. Two bites burned off every last one of my taste buds. Local food in Bhutan is spicy AF.

My time in Bhutan was truly magical. There is so much more I could talk about: seeing the giant golden Buddha statue for the first

Located atop a hill in Thimphu, the giant Buddha Dordenma statue stands 169 feet (52 m) tall and houses an additional 125,000 miniature Buddhas.

time or singing Sia at the top of my lungs in a nightclub in Thimphu; the intricacy of the architecture or all of the astounding views during extended drives that left me wondering how the entirety of one country could be so beautiful. I could laugh with you at my futile attempts at archery, the national sport—though I eventually got two arrows on the board. Or I could wax poetic about the local artist Pema Tshering, who was born with cerebral palsy but with a sponsorship from the Queen Mother became a renowned painter and carver using only his feet. I could describe the stunning majesty of Punakha Dzong, the second largest dzong in the country. I could describe the intensity of the heat as we walked to the rope bridge that prompted Tshewang to drop the top of his gho, revealing his camouflage undershirt. These moments, and more, made Bhutan a country I will visit time and time again. More than anything, though, what I hold most from Bhutan is the peace that came over me while in the country.

My adventure in Bhutan felt like it reflected my entire journey so far: beauty, pain, frustration, joy, relaxation, reflection, and a little bit of spice. What a life I was living. As we reached cruising altitude on my departing flight, I looked out the window as Mount Everest came into view, waving me off to my five remaining countries.

Located in western Bhutan, the stunningly majestic Punakha Dzong is the second largest *dzong*, or fortress, in the country.

pakistan

I LEFT BHUTAN FOR ✈ PAKISTAN, which was no easy feat. It took me 19 hours, three flights, a 10-hour layover in Delhi, India, and an overnight stay in Muscat, Oman, to get from Paro to Islamabad. If I'd had a private jet, the nonstop flight would've been two and a half hours. When I arrived at the Muscat airport to check in for my flight to Islamabad, I was surprised to see only men in line. I have been socialized to believe

women should not be in a space where there are only men and felt a bit nervous as I approached the desk. I was asked where I was traveling to at least four times, even though the line was only for flights to Islamabad. People were shocked that a woman was traveling to Pakistan alone.

To make myself more comfortable, I asked to be seated near the front of the plane in a row by myself. The kind gentlemen at the desk obliged. I put on my head scarf as I approached the boarding gate, knowing that Pakistan is a conservative Muslim country.

I began to feel more at ease when a male passenger struck up polite small talk, asking me about my travels to his country. My being there for tourism piqued his curiosity. He asked what I had planned (not much; I like to let things unfold organically), then offered his contact info should I need anything. Without asking, he brought me a luggage cart when we reached the baggage claim. So far, so good.

My visit coincided with the 72nd anniversary of Pakistan's independence, and national pride was on full display. Vendors were selling flags along the main thoroughfares and people drove by with flags attached to cars and motorcycles.

While I was touring the country, I found that my nerves at the Muscat airport had been mostly unfounded. I was grateful for the kindness of Pakistani men. I met Imran at a flag ceremony, and he invited me to his home for lunch, where we feasted on chicken, leg of lamb, and okra with his mom and other family members. I had the pleasure of explor-

A S I A

While traveling, I often buy clothes locally to add to my colorful wardrobe. This tunic, purchased in Lahore, features handmade embroidery.

Located in Lahore, the Mughal-era Badshahi Mosque, seen here at sunset, is the second largest in Pakistan.

ing Islamabad with photographers Danish and Usman, who took me to see their favorite sites.

Faisal Mosque—one of the largest mosques in the world—was built in 1986 to accommodate 300,000 worshippers. Men were wearing *shalwar kameez,* a long, brilliantly colored tunic and matching pants combination. I caught some of these men lying on the outer wall, posing for their friends' cameras. Though the mosque was closed, it gave me a glimpse into local life.

I took a four-hour taxi ride to Lahore, a colorful and vibrant city in the Punjab Province of eastern Pakistan that quickly drew me in. Given the extensive history of Lahore, which dates back to the end of the first century, I felt more of Pakistan's true culture there than in the capital. Lahore felt like the pulse of the nation.

On the first day, a torrential downpour flooded the city. As my guide and I took refuge in a shop, I watched as unbothered people waded in the waters, motorcycles continued on their missions, and no one used umbrellas. Life goes on. After waiting for nearly an hour for the rain to cease, we escaped via rickshaw and I traded a rainy day for a warm bed and room service. Sometimes, a rained-out lazy day is exactly what you need to refresh and recharge.

The following day, the sun came out and I connected with Hamd and Belal, whom I was put in touch with through an Instagram friend. We visited Masjid Wazir Khan, where Persian influence was present in the entryway tiling and courtyard. We climbed to the top of the minaret to see the city views. At the top, the 95°F (35°C) temperature, coupled with dehydration, humidity, long sleeves, and a lack of calories, made my heart start racing. The world around me spun. I warned Hamd and Belal that I might pass out, but they didn't believe me. Finally, I said, "I'm going to pass out; make sure I don't hit my head!" They kicked into gear. Belal laid me down on the floor, and gave me water; Hamd was sure to catch the embarrassing moment on camera. Even after 191 countries, I was still facing some travel woes! After water and rest, I was able to enjoy the views of the densely populated old city center from the minaret.

We then headed to a very packed Badshahi Mosque just before sunset. One of the most iconic locations in Pakistan, the building is made of red sandstone and marble and was built in 1671. The courtyard was filled with locals, tourists, couples taking wedding pictures, and worshippers. At a restaurant overlooking the mosque, we watched the sun descend below the horizon.

In Lahore, I visited the Liberty Market with Hajra, whom I met through Instagram. As she navigated me through the labyrinth of shops, I was

MUST-EAT:
STREET FOOD

Pakistan is street food heaven. I loved *gol gappa,* chickpeas served in a little fried dough cup that you dip into a tamarind sauce and then devour. There was also regional fare, including beef kebabs, chicken tikka, naan, and biryani. And all the street food was cheap. In Lahore, I watched a man on the street make puri, a flatbread made from white flour. He spun the small disk of dough as he tossed it into the oil. Twelve seconds later, it was served piping hot with chana, a mix of chickpeas, onion, ginger, garlic, and coriander. My host said it would upset my stomach and suggested I skip a tasting, but given the number of people in line, I decided to give it a try. I happily snacked on it in the car, my stomach unbothered.

While I was visiting Lahore, the old city was flooded by torrential rains. We waited out the wet weather in a small shop.

enchanted by the hand-beaded clothing, gold purses, and costume jewelry. I bought a bracelet made of brass and a piece of Farsi *kundan,* a traditional form of gemstone jewelry thought to have originated in the royal courts of Rajasthan and Gujarat.

I also went to the Wagah border at the frontier of India, about 45 minutes from the city center. After bumper-to-bumper traffic we arrived at the border about an hour before the daily military event. Directly on the border were spectators on both sides—locals well outnumbered foreigners. Huge flags waved on both sides of the border. Two years before my visit, Pakistan had lengthened its flagpole so its flag would be higher than the Indian flag. I am assuming funding came from the Bank of Petty.

As starting time neared, an amputee flag bearer made his way to the main stage and spun in circles, the flag following suit. The crowd got excited, and on the Indian side a giant flag began moving about the stands. Not to be outdone, a huge Pakistani flag appeared on the other side of the border, making its way across the sea of people. As I took in the national pride, I thought, This must be what the Olympics or World Cup feel like. It was better than any sporting event I had ever been to. The Pakistan Rangers, an abnormally tall paramilitary force, began the ceremony. They put on a show for the crowd with marching, high kicks, and precise formations. The maneuvers were mirrored on the Indian side. Eventually, the gate of the border opened and both sides came together to ceremoniously lower the flags.

At 2:35 a.m. I headed to the airport to start a 28-hour journey back to Detroit. I was tired but used to these middle-of-the-night flights after nearly 20 of them in one year. I didn't expect what came next.

At the security checkpoint, I was asked to step to the side for an extra luggage screening. No big deal. Officers went through my bags, meticulously unzipping everything. Then, three additional officers approached and asked, "Where are you from?" I replied that I'm American—even though they were holding my passport that clearly stated the fact. They then asked where I was born, to which I replied the United States—also listed on my passport. They asked if I had another passport; I lied and said no, because my Ugandan passport was irrelevant. They continued with a barrage of questions: "When did you come?" "Who do you work for?" "If you flew into Islamabad, why are you flying out of Lahore?"

I was led to an x-ray machine. It wasn't typical of the ones found in airports but like an x-ray machine that you would expect to find in a doctor's office. I was told, "People usually keep the drugs in their stomachs." Once the x-ray showed that I was not, in fact, smuggling drugs in my stomach, I was allowed to proceed to the airline check-in.

In many Muslim countries, airport screenings are separate for men and women. Women are screened inside a small room. I walked through the metal detector, then into the designated room. The female security officer groped my vagina in a way that I had never been subjected to before. Then she asked me to spread my legs and violated me again. I was shocked, shaken, and in tears.

This happened to me because I am Black. More specifically because I am visibly African. From the moment I entered the airport, I was judged and treated horribly based on my appearance. Without a doubt, this was the most traumatizing experience I have had traveling after 37 years of living and visiting 195 countries and 10 territories. It still brings me to tears.

And yet, I still look upon my time in Pakistan with fondness. I remember the kindness of strangers in the market, the beauty of the mosques in Lahore, the orange of the sunset, the green-and-white flags flailing in the winds on Independence Day, and the pride of Pakistani soldiers and spectators at the Wagah border. I had been through a lot over these 191 countries. I knew how to compartmentalize the good and the bad. I will not let the racism at the airport color my entire experience in the country. I will still gladly return to explore more of this beautiful nation.

I visited Islamabad, Pakistan's capital, on Independence Day, and people all over the city were selling and flying flags in celebration.

venezuela

I HAD BEEN GONE SIX WEEKS—and had visited at least as many countries—when I finally returned home. It was a welcome break and chance to breathe. I spent three weeks in the States, bouncing between Detroit and NYC, applying for my last visa, and enjoying some much needed time with family and friends. With four countries left across three continents, I had less than a month to reach my goal.

SOUTH
AMERICA

The islands of Los Roques gave me a front-row seat to the extensive beauty of Venezuela, which is never seen in mainstream media.

In January 2019, along with the rest of the world, I watched as President Nicolás Maduro of Venezuela announced a severing of diplomatic relations with the United States. At that time, I had 44 countries left in my journey, and Venezuela was one of them. A slight panic set in, but, always thinking ahead, I looked at the list of Venezuelan embassies around the world and found one in Russia, which was on the list of remaining countries. I applied for my visa to Venezuela using my Ugandan passport and received it in a single day thanks to the kindness of a woman at the Venezuelan Embassy in Moscow. There is always a way.

I landed in Caracas by way of Bogotá and welcomed the decrease in elevation but not the passport discrimination. I was the first to enter immigration and the last to leave. My passport changed hands five times and I was asked the same questions repeatedly. Apparently, my being there on a tourist visa was incomprehensible. I had made it this far, even with diplomatic hurdles trying to stop me—I would not be deterred.

The following day, I met my handler, Johan, on the domestic side of Simón Bolívar International Airport. Thankfully, he knew more English than I knew Spanish.

Johan was young and had a kind energy. After we checked my bags, I gave him a $5 tip for his help and asked him to point me toward the gate for my flight to Los Roques. Johan insisted on walking me to the gate, and a conversation ensued. We landed on the economic situation in Venezuela, an oil-rich country full of people who are not making a livable wage. He had what was considered a good job and was

making around 100,000 bolivares a month, roughly $5. I was flabbergasted. I had just tipped him what was considered a *full month's salary* without even giving it a second thought. He was saddened by the global image of his country. He told me this should be the best time in his life because he was a young man—22 at the time—and full of dreams, namely to learn English and move to London.

At no point in our discussion was Johan asking me for a handout or for favors. He was simply sharing the reality of life in his country. When our conversation was cut short by my boarding call, Johan shook my hand and thanked me. I thanked him back, then rolled up a $20 bill and put it in his hand. He was so grateful that he began to cry, uncontrollably. Tears ran down my own cheeks. I gave him a hug and headed to the bus that would take me to the small plane to Los Roques. I turned back and sent air kisses as the doors closed and the movement of the bus jerked me forward.

After visiting 195 countries I have found that tourism and politics exist on two different planes. Stepping foot in a country does not mean that one is supporting a government. Rather, you are supporting the people. Should I have decided not to visit Venezuela because of its political climate, Johan and several others I met would not have had a boost in their income that month. That short interaction with Johan allowed him to feed his family a little longer, to pay rent for another month. If we write off countries because of their governments, what happens to their citizens? I, for one, will continue to travel to these countries, continue to experience life behind borders some believe are impenetrable, continue to tell the stories of the people living there.

As I boarded the small 12-seater plane to Los Roques, I laughed, thinking of all the adventures I've done solo. Most of my friends would have protested the small, old, rickety planes I've flown on—along with other questionable modes of transportation—to reach my destinations. For me, it was all in a day's work.

I wasn't focused on the size of the plane. My attention sat squarely on the expansive views of the lush mountains of Cerro El Ávila. Within seconds of takeoff, the Caribbean Sea revealed itself, lapping the shores of the mainland before reaching the large grouping of islands that is Los Roques.

We landed at the small airport on Isla el Gran Roque, the largest of roughly 350 islands. I came here on the recommendation of the doorman at my hotel in Santiago de Chile a year prior. I knew nothing of the national park's entrance fee, nor the fact that there are no passenger cars on the island, only a garbage and water truck.

Caracas is full of street art and pro-government propaganda, paired with a sense of heaviness in the air.

After a seven-or-so-minute walk, I made it to my *posada,* a quaint guesthouse surrounded by trees and run by a little old lady named Mama Nelly. Mama Nelly was a legend as the island's first bartender. She packed me a bagful of water and sunscreen and I made my way to the dock to procure a trip to the surrounding islands. After much back-and-forth, I decided I would go to Cayo de Agua. A few other people, all Venezuelans, were doing the same excursion.

As the speedboat cut across jewel-toned blue waters, we watched birds dive into the sea to capture their unsuspecting meals. At Cayo de Agua, I could barely believe my eyes. The small island had some of the whitest sand and some of the bluest waters I had ever seen—even more unbelievable in that I had never heard of this place. I wondered how many beautiful parts of this earth remain largely unknown because the mainstream travel industry hasn't declared them winners. I am not complaining, though; it means more unspoiled beaches for me!

I walked across the shallow waters to a nearby island with some Venezuelans in my tour group and we talked about the great disparities between the haves and have-nots in the country. This group was part of the haves, their daily experiences a stark contrast to Johan's. We stopped by another island, where I devoured fresh ceviche served with *arepitas* (smaller versions of the traditional grilled corn-meal cakes).

My tour guide, Ronald, and his mother, Marianela, made me feel like family as we explored the streets, art, and history of Caracas.

I spent a lot of my short time on Gran Roque observing the simplicity of life. I watched as freshly caught fish were brought to shore, then purchased by Mama Nelly's helper after I asked for fish for lunch. I drank the caipirinhas Mama Nelly is famous for and dined on grilled octopus, rice, and fried fish on the beach at sunset. I talked to strangers about their love of the island.

More than anything, I sat in gratitude for my bravery in this journey. With just three countries until the finish line, I was savoring the simple moments even more. This part of my life would all be over soon. I was soaking it in.

Back in Caracas, I met my tour guide, Ronald, and his mother, Marianela. They gave me a nighttime tour of the city, taking me to major monuments such as Los Próceres, built in honor of the independence struggles of Colombia,

Bolivia, Ecuador, Peru, and Venezuela. As we drove around, they gave me a rundown of the country's history and a better understanding of its economy.

Before taking me to my hotel, the pair kindly invited me to their home, something they said they had never done before with a client. We sat in the backyard and drank mango smoothies made from fruit picked fresh from the tree. I had found my Venezuelan family. I pride myself on my ability to connect with strangers. It has enriched this journey with immersive experiences and the memories I treasure most.

The economic crisis in Venezuela is very bad. But there is a disparity. You still see people eating in restaurants and enjoying beaches, but those who are most affected by the crisis are desperately struggling to survive. The city is full of beautiful street art and also pro-government propaganda. A sense of heaviness fills the air, but I never felt unsafe, because I was moving around with locals. Still, I was acutely aware of hardships, both visible and beneath the surface.

Overall, I felt the heart of the country. My departure from Venezuela was a sad one. Ronald, Marianela, and I exchanged several hugs and I promised a return trip. When I return, it will be to see my family again. No government, no economy, can take away that type of kindness.

Cayo de Agua is one of roughly 350 islands that make up Los Roques, an island group off the coast of Caracas.

algeria

I APPLIED FOR my Algerian visa at the consulate in New York City and was told it would be ready in 10 days. Twelve days later, it wasn't. On the last day before my trip, a very kind man at the consulate told me that I absolutely would not get it on time. I protested and groveled. I told someone else at the consulate how I was just under a month away from touching down in country 195; he wouldn't want to

AFRICA

be the guy that ruined everything for me. Am I dramatic? Yes, yes I am. But it worked. He agreed to help me obtain my visa in Ghana. Luckily, I was already going to Ghana for a festival and was flying to Algeria from there. If the kind man at the Algerian Consulate in NYC is reading this: *Saha.*

Even with a visa secured, nothing is ever easy. I arrived in Algeria and watched as passengers in front of me moved through immigration quickly. I assumed it would be a smooth process. I was wrong. I handed my passport to the immigration officer and watched it switch hands multiple times. I was the only Black African in the airport. I had seen this play out before. Another officer came over and asked where I was from—despite having my American passport in his hand—and what I was doing in the country. I replied, "I'm American and I am here for tourism." Dissatisfied and suspicious, he left with my passport again. Only after the fourth officer was I granted entry. I did some deep breathing to let it go. After all, I was in country 193!

At lunch, I felt a slight but familiar pain in my stomach. My period was starting. Unprepared, I told my tour guide that I needed to go to a pharmacy. (Note: When you travel abroad, you can always find menstrual products at a pharmacy.) I grabbed my preferred tampons and pulled out my credit card, only to be told they took cash only. I had to ask my guide to buy them for me. I'm sure that was a first for him, but a girl gotta do what a girl gotta do! After all the work to get into Algeria, I spent the rest of the day in bed, nursing my cramps.

Inside Constantine's Palais Ahmed Bey, you are immediately transported to the opulence of 1835.

The following morning, feeling a bit better, I met my new guide, Zaki. He had a calm and kind energy and was equal parts witty, intelligent, and introspective. When we stopped at city hall, I noticed Arabic with another script below called Amazigh. Zaki explained it was a language of the Indigenous Berber people. Most Algerians can trace their lineage to one of five major Berber tribes still easily identifiable today.

In the middle of the city, we came upon a huge protest where people were chanting "Bring down the general" as they marched for democracy over the current military dictatorship. With military planes flying above and foot soldiers on the ground, Zaki remarked, "Ah, this is dangerous." Unafraid, I continued watching as people used their voices to affect change.

I took out my DSLR to photograph the protest. Unbeknownst to me, a police officer tapped Zaki on the shoulder to ask if I was a journalist. Zaki, nervous, explained that I was a tourist and showed him his guide badge. The officer asked me if I was a journalist. I quickly responded, *"Non, non, je suis une touriste seulement!"* I knew military governments are not fond of foreign journalists.

A little shaken, we hopped in a shared taxi to explore the Casbah, the traditional area of the city that dates back to the 10th century. It was all fun and games until I had to change my tampon in a bathroom with a squat toilet and a bucket of water. Oh, the joys of being a female traveler. My experience is *so* different from my globe-trotting male counterparts.

The Casbah reminded me of other North African cities. The archways, intricate hand-carved doors, and narrow cobblestone alleys took me back to Tunis. There were dilapidated buildings of washed-out pastels, adorned with shutters, opened and exposing rusted and barred windows with lace curtains. Inside a small tea shop, the walls were decorated with Moroccan tile that reminded me of the madrassa in Marrakech.

The best part of the day was my conversation with Zaki. When I asked what his life goals were, he gave a slight chuckle before responding, "I'm just living for the sake of living. You can't have wild ambitions around here, especially if you're the eldest." While I understood what he was saying—the cultural oppression of it all—it really got me thinking how much wasted potential and unrealized dreams there are in the world.

I recognize that I won the lottery of birth, being born in the U.S., especially when I have more than 100 first cousins born in Uganda, many in a village without running water or electricity. Having access to an American passport and the childhood

While walking around Algiers, I came upon protesters, fighting for democracy rather than the current military dictatorship.

that my parents crafted, one without limits, allowed me to dream.

Achieving any dream is rooted in an understanding that you have every single thing inside of you to reach your goals. Only once you believe that will it manifest into reality—no matter where you were born, no matter your circumstances, and no matter your family pressures. I shared this belief with Zaki. I hope it made him feel differently about his own circumstances.

After two days in Algiers, I hopped on a short flight to Constantine. The ancient city, which dates back to 203 B.C., reminded me of the Italian countryside. My guide, Ouided, took me to the Palais Ahmed Bey. Though the outside of the building leaves a lot to be desired, the interior immediately transports you to the opulence of 1835, when the palace first opened. A quilt of tile in clashing colors and designs was beautifully strewn together throughout. On the walls were intricate paintings detailing the journey of Ahmed Bey crossing the Red Sea to visit Medina and Mecca in Saudi Arabia.

Always on a quest to find cultural similarities and differences, I try to ask the people I meet questions that provoke answers that tell about a place and its people. I asked Ouided what love feels like. She replied, "Everything beautiful."

As we zigzagged our way through traffic to the airport, traditional Algerian music blasting through speakers, I couldn't help but smile. I loved Algeria. Its people were everything that is beautiful.

Algiers is an idyllic city with both Arab and French influences, perched on the shores of the Mediterranean.

Syria

ACROSS ALL 195 UN-RECOGNIZED COUNTRIES and 10 territories, I was only denied a visa one time, and that was for my visit to Syria. Until this second to last country on my list, I had been grateful for my dual citizenship, which allowed me to easily visit every country in the world. I used my American passport in countries where U.S. citizens did not need a visa and my Ugandan passport in countries where

ASIA

Majid Tarabe shared that his orchard was started by his grandfather, whom he last saw in 1967 when the war started because they lived on separate sides of the fence.

Ugandan citizens did not need a visa. Out of the world's 195 countries, I only had to apply for 18 visas in advance. I used my U.S. passport for 13 of those countries and my Ugandan passport for five.

When I initially applied in early 2019, Americans were not being given Syrian visas, so I applied as a Ugandan. Two months later, I was told that my application was denied without explanation. Someone told me they often deny African passports because they do not want African travelers to overstay their visas to work in the country. To be fair, that comment did not come from the Syrian government but from a Syrian visa agent, but I still thought it was an absolutely ridiculous rationale. Plus, a quick Google search of my name would prove I was highly unlikely to overstay my visa in Syria. At the time, only European and Japanese passport holders were being granted visas into Syria—suddenly I was really wishing things had worked out with the Italian. I had to find another way.

As a crazy plan B, concocted in real time, I decided to visit the Golan Heights instead of Damascus.

The geopolitical area of the Golan Heights lies in eastern Syria and is bordered by Israel and Jordan. In 1967, during the Six-Day War, Israel captured the territory and has occupied it ever since. Internationally, this has been condemned and is considered illegal under international law. As such, the United Nations considers the Golan Heights part of Syria.

With the help of my trusty friend and logistics coordinator, Anna, I booked a flight from Algiers to Tel Aviv. Then, I reached out to my driver from Palestine, who connected me with his brother Gassan.

From this overlook you can see both the Golan Heights and the rest of Syria.

Gassan, a Jerusalem-born Palestinian, agreed to take me on a tour of the Golan Heights.

Though I lost money on my original flight, I had enough credit card points to buy a very last-minute flight to Tel Aviv and the flight home to Detroit for $25. Credit card points are a real thing. Use them!

As much as I would like you to believe that things went off without a hitch, of course they didn't. An Israeli man refused to sit next to me on the flight to Tel Aviv because I am a woman. His protest caused a delay in takeoff. To top it off, the ATM in Tel Aviv ate my debit card, and, upon departure, I was shortly detained at the Jordanian border because of my drone. But, I made it!

My goal is to have deep cultural experiences and make authentic connections in every country that I visit. I was worried that by visiting the Golan Heights, I wasn't going to experience the *real* Syria. The trip far exceeded my expectations.

Gassan had been working as a tour guide for several years. As we started our two-hour drive to the Golan Heights, I explained this mission to him—and, of course, the context of my journey around the world—and told him we had to figure out how to experience *real* Syria during this short trip. He was the perfect person to show me around. He truly brought the country to life for me.

We visited Majdal Shams, a Syrian-Druze town at the foothills of Mount Hermon. Though this area has been occupied by Israel since 1967, the town remains Arab, even down to its name. Most of the signage is in Arabic, though here and there you will see some is in Hebrew. The lingua franca remains Syrian Arabic, but the younger generation is beginning to speak Hebrew more often. It is a reflection of the dynamic of the occupation.

As we drove through the small town, I spotted an older woman tending to her plants and asked to chat with her. She was living in Majdal Shams in 1967 when the war started. Overnight she and others in the town were completely separated from their families. In the beginning, they used bullhorns to communicate with their families on the other side of the fence that separates the Golan Heights from Syria. When they saw movements signaling a funeral, they would use the bullhorn to find out who died. She was very happy when the internet was invented because it made communication much easier.

Later, while in town, a young girl wearing a shirt that said "Celebrate the little things" gifted me a few Syrian apples, which are deliciously sweet and incredibly popular in the area. Gassan took me to an apple orchard where we met Majid Tarabe, whose grandfather had planted the orchard decades ago. It broke my heart when he told me that he hadn't seen his grandfather since the day the war began. He was on the other side of the fence.

We heard many similar stories about the war and the separation it caused for so many families. My heart broke again and again listening to each one. The most poignant story was of a man who was visiting his family in another village the day the war started. He was not able to return to his pregnant wife. His son was 45 the first time they met when they finally reunited in Jordan.

Over a lunch of chicken shawarma, Gassan told me that he had been to the Golan Heights hundreds of times and had never heard those stories before. No tourist had ever asked. He had never thought to ask. I was honored that he made it possible for me to hear the stories of the Syrian people. The stories are tragic, heartwarming, and, despite the hardship, full of love and optimism.

In many ways, visiting the Golan Heights was the perfect trip to Syria. It may not have been in its major cities. It may not have been a trip to its most famous monuments. But the people I met shared a pride for their country and their unique experience—one I may not have considered before this journey and one many don't give a second thought. Those people in the Golan Heights consider themselves to be Syrian, and they want to be reunited with their country, with their families. Nothing more.

seychelles

"WE ARE NOW BEGINNING OUR INITIAL DESCENT . . ." Words that I had heard hundreds of times before took on a different meaning as I looked out the window: Small islands encircled by the blue waters of the Indian Ocean came into view. The Seychelles, an archipelago of 115 islands, is Africa's smallest and least populated country, and it was the final one on my journey to every country in the world. The wheels touched down

AFRICA

and the plane erupted in cheers—28 of my friends and family, who took the same flight as me, were celebrating the milestone. I opened my tracking app and ticked off the island nation, bringing the official count to 195. I exited the plane and walked out onto cloud nine.

I landed in the Seychelles on October 6, my father's birthday. My father had been murdered two days after my 19th birthday. Though he couldn't be part of this journey, he had contributed to it in so many ways: exposing me to the world, challenging me intellectually, and building my confidence so I could dream so big that I thought I could visit every country in the world—and I did. He was with me on every step of this journey. Though I had initially planned to visit every country by my 35th birthday, landing in country 195 a few months later on what would have been *his* 82nd birthday helped me feel that he was right there with me.

After receiving that final stamp in my Ugandan passport, I was met by representatives of the Seychelles government. They gifted me with the nut of a coco de mer, a rare species of palm tree native to the island. The nut is the largest seed in the plant kingdom and resembles the bottom half of a woman. They also gave me a bottle of local rum, which I have been sipping slowly for more than two years.

In total, 55 people celebrated with me in the Seychelles. We laughed, ate, drank, and danced. We rented a huge catamaran and sailed to La Digue, a beautiful Seychellois island with huge rock formations that made it feel otherworldly. On the island, we rented clear-bottom kayaks, and even as the rain poured down on us, our joy was not dampened.

Back on Mahé, we organized ourselves into four teams for "beach Olympics." There was a relay race, potato sack race, and tug-of-war. We played our version of Family Feud, dividing up into teams by how I knew people. There was "The Real Family," "Not From Detroit," "15+ Years," and "New Kids on the Block." I played host.

At our final dinner, which everyone joked was basically my wedding reception, many of my guests spoke of how we met and what my friendship and journey meant to them. As I listened to my older sisters and closest friends share special memories, I realized that nothing happens by chance. Those celebrating with me were just as excited that I had completed this journey as I was. I was officially the first Black woman to visit every country in the world. And their shared joy proved just what an impact that could have on others.

Here I was, in one of the world's most beautiful countries, surrounded by people I love and who love me, celebrating a feat that fewer than 200 people had accomplished. I realized the universe hand-selected me for this. That is the only way to explain the resilience required to reach the finish line and the circumstances that led to each and every one of these people being in my life. We closed the final night dancing to Detroit mix music played by my friend DJ B-Hen, then a few of us shed our gowns and suits and skinny-dipped under the full moon in the Indian Ocean. How lucky am I?

A lot of my visit to the Seychelles is a blur. It was truly a celebration of the feat I had accomplished. Running on adrenaline and champagne for six days straight makes for a memory haze of love, joy, and awe. When I really sit with the fact that I visited every country in the world, even two and a half years after the monumental feat, I find it to be unbelievable. Did I really see the pyramids in Egypt? Did I really sleep in a yurt on a mountaintop in Kyrgyzstan? Did I really drive to Guinea with two men I barely knew? Did I really travel 244,547 air miles (393,560 km) in 2019? Did I really fill up three passports in less than five years? Did I really swim with a humpback whale in Tonga?

The answer is yes. Yes to it all—195 countries, 35 years, 12 passports, 45 countries entered on a Ugandan passport, 89 countries traveled solo, 17 advanced visas, 44 countries visited more than once, 46 countries visited by car or on foot. What a journey.

Celebrating the end of the journey on the shores of Beau Vallon beach with my sisters, Joyce and Christina, and my mother, Rose

epilogue

FIVE MONTHS AFTER completing my journey, the coronavirus pandemic brought everything to a screeching halt. Borders shut down, international flights were grounded, and countries around the world were in chaos as we collectively battled a virus that locked us in our homes and took millions of lives. Simultaneously, a racial reckoning boiled over in the U.S. and protests erupted at home and abroad. As I write this, the virus still rages, refugees are fleeing Afghanistan, an underwater volcanic eruption has devastated Tonga, and Haiti is dealing with the aftermath of yet another earthquake.

Though heartbreaking, these circumstances have been reminders of just how connected the world is and how similar we all are. My extended period at home—the longest since 2011—was difficult, but it allowed me to take a pause, to reflect on an amazing, though often hectic, journey of a lifetime. My travel memories held me over as my passport sat unused.

Of course, I couldn't stay entirely planted. When it was safe, I took road trips around the U.S. I celebrated the coming of 2021 in Dakar, Senegal. I enjoyed the beaches of Bahia, Brazil, I was awed by the shores of Anguilla, I took my first trip to Venice, Italy, and I visited France to speak on climate change at the IUCN Congress.

I am more grateful than ever for the privilege to travel, my freedom, and the life I've created. I am thankful for the beauty the world has to offer, the kind people I have encountered and have yet to meet, and all of the places I have yet to see.

The pandemic reminded us how quickly life can be taken away. I for one don't want to miss living mine to the fullest. I want to see every bit of the planet that I can. And I also want to leave it a little bit better than I found it. During my forced time-out from traveling, I spent a lot of time thinking about what comes next: I want to inspire others to safeguard our world and to treasure it. I want to implore travelers to take chances on seldom considered destinations. I want to change how the world sees travelers of color.

It took more than 450 flights across more than one million air miles, but I made it to 195 countries in the world—I met my goal. Now I have others. The journey is just beginning. I hope to see you out there.

The soft golden sands of the Sahara near Meroë, Sudan, the former capital of the Kingdom of Kush, whisper stories of the past.

the 195 by year visited

Bold indicates countries featured in this book.

Born 1984
1. The United States

1988
2. Canada

1991
3. United Kingdom
4. Uganda

1994
5. Jamaica

1999
6. Mexico

2000
7. The Bahamas

2007
8. France
9. Spain

2008
10. Japan

2009
11. Honduras
12. Australia
13. Fiji
14. Costa Rica
15. Netherlands
16. Turkey
17. Egypt

2010
18. Belgium
19. Malta
20. Switzerland
21. Czechia
22. Croatia
23. Montenegro
24. Sweden
25. Italy
26. Vatican City
27. Benin
28. Togo
29. Ghana

2011
30. Greece
31. Germany
32. Hungary

2012
33. Oman

2013
34. Argentina
35. Uruguay
36. Brazil
37. Ethiopia
38. Kenya
39. Iceland

2014
40. Portugal
41. Senegal
42. Panama
43. St. Lucia
44. Colombia

45. Denmark

2015
46. Haiti
47. United Arab Emirates
48. Thailand
49. Laos
50. Cambodia
51. Vietnam
52. Singapore
53. Finland
54. Rwanda

2016
55. Peru
56. Cuba
57. Luxembourg
58. Ireland
59. Norway

2017
60. Indonesia
61. Malaysia
62. Morocco
63. Grenada
64. Djibouti
65. Tanzania
66. Bahrain
67. Qatar
68. Liechtenstein
69. Austria
70. Slovakia
71. Ukraine
72. Moldova
73. Romania
74. Serbia

75. Slovenia
76. Tunisia
77. San Marino
78. Bulgaria
79. North Macedonia
80. Albania
81. Bosnia and Herzegovina
82. Belize
83. Guatemala
84. El Salvador
85. Nicaragua
86. Sri Lanka
87. Maldives
88. India
89. Nepal
90. Bangladesh
91. South Africa
92. Mozambique
93. Zimbabwe
94. Zambia
95. Namibia
96. Sudan

2018

97. Botswana
98. Lesotho
99. Eswatini
100. Antigua and Barbuda
101. St. Kitts and Nevis
102. Dominican Republic
103. Philippines
104. Brunei
105. Timor-Leste
106. Gambia
107. Côte d'Ivoire
108. Nigeria
109. Guyana
110. Suriname
111. Barbados
112. Dominica
113. St. Vincent and the Grenadines
114. Andorra

115. Monaco
116. Poland
117. Lithuania
118. Estonia
119. Latvia
120. Kyrgyzstan
121. Kazakhstan
122. Uzbekistan
123. Afghanistan
124. Tajikistan
125. Armenia
126. Ecuador
127. Bolivia
128. Paraguay
129. Chile
130. Papua New Guinea
131. Solomon Islands
132. Nauru
133. Marshall Islands
134. Kiribati
135. Lebanon
136. Cyprus
137. Israel
138. Palestine
139. Jordan
140. Kuwait
141. China
142. North Korea
143. Mauritius
144. Madagascar
145. Comoros
146. Saudi Arabia
147. Somalia
148. Eritrea
149. Burundi

2019

150. South Sudan
151. Malawi
152. Libya
153. Mauritania
154. Mali
155. Niger

156. Burkina Faso
157. Trinidad and Tobago
158. Myanmar
159. Iran
160. Iraq
161. Yemen
162. Central African Republic
163. Turkmenistan
164. Azerbaijan
165. Georgia
166. Belarus
167. Russia
168. Guinea-Bissau
169. Guinea
170. Cabo Verde
171. Chad
172. Cameroon
173. Equatorial Guinea
174. Gabon
175. Congo
176. Democratic Republic of the Congo
177. Angola
178. Sao Tome and Principe
179. Sierra Leone
180. Liberia
181. Samoa
182. Tonga
183. New Zealand
184. Vanuatu
185. Tuvalu
186. Federated States of Micronesia
187. Palau
188. South Korea
189. Mongolia
190. Bhutan
191. Pakistan
192. Venezuela
193. Algeria
194. Syria
195. Seychelles

my bucket list for you

- ☐ **Afghanistan:** Visit Hazrat Ali Mazar.
- ☐ **Benin:** Visit Ganvie lake village.
- ☐ **Bhutan:** Hike to Tiger's Nest.
- ☐ **Bolivia:** Watch the sun set in the Salar de Uyuni (salt flat).
- ☐ **Bosnia and Herzegovina:** Visit Blagaj.
- ☐ **Brazil:** Wander around Pelourinho.
- ☐ **Burkina Faso:** Visit Tiébélé.
- ☐ **Canada:** Visit Banff during winter.
- ☐ **Colombia:** People-watch in Plaza de la Trinidad.
- ☐ **Cuba:** Wander through the streets of Habana Vieja.
- ☐ **Cuba:** Take a salsa class at La Casa del Son.
- ☐ **Djibouti:** Float in Lake Assal.
- ☐ **Egypt:** Eat falafel sandwiches.
- ☐ **Eritrea:** Visit Massawa.
- ☐ **Finland:** Dogsled in northern Finland.
- ☐ **Georgia:** Eat lunch at Pheasant's Tears.

- ☐ **Georgia:** Get a body scrub at Orbeliani Baths.
- ☐ **Ghana:** Visit—and party—during Festive Season.
- ☐ **Grenada:** Explore the underwater sculpture park.
- ☐ **Guatemala:** Visit Tikal.
- ☐ **Guyana:** Visit Kaieteur Falls.
- ☐ **Guyana:** Have lunch at Backyard Café.
- ☐ **Haiti:** Visit Anse-à-Galets.
- ☐ **Honduras:** Go snorkeling on Roatán.
- ☐ **Iceland:** Hike a glacier.
- ☐ **Iran:** Visit Sheikh Lotfollah Mosque in Isfahan.
- ☐ **Ireland:** Stay in a castle.
- ☐ **Italy:** Rent a Fiat 500 and visit small Tuscan villages.
- ☐ **Italy:** View the Vatican through the keyhole in Giardino degli Aranci.
- ☐ **Jamaica:** Eat pan chicken from a roadside vendor in Kingston.
- ☐ **Japan:** Visit Fushimi Inari-taisha.
- ☐ **Jordan:** Climb to the top of the hill and snap a Petra money shot.

- ☐ **Kazakhstan:** Visit Big Almaty Lake.
- ☐ **Kenya:** Take a sunset dhow ride off the coast of Lamu.
- ☐ **Kyrgyzstan:** Sleep in a yurt on a mountaintop.
- ☐ **Kyrgyzstan:** Try fermented horse milk.
- ☐ **Laos:** Watch almsgiving in Luang Prabang.
- ☐ **Libya:** Explore Leptis Magna.
- ☐ **Madagascar:** Visit the Avenue of the Baobabs.
- ☐ **Maldives:** Splurge on an overwater bungalow.
- ☐ **Mali:** Buy *bogolan* fabric from the source.
- ☐ **Mauritania:** Visit Chinguetti.
- ☐ **Mongolia:** Spend the night with a nomadic family.
- ☐ **Morocco:** Shop in a souk in Marrakech.
- ☐ **Myanmar:** Take a hot air balloon ride in Bagan.
- ☐ **Myanmar:** Visit Kakku Pagodas.
- ☐ **Namibia:** Visit Deadvlei.
- ☐ **Namibia:** Enjoy stargazing.

- ☐ **Nauru:** Explore the entire country on a scooter.
- ☐ **Nigeria:** Go shopping in Lekki Market.
- ☐ **Nigeria:** Visit and party in Dezemba.
- ☐ **North Korea:** Watch the Mass Games.
- ☐ **North Macedonia:** Visit Lake Ohrid.
- ☐ **Pakistan:** Watch the Wagah border ceremony.
- ☐ **Palestine:** Eat *knafeh* at Al Aqssa Sweets.
- ☐ **Peru:** Go surfing in Lima.
- ☐ **Russia:** Have champagne and caviar at Four Seasons Hotel Lion Palace.
- ☐ **Samoa:** Swim in To Sua ocean trench.
- ☐ **Sao Tome and Principe:** Visit the center of the world.
- ☐ **Saudi Arabia:** Visit the Edge of the World.
- ☐ **Senegal:** Go surfing in Yoff.
- ☐ **Senegal:** Eat *thieboudienne* and *yassa poisson*.
- ☐ **Seychelles:** Buy a coco de mer.
- ☐ **Sierra Leone:** Eat pepper soup with goat on the beach.
- ☐ **Somaliland:** Drink fresh camel's milk.
- ☐ **South Africa:** Visit Johannesburg's Neighbourgoods Market.
- ☐ **South Africa:** Take a helicopter above Cape Town.
- ☐ **Sri Lanka:** Take the train from Colombo to Galle.
- ☐ **Sudan:** Visit the pyramids of Meroë.
- ☐ **Suriname:** Ride down the Amazon River.
- ☐ **Tanzania:** Visit the Serengeti during the great migration.
- ☐ **Tanzania:** Swim at Zanzibar's Nungwi Beach.
- ☐ **Tonga:** Swim with humpback whales.
- ☐ **Trinidad and Tobago:** Eat *all* the street food.
- ☐ **Tunisia:** Hang out in Sidi Bou Said.
- ☐ **Turkey:** Drink apple tea in the Grand Bazaar.
- ☐ **Turkmenistan:** Spend the night at Darvaza gas crater.
- ☐ **Tuvalu:** Take a picture in the middle of the airport's runway.
- ☐ **Uganda:** Eat fresh roasted pork from a pork joint on Entebbe Road.
- ☐ **Uganda:** Go white-water rafting on the Nile.
- ☐ **United States:** Visit seven states on a single road trip.
- ☐ **United States:** Learn how to lasso from a Black cowboy.
- ☐ **Uzbekistan:** Take the train from Tashkent to Samarkand.
- ☐ **Venezuela:** Visit Cayo de Agua.
- ☐ **Zambia:** Wade in Devil's Pool.

☐ _____
☐ _____
☐ _____
☐ _____
☐ _____
☐ _____
☐ _____
☐ _____
☐ _____
☐ _____
☐ _____
☐ _____
☐ _____
☐ _____
☐ _____
☐ _____
☐ _____
☐ _____
☐ _____
☐ _____
☐ _____
☐ _____
☐ _____
☐ _____
☐ _____
☐ _____
☐ _____
☐ _____
☐ _____
☐ _____
☐ _____
☐ _____
☐ _____
☐ _____

acknowledgments

This book was made possible by my selfless parents, who left their home country of Uganda and moved to the United States. This book is for immigrants and their children because without the bravery of our parents, we would be nothing.

To my editor, Allyson, thank you for helping me write the book that I wanted to write. And to the entire team at Nat Geo books—especially Nicole, Krista, Elisa, Lisa G., and Lisa T.—thank you for your patience in getting this book to the finish line.

To my mother, Rose, you are the best mommy to ever mommy and I thank you for that. To my sisters, Joyce and Christina, thank you for always putting up with me and for a lifetime of support. To my entire family and extended family in the U.S., Uganda, and the U.K.: *Mwebale nnyo bassebo ne banyabo!* Extra special thanks to Cedric.

Nyanquoi, thank you for putting up with my ridiculousness on a daily basis and for playing a multitude of roles in my life. Wes, I definitely knew you in a past life. I'm thrilled we get to hang in this life, and I look forward to seeing you in the next. It is difficult to put in words the depth of our friendship. I am just grateful. Melissa, thank you for constantly pushing me forward and telling me what I don't want to hear, but need to hear, without remorse. James, thank you for your wisdom and advice, and our praise reports. Kateri, you are a pure light, and you've given me so many gems that played continuously in my head during the writing of this book. Sarah, thank you for always answering my calls and being my forever cheerleader.

To my tribe, my blue marbles, most of whose names are sprinkled throughout the book, you know who you are because your number is in my phone, and though you do not always answer my random FaceTimes, just know I do it because I love you. Extra special thanks to Anthony, Ashley M., Kam, Katie, Rahsaan, Serena, Sheree, Tosin, Will, Wintta, and Xiomara.

Anna, this journey would've taken a lot longer without you! I will never delete our Google Docs and spreadsheets. Hajni, thank you for working in my time zone despite not living in it, and for always keeping me laughing. Luvvie, thank you for giving me advice so many times over the years; it meant more than you will ever know. And thank you for connecting me with Lisa, without whom this deal would not have closed!

To my family at Four Seasons Punta Mita, thank you for making me feel at home for seven weeks while writing this book. I am not sure there could have been a more perfect place to write. Miguel, you are stuck with me. And to John, oh John, words escape me, but I feel like we don't need them. To the entire staff: *Muchas gracias por todo.*

To the more than 200 people who supported my journey financially, most of whom were strangers, thank you. Each person who donated can be found at *thecatchmeifyoucan.com/support.* I wanted to list all the names in the book, but the word count said no.

To the strangers who became friends during my travels, thank you for making me feel at home and opening up your countries to me.

To my community, you have cheered me on, cried with me, laughed with me, and reminded me that this journey is so much bigger than me. Thank you.

about the author

JESSICA NABONGO is a writer, photographer, entrepreneur, travel expert, influencer, and public speaker. She completed her journey as the first Black woman on record to travel to all 195 countries of the world in October 2019. At her core, Jessica is a dreamer looking to craft a life and career that connects her passions and talents. She wants to use her story to educate and inspire others to travel and experience the world around them. A first-generation American, Jessica was born and raised in Detroit by Ugandan parents. She attended St. John's University in New York, where she earned a degree in English literature, later completing a graduate degree in development studies at the London School of Economics. She uses her blog, The Catch Me If You Can, to share her travel adventures and to build a global community. She is also founder of the lifestyle brand The Catch. When she's not on a plane, she is home tending to her plants in Detroit, Michigan.

illustrations credits

Since 1888, the National Geographic Society has funded more than 14,000 research, conservation, education, and storytelling projects around the world. National Geographic Partners distributes a portion of the funds it receives from your purchase to National Geographic Society to support programs including the conservation of animals and their habitats.

Get closer to National Geographic Explorers and photographers, and connect with our global community. Join us today at nationalgeographic.org/joinus

For rights or permissions inquiries, please contact National Geographic Books Subsidiary Rights: bookrights@natgeo.com

Library of Congress Cataloging-in-Publication Data
Names: Nabongo, Jessica, author.
Title: The catch me if you can : one woman's journey to every country in the world / Jessica Nabongo.
Description: Washington, DC : National Geographic, 2022. | Summary: "Celebrated traveler and photographer Jessica Nabongo-the first documented Black woman to visit all 195 countries in the world-shares her journey around the globe with fascinating stories of adventure, culture, travel musts, and human connections"-- Provided by publisher.
Identifiers: LCCN 2021062584 (print) | LCCN 2021062585 (ebook) | ISBN 9781426222269 (hardcover) | ISBN 9781426222467 (ebook)
Subjects: LCSH: Nabongo, Jessica--Travel. | International travel. | African American women travelers--Biography. Classification: LCC G154.5.N34 A3 2022 (print) | LCC G154.5.N34 (ebook) | DDC 910.4/1092 [B]--dc23/eng20220207 LC record available at https://lccn.loc.gov/2021062584

LC ebook record available at https://lccn.loc gov/2021062585

ISBN: 978-1-4262-2226-9

Printed in the United States of America

22/WOR/1